Financial Crisis, Labour Markets and Institutions

This book seeks to explain the global financial crisis and its wider economic, political, and social repercussions, arguing that the 2007–9 meltdown was in fact a systemic crisis of the capitalist system.

The volume makes these points through the exploration of several key questions:

- What kind of institutional political economy is appropriate to explain crisis periods and failures of crisis-management?
- Are different varieties of capitalism more or less crisis-prone, and can the global financial crisis can be attributed to one variety more than others?
- What is the interaction between the labour market and the financialization process?

The book argues that each variety of capitalism has its own specific crisis tendencies, and that the uneven global character of the crisis is related to the current forms of integration of the world market. More specifically, the 2007–9 economic crisis is rooted in the uneven income distribution and inequality caused by the current financial-led model of growth.

The book explains how the introduction of more flexibility in the labour markets and financial deregulation affected everything from wages to job security to trade union influence. Uneven income distribution and inequality weakened aggregate demand and brought about structural deficiencies in aggregate demand and supply. It is argued that the process of financialization has profoundly changed how capitalist economies operate. The volume posits that financial globalization has given rise to growing international imbalances, which have allowed two growth models to emerge: a debt-led consumption growth model and an export-led growth model. Both should be understood as reactions to the lack of effective demand due to the polarization of income distribution.

Sebastiano Fadda is Professor of Labour Economics and Economic Growth at the University of Roma Tre, Italy. He is also Director of the ASTRIL Research Centre at the University of Roma Tre.

Pasquale Tridico is Professor of Labour Economics at the University of Roma Tre, Italy, and Research Associate at Trinity College Dublin, Ireland. He is currently General Secretary of the European Association for Evolutionary Political Economy.

Routledge frontiers of political economy

1 **Equilibrium Versus Understanding**
  Towards the rehumanization of economics within social theory
  Mark Addleson

2 **Evolution, Order and Complexity**
  Edited by Elias L. Khalil and Kenneth E. Boulding

3 **Interactions in Political Economy**
  Malvern after ten years
  Edited by Steven Pressman

4 **The End of Economics**
  Michael Perelman

5 **Probability in Economics**
  Omar F. Hamouda and Robin Rowley

6 **Capital Controversy, Post Keynesian Economics and the History of Economics**
  Essays in honour of Geoff Harcourt, volume one
  Edited by Philip Arestis, Gabriel Palma and Malcolm Sawyer

7 **Markets, Unemployment and Economic Policy**
  Essays in honour of Geoff Harcourt, volume two
  Edited by Philip Arestis, Gabriel Palma and Malcolm Sawyer

8 **Social Economy**
  The logic of capitalist development
  Clark Everling

9 **New Keynesian Economics/Post Keynesian Alternatives**
  Edited by Roy J. Rotheim

10 **The Representative Agent in Macroeconomics**
   James E. Hartley

11 **Borderlands of Economics**
   Essays in honour of Daniel R. Fusfeld
   Edited by Nahid Aslanbeigui and Young Back Choi

12 **Value, Distribution and Capital**
   Essays in honour of Pierangelo Garegnani
   Edited by Gary Mongiovi and Fabio Petri

13 **The Economics of Science**
   Methodology and epistemology as if economics really mattered
   James R. Wible

14 **Competitiveness, Localised Learning and Regional Development**
   Specialisation and prosperity in small open economies
   Peter Maskell, Heikki Eskelinen, Ingjaldur Hannibalsson, Anders Malmberg and Eirik Vatne

15 **Labour Market Theory**
   A constructive reassessment
   Ben J. Fine

16 **Women and European Employment**
    Jill Rubery, Mark Smith, Colette Fagan and Damian Grimshaw

17 **Explorations in Economic Methodology**
    From Lakatos to empirical philosophy of science
    Roger Backhouse

18 **Subjectivity in Political Economy**
    Essays on wanting and choosing
    David P. Levine

19 **The Political Economy of Middle East Peace**
    The impact of competing trade agendas
    Edited by J.W. Wright, Jnr

20 **The Active Consumer**
    Novelty and surprise in consumer choice
    Edited by Marina Bianchi

21 **Subjectivism and Economic Analysis**
    Essays in memory of Ludwig Lachmann
    Edited by Roger Koppl and Gary Mongiovi

22 **Themes in Post-Keynesian Economics**
    Essays in honour of Geoff Harcourt, volume three
    Edited by Claudio Sardoni and Peter Kriesler

23 **The Dynamics of Technological Knowledge**
    Cristiano Antonelli

24 **The Political Economy of Diet, Health and Food Policy**
    Ben J. Fine

25 **The End of Finance**
    Capital market inflation, financial derivatives and pension fund capitalism
    Jan Toporowski

26 **Political Economy and the New Capitalism**
    Edited by Jan Toporowski

27 **Growth Theory**
    A philosophical perspective
    Patricia Northover

28 **The Political Economy of the Small Firm**
    Edited by Charlie Dannreuther

29 **Hahn and Economic Methodology**
    Edited by Thomas Boylan and Paschal F. O'Gorman

30 **Gender, Growth and Trade**
    The miracle economies of the postwar years
    David Kucera

31 **Normative Political Economy**
    Subjective freedom, the market and the state
    David Levine

32 **Economist with a Public Purpose**
    Essays in honour of John Kenneth Galbraith
    Edited by Michael Keaney

33 **Involuntary Unemployment**
    The elusive quest for a theory
    Michel De Vroey

34 **The Fundamental Institutions of Capitalism**
    Ernesto Screpanti

35 **Transcending Transaction**
    The search for self-generating markets
    Alan Shipman

36 **Power in Business and the State**
    An historical analysis of its concentration
    Frank Bealey

37 **Editing Economics**
    Essays in honour of Mark Perlman
    Edited by Hank Lim, Ungsuh K. Park and Geoff Harcourt

38 **Money, Macroeconomics and Keynes**
Essays in honour of Victoria Chick, volume one
Edited by Philip Arestis, Meghnad Desai and Sheila Dow

39 **Methodology, Microeconomics and Keynes**
Essays in honour of Victoria Chick, volume two
Edited by Philip Arestis, Meghnad Desai and Sheila Dow

40 **Market Drive and Governance**
Reexamining the rules for economic and commercial contest
Ralf Boscheck

41 **The Value of Marx**
Political economy for contemporary capitalism
Alfredo Saad-Filho

42 **Issues in Positive Political Economy**
S. Mansoob Murshed

43 **The Enigma of Globalisation**
A journey to a new stage of capitalism
Robert Went

44 **The Market**
Equilibrium, stability, mythology
S.N. Afriat

45 **The Political Economy of Rule Evasion and Policy Reform**
Jim Leitzel

46 **Unpaid Work and the Economy**
Edited by Antonella Picchio

47 **Distributional Justice**
Theory and measurement
Hilde Bojer

48 **Cognitive Developments in Economics**
Edited by Salvatore Rizzello

49 **Social Foundations of Markets, Money and Credit**
Costas Lapavitsas

50 **Rethinking Capitalist Development**
Essays on the economics of Josef Steindl
Edited by Tracy Mott and Nina Shapiro

51 **An Evolutionary Approach to Social Welfare**
Christian Sartorius

52 **Kalecki's Economics Today**
Edited by Zdzislaw L. Sadowski and Adam Szeworski

53 **Fiscal Policy from Reagan to Blair**
The left veers right
Ravi K. Roy and Arthur T. Denzau

54 **The Cognitive Mechanics of Economic Development and Institutional Change**
Bertin Martens

55 **Individualism and the Social Order**
The social element in liberal thought
Charles R. McCann Jnr

56 **Affirmative Action in the United States and India**
A comparative perspective
Thomas E. Weisskopf

57 **Global Political Economy and the Wealth of Nations**
Performance, institutions, problems and policies
Edited by Phillip Anthony O'Hara

58 **Structural Economics**
Thijs ten Raa

59 **Macroeconomic Theory and Economic Policy**
Essays in honour of Jean-Paul Fitoussi
Edited by K. Vela Velupillai

60 **The Struggle over Work**
The "end of work" and employment alternatives in post-industrial societies
Shaun Wilson

61 **The Political Economy of Global Sporting Organisations**
John Forster and Nigel Pope

62 **The Flawed Foundations of General Equilibrium Theory**
Critical essays on economic theory
Frank Ackerman and Alejandro Nadal

63 **Uncertainty in Economic Theory**
Essays in honor of David Schmeidler's 65th birthday
Edited by Itzhak Gilboa

64 **The New Institutional Economics of Corruption**
Edited by Johann Graf Lambsdorff, Markus Taube and Matthias Schramm

65 **The Price Index and its Extension**
A chapter in economic measurement
S.N. Afriat

66 **Reduction, Rationality and Game Theory in Marxian Economics**
Bruce Philp

67 **Culture and Politics in Economic Development**
Volker Bornschier

68 **Modern Applications of Austrian Thought**
Edited by Jürgen G. Backhaus

69 **Ordinary Choices**
Individuals, incommensurability, and democracy
Robert Urquhart

70 **Labour Theory of Value**
Peter C. Dooley

71 **Capitalism**
Victor D. Lippit

72 **Macroeconomic Foundations of Macroeconomics**
Alvaro Cencini

73 **Marx for the 21st Century**
Edited by Hiroshi Uchida

74 **Growth and Development in the Global Political Economy**
Social structures of accumulation and modes of regulation
Phillip Anthony O'Hara

75 **The New Economy and Macroeconomic Stability**
A neo-modern perspective drawing on the complexity approach and Keynesian economics
Teodoro Dario Togati

76 **The Future of Social Security Policy**
Women, work and a citizens' basic income
Ailsa McKay

77 **Clinton and Blair**
The political economy of the third way
Flavio Romano

78 **Marxian Reproduction Schema**
Money and aggregate demand in a capitalist economy
A.B. Trigg

79 **The Core Theory in Economics**
Problems and solutions
Lester G. Telser

80 **Economics, Ethics and the Market**
Introduction and applications
Johan J. Graafland

81 **Social Costs and Public Action in Modern Capitalism**
Essays inspired by Karl William Kapp's theory of social costs
Edited by Wolfram Elsner, Pietro Frigato and Paolo Ramazzotti

82 **Globalization and the Myths of Free Trade**
History, theory and empirical evidence
Edited by Anwar Shaikh

83 **Equilibrium in Economics**
Scope and limits
Edited by Valeria Mosini

84 **Globalization**
State of the art and perspectives
Edited by Stefan A. Schirm

85 **Neoliberalism**
National and regional experiments with global ideas
Edited by Ravi K. Roy, Arthur T. Denzau and Thomas D. Willett

86 **Post-Keynesian Macroeconomics**
Essays in honour of Ingrid Rima
Edited by Mathew Forstater, Gary Mongiovi and Steven Pressman

87 **Consumer Capitalism**
Anastasios S. Korkotsides

88 **Remapping Gender in the New Global Order**
Edited by Marjorie Griffin Cohen and Janine Brodie

89 **Hayek and Natural Law**
Eric Angner

90 **Race and Economic Opportunity in the Twenty-First Century**
Edited by Marlene Kim

91 **Renaissance in Behavioural Economics**
Harvey Leibenstein's impact on contemporary economic analysis
Edited by Roger Frantz

92 **Human Ecology Economics**
A new framework for global sustainability
Edited by Roy E. Allen

93 **Imagining Economics Otherwise**
Encounters with identity/difference
Nitasha Kaul

94 **Reigniting the Labor Movement**
Restoring means to ends in a democratic labor movement
Gerald Friedman

95 **The Spatial Model of Politics**
Norman Schofield

96 **The Economics of American Judaism**
Carmel Ullman Chiswick

97 **Critical Political Economy**
Christian Arnsperger

98 **Culture and Economic Explanation**
Economics in the US and Japan
Donald W. Katzner

99 **Feminism, Economics and Utopia**
Time travelling through paradigms
Karin Schönpflug

100 **Risk in International Finance**
Vikash Yadav

101 **Economic Policy and Performance in Industrial Democracies**
Party governments, central banks and the fiscal–monetary policy mix
Takayuki Sakamoto

102 **Advances on Income Inequality and Concentration Measures**
Edited by Gianni Betti and Achille Lemmi

103 **Economic Representations**
Academic and everyday
Edited by David F. Ruccio

104 **Mathematical Economics and the Dynamics of Capitalism**
Goodwin's legacy continued
Edited by Peter Flaschel and Michael Landesmann

105 **The Keynesian Multiplier**
Edited by Claude Gnos and Louis-Philippe Rochon

106 **Money, Enterprise and Income Distribution**
Towards a macroeconomic theory of capitalism
John Smithin

107 **Fiscal Decentralization and Local Public Finance in Japan**
Nobuki Mochida

108 The 'Uncertain' Foundations of Post-Keynesian Economics
Essays in exploration
Stephen P. Dunn

109 Karl Marx's *Grundrisse*
Foundations of the critique of political economy 150 years later
Edited by Marcello Musto

110 Economics and the Price Index
S.N. Afriat and Carlo Milana

111 Sublime Economy
On the intersection of art and economics
Edited by Jack Amariglio, Joseph W. Childers and Stephen E. Cullenberg

112 Popper, Hayek and the Open Society
Calvin Hayes

113 The Political Economy of Work
David Spencer

114 Institutional Economics
Bernard Chavance

115 Religion, Economics and Demography
The effects of religion on education, work, and the family
Evelyn L. Lehrer

116 Economics, Rational Choice and Normative Philosophy
Edited by Thomas A. Boylan and Ruvin Gekker

117 Economics Versus Human Rights
Manuel Couret Branco

118 Hayek Versus Marx and Today's Challenges
Eric Aarons

119 Work Time Regulation as Sustainable Full Employment Policy
Robert LaJeunesse

120 Equilibrium, Welfare and Uncertainty
Mukul Majumdar

121 Capitalism, Institutions and Economic Development
Michael Heller

122 Economic Pluralism
Robert Garnett, Erik Olsen and Martha Starr

123 Dialectics of Class Struggle in the Global Economy
Clark Everling

124 Political Economy and Globalization
Richard Westra

125 Full-Spectrum Economics
Toward an inclusive and emancipatory social science
Christian Arnsperger

126 Computable, Constructive and Behavioural Economic Dynamics
Essays in honour of Kumaraswamy (Vela) Velupillai
Stefano Zambelli

127 Monetary Macrodynamics
Toichiro Asada, Carl Chiarella, Peter Flaschel and Reiner Franke

128 Rationality and Explanation in Economics
Maurice Lagueux

129 The Market, Happiness, and Solidarity
A Christian perspective
Johan J. Graafland

130 Economic Complexity and Equilibrium Illusion
Essays on market instability and macro vitality
Ping Chen

131 Economic Theory and Social Change
Problems and revisions
Hasse Ekstedt and Angelo Fusari

132 **The Practices of Happiness**
Political economy, religion and wellbeing
Edited by John Atherton, Elaine Graham and Ian Steedman

133 **The Measurement of Individual Well-Being and Group Inequalities**
Essays in memory of Z. M. Berrebi
Edited by Joseph Deutsch and Jacques Silber

134 **Wage Policy, Income Distribution, and Democratic Theory**
Oren M. Levin-Waldman

135 **The Political Economy of Bureaucracy**
Steven O. Richardson

136 **The Moral Rhetoric of Political Economy**
Justice and modern economic thought
Paul Turpin

137 **Macroeconomic Regimes in Western Industrial Countries**
Hansjörg Herr and Milka Kazandziska

138 **The Political Economy of the Environment**
Edited by Simon Dietz, Jonathan Michie and Christine Oughton

139 **Business Ethics and the Austrian Tradition in Economics**
Hardy Bouillon

140 **Inequality and Power**
The economics of class
Eric A. Schutz

141 **Capital as a Social Kind**
Definitions and transformations in the critique of political economy
Howard Engelskirchen

142 **Happiness, Ethics and Economics**
Johannes Hirata

143 **Capital, Exploitation and Economic Crisis**
John Weeks

144 **The Global Economic Crisis**
New perspectives on the critique of economic theory and policy
Edited by Emiliano Brancaccio and Giuseppe Fontana

145 **Economics and Diversity**
Carlo D'Ippoliti

146 **Political Economy of Human Rights**
Rights, realities and realization
Bas de Gaay Fortman

147 **Robinson Crusoe's Economic Man**
A construction and deconstruction
Edited by Ulla Grapard and Gillian Hewitson

148 **Freedom and Happiness in Economic Thought and Philosophy**
From clash to reconciliation
Edited by Ragip Ege and Herrade Igersheim

149 **Political Economy After Economics**
David Laibman

150 **Reconstructing Keynesian Macroeconomics Volume 1**
Partial perspectives
Carl Chiarella, Peter Flaschel and Willi Semmler

151 **Institutional Economics and National Competitiveness**
Edited by Young Back Choi

152 **Capitalist Diversity and Diversity within Capitalism**
Edited by Geoffrey T. Wood and Christel Lane

153 **The Consumer, Credit and Neoliberalism**
Governing the modern economy
Christopher Payne

154 **Order and Control in American Socio-Economic Thought**
U.S. social scientists and progressive-era reform
Charles McCann

155 **The Irreconcilable Inconsistencies of Neoclassical Macroeconomics**
A false paradigm
John Weeks

156 **The Political Economy of Putin's Russia**
Pekka Sutela

157 **Facts, Values and Objectivity in Economics**
José Castro Caldas and Vítor Neves

158 **Economic Growth and the High Wage Economy**
Choices, constraints and opportunities in the market economy
Morris Altman

159 **Social Costs Today**
Institutional analyses of the present crises
Edited by Wolfram Elsner, Pietro Frigato and Paolo Ramazzotti

160 **Economics, Sustainability and Democracy**
Economics in the era of climate change
Christopher Nobbs

161 **Organizations, Individualism and Economic Theory**
Maria Brouwer

162 **Economic Models for Policy Making**
Principles and designs revisited
S. I. Cohen

163 **Reconstructing Keynesian Macroeconomics Volume 2**
Integrated approaches
Carl Chiarella, Peter Flaschel and Willi Semmler

164 **Architectures of Economic Subjectivity**
The philosophical foundations of the subject in the history of economic thought
Sonya Marie Scott

165 **Support-Bargaining, Economics and Society**
A social species
Patrick Spread

166 **Inherited Wealth, Justice and Equality**
Edited by Guido Erreygers and John Cunliffe

167 **The Charismatic Principle in Social Life**
Edited by Luigino Bruni and Barbara Sena

168 **Ownership Economics**
On the foundations of interest, money, markets, business cycles and economic development
Gunnar Heinsohn and Otto Steiger; translated and edited with comments and additions by Frank Decker

169 **Urban and Regional Development Trajectories in Contemporary Capitalism**
Edited by Flavia Martinelli, Frank Moulaert and Andreas Novy

170 **Social Fairness and Economics**
Economic essays in the spirit of Duncan Foley
Edited by Lance Taylor, Armon Rezai and Thomas Michl

171 **Financial Crisis, Labour Markets and Institutions**
Edited by Sebastiano Fadda and Pasquale Tridico

Financial Crisis, Labour Markets and Institutions

Edited by Sebastiano Fadda and
Pasquale Tridico

LONDON AND NEW YORK

First published 2013
by Routledge
2 Park Square, Milton Park, Abingdon, Oxon OX14 4RN

Simultaneously published in the USA and Canada
by Routledge
711 Third Avenue, New York, NY 10017

Routledge is an imprint of the Taylor & Francis Group, an informa business

© 2013 selection and editorial material, Sebastiano Fadda and Pasquale Tridico; individual chapters, the contributors

The right of Sebastiano Fadda and Pasquale Tridico to be identified as the authors of the editorial material, and of the authors for their individual chapters, has been asserted in accordance with sections 77 and 78 of the Copyright, Designs and Patents Act 1988.

All rights reserved. No part of this book may be reprinted or reproduced or utilised in any form or by any electronic, mechanical, or other means, now known or hereafter invented, including photocopying and recording, or in any information storage or retrieval system, without permission in writing from the publishers.

Trademark notice: Product or corporate names may be trademarks or registered trademarks, and are used only for identification and explanation without intent to infringe.

British Library Cataloguing in Publication Data
A catalogue record for this book is available from the British Library

Library of Congress Cataloging in Publication Data
Financial crisis, labour markets, and institutions / edited by Sebastiano Fadda and Pasquale Tridico.
    p. cm.
    Includes bibliographical references and index.
    1. Financial crises. 2. Labor market. 3. Capitalism. 4. Global Financial Crisis, 2008–2009. I. Fadda, Sebastiano. II. Tridico, Pasquale, 1975–
HB3722.F555 2013
330.9'0511–dc23   2012030584

ISBN: 978-0-415-53860-2 (hbk)
ISBN: 978-0-203-10913-7 (ebk)

Typeset in Times New Roman
by Wearset Ltd, Boldon, Tyne and Wear

Contents

Notes on the authors   xv
Acknowledgements   xvii

Introduction   1
SEBASTIANO FADDA AND PASQUALE TRIDICO

PART I
Capitalism in crisis: nature and origins   17

1 **Capitalism in deep trouble**   19
   RICHARD WOLFF

2 **The North Atlantic financial crisis and varieties of capitalism: a Minsky and/or Marx moment? And perhaps Max Weber too?**   40
   BOB JESSOP

3 **Beyond the political economy of Hyman Minsky: what financial innovation means today**   60
   ANASTASIA NESVETAILOVA

4 **The problematic nature of the Economic and Monetary Union**   79
   MALCOLM SAWYER

5 **Financialization, income distribution and the crisis**   98
   ENGELBERT STOCKHAMMER

PART II
Impact and consequences of the crisis 121

6 Labour market institutions and the crisis: where we come from and where we are going 123
SEBASTIANO FADDA

7 Financial crisis, labour markets and varieties of capitalism: a comparison between the European social model and the US model 143
PASQUALE TRIDICO

8 Labour market rigidities can be useful: a Schumpeterian view 175
ALFRED KLEINKNECHT, C.W.M. NAASTEPAD, SERVAAS STORM AND ROBERT VERGEER

9 The unemployment impact of financial crises 192
ENRICO MARELLI AND MARCELLO SIGNORELLI

Index 212

Authors

Editors

Sebastiano Fadda is Professor of Labour economics and of Economic growth at the University of Roma Tre where he is also director of a two-year Master's degree course in "Labour Market, Industrial Relations and Welfare Systems" and director of the Research Centre ASTRIL (Associazione Studi e Ricerche Interdisciplinari sul Lavoro).

Pasquale Tridico is Professor of Labour economics at the University of Roma Tre. He is also research associate at the IIIS – Trinity College Dublin. In the academic year 2010–11 he was Fulbright Scholar at New York University. He is currently General Secretary of the EAEPE (European Association for Evolutionary Political Economy) www.eaepe.org.

Contributors

Bob Jessop is Distinguished Professor of Sociology and Co-Director of the Cultural Political Economy Research Centre at Lancaster University and a Senior Fellow at the Rosa Luxemburg Stiftung (Berlin). He currently holds a three-year ESRC Professorial Fellowship to study crises of crisis management in the North Atlantic Financial Crisis.

Alfred Kleinknecht is Professor of the Economics of Innovation at TU Delft. He has worked at the Berlin Wissenschaftszentrum, the two Amsterdam universities and the University of Maastricht.

Enrico Marelli is Professor of Economic Policy at the University of Brescia, where he is Head of the Teaching Board for the degree in Economics. He has also taught or carried out research at LSE, University of Pennsylvania, Bocconi University and other universities in Italy.

C.W.M. Naastepad obtained her PhD degrees in economics at Erasmus University, Rotterdam. She is now Lecturer in Economics at TU Delft.

Anastasia Nesvetailova is Reader in International Political Economy at City University London. She is the author of *Fragile Finance: Debt, Speculation* *and Crisis in the Age of Global Credit* (2007, Palgrave) and *Financial Alchemy in Crisis: the Great Liquidity Illusion* (2010, Pluto).

Malcolm Sawyer is Emeritus Professor of Economics at the University of Leeds. He is Principal Investigator for Financialisation, Economy, Society and Sustainable Development (FESSUD), funded by European Union Framework Programme 7, and Managing Editor of the *International Review of Applied Economics*.

Marcello Signorelli is Professor of Economic Policy and of Labour Institutions and Policies at the University of Perugia. He is also President of the European Association for Comparative Economic Studies (EACES).

Engelbert Stockhammer is Professor of Economics at Kingston University. He is also research associate at the Political Economy Research Institute at the University of Massachusetts at Amherst and a member of the coordination committee of the Research Network Macroeconomics and Macroeconomic Policies (FMM).

Servaas Storm obtained his PhD degree in economics at Erasmus University, Rotterdam. He is now lecturer in economics at TU Delft.

Robert Vergeer first worked at the research institute of the Association of Dutch Municipalities and then became a PhD fellow at TU Delft. After a period as policy advisor at the Dutch parliament, he became a researcher at TNO-Labour, a public institute for applied research.

Richard Wolff is Professor of Economics Emeritus at the University of Massachusetts at Amherst and Visiting Professor at the New School, New York. For books, articles and videos, see www.rdwolff.com.

Acknowledgements

This book is an outcome of the 2011 EAEPE Summer School which was held in July 2011 at the University Roma Tre, Rome, Italy. The editors are very grateful to the EAEPE (European Association for Evolutionary Political Economy), to the authors of this book, who presented firstly their papers at the summer school, and to the many PhD students who participated in the summer school and commented with great interest lecturers' contributions. The editors acknowledge also the financial support of the COST action IS0902 ("Systemic Risks, Financial Crises and Credit – the roots, dynamics and consequences of the Subprime Crisis") for the organization of the Summer School and the support of the Department of Economics at the University Roma Tre.

Introduction

From the financial meltdown to the current economic crisis: roots and consequences

Sebastiano Fadda and Pasquale Tridico

Book objectives and crisis background

The objective of this book is to show that the 2007–9 crisis which started in the US financial sector is a systemic crisis of the capitalist system. The crisis is fundamentally explained by the uneven income distribution and inequality caused by the current financial-led model of growth, which weakened aggregate demand and brought about structural deficiencies in the aggregate demand and supply. However, there is a mutual interaction between the financial sector and income distribution. In fact, the explosion of financial activities and of financial innovation was pulled out by the need of the middle class, whose income was squeezed by the fall in the wage share over GDP. Consumption credit and loans contributed to the reinforcing of financial innovation and to the financialization process. We argue that the process of financialization has profoundly changed how capitalist economies operate. We demonstrate that the financial globalization has given rise to growing international imbalances, which have allowed two growth models to emerge: a debt-led consumption growth model and an export-led growth model. Both should be understood as reactions to the lack of effective demand due to the polarization of income distribution.

This book tries to answer a set of questions that would explain the global financial crisis and its wider economic, political, and social repercussions. First of all, what kind of institutional political economy is appropriate to explain crisis periods and failures of crisis-management. Second, it considers whether different varieties of capitalism are more or less crisis-prone and whether the global financial crisis can be attributed to one or another variety more than others. We assume that each variety of capitalism has its own specific crisis-tendencies and the uneven global character of the crisis is related to the current forms of integration of the world market. More specifically, the 2007–9 economic crisis is rooted in the uneven income distribution and inequality caused by the current financial-led model of growth.

In addition, we look at the interaction between the labour market and the financialization process: since the 1980s advanced economies introduced more flexibility in the labour markets and financial deregulation. This brought about lower minimum wages, modest social benefits, easier firing, reduced power of trade unions, profit soar and extra compensation in the financial sector. We show that more flexible labour market regimes lead to a substantially lower labour productivity growth and have a negative impact on innovation and learning. The flexibility agenda of the labour market and the end of wage increases, along with the contraction of indirect wage (i.e. public social expenditure) diminished workers' purchasing power. This was partly compensated with increasing borrowing opportunities and the boom of credit consumption, which helped workers to maintain some unstable consumption capacity. However, in the long term such an unstable consumption derived from precarious job creation, job instability, and poor wages weakens the aggregate demand.

Meanwhile, rising economic inequality realigned US politics after the 1970s, substituting neo-liberalism for the welfare state inherited from the 1930s New Deal. To overcome crisis, neo-liberal regimes borrowed heavily to unfreeze credit by bailing out banks. That shifted private sector debt onto governments' balance sheets. In fact, in particular after the Greek economic crisis in May 2010, governmental policies shifted towards austerity measures, balanced budgets; and as a result, the consensus which had allowed for partial recovery, monetary liquidity, and the bail-out of banks and financial institutions almost dissipated. Fiscal stimuli are no longer unanimously accepted, and the main concerns of industrialized nations became sovereign debt crises, budget sustainability, and public spending cuts. All this, in our view, exacerbated even further the economic crisis, and the negative impact on the labour market in terms of unemployment which became massive both in the US and in Europe.

The financial meltdown: an overview

As we all know now, the background of the crisis is the increase of household debt in advanced economies (like the US) and the bubble in the housing sector created by low interest rates. This is coupled with global imbalances which occur when a saving glut in Asia is not compensated by increased investments in the US and other developed economies. Price bubbles, both in the housing and in the commodity sectors, emerged in the economy. Prices in the US housing sector rose almost 200 per cent since 1997. The situation in other countries is even worse: in Ireland, the increase in housing prices over the same period is about 300 per cent and about 225 per cent in the UK and Spain. In Australia, Norway, Sweden, France, Denmark, Italy, Canada, and the Netherlands, housing prices increased around 200 per cent.

The loosening of monetary policies and the resulting cheap money favoured the financial bubble. Nevertheless, the fall of interest rates was not followed by an increase of investments, according to a classical "Keynesian effect". On the contrary, high asset capitalization allowed only for portfolio movements and financial investments. In contrast the financial sector, supported by general enthusiasm and an excess of liquidity, manufactured a revolution; inventing financial instruments and financial packages for everybody, promising high returns to all. Financial innovation allowed for an impressive variety of instruments, securitization, derivatives, and speculative funds such collateralized debt obligations (CDO), mortgage-backed securities (MBS), mortgage-backed bonds (MBB), credit default swaps (CDS), asset-backed securities (ABS), hedge funds, futures, etc. The result was an explosion in the availability of financing, in particular mortgage financing (Lowenstein 2010). Financial institutions and banks, in order to protect themselves against NINJA and other weak borrowers, securitized mortgages with financial tools which were traded with customers and others banks and institutions in order to spread the high risk. Obviously, high risk investments were associated with high returns and vice versa. Customers could choose from a menu, as if they were in a casino. The camouflaging of toxic assets and securities, along with collusion with the Credit Rating Agencies (CRA), completed the picture.

Perverse incentive schemes within financial institutions and extra bonuses for managers and brokers contributed to excessive risk-taking. Increasing risky trades made fortunes for financial intermediaries, who were rewarded according to the short-term expansion generated by these risky activities, rather than the long-term profitability of investments. Benchmarks became the delivery of exceedingly high expected quarterly earnings in terms of dividends and share prices for investors. This hugely increased financial pressure generated manias and reinvigorated the bubble. But banks are not casinos, and a crisis could potentially, and actually did, emerge when only a small fraction of mortgage holders declared default, causing a so-called *default correlation*. As a matter of fact, these defaults actually caused the value of the most risky instruments to fall to zero. In turn, investors in the securities tools (MBS, CDO, ABS, etc.) demanded now, with higher levels of risk, higher compensatory interests, paid again by mortgage owners, causing further defaults. The fact that these instruments were spread out across the world only increased the level of panic, because nobody could actually know precisely where the toxic assets were. Paraphrasing Kindleberger (2005), panic follows mania. As a result, the American housing bubble burst. Banks started to worry seriously and drastically limited the levels at which they were willing to lend to each other, causing a huge increase in the intra-bank rate of lending, therefore worsening the position of many creditors. This caused even more default correlation as an increasing number of borrowers could not repay their debts. Simultaneously, a crisis of solvency (for borrowers) and a crisis of liquidity (for banks) emerged at the end 2007 and beginning of 2008 (Chorafas, 2009).

However, beside the financial irresponsibility and the greedy behaviour of speculators, mostly important was the lack of adequate regulation and institutions able to cope with perverse behaviour and to channel and limit speculation and greedy actions. The case of the CRA is emblematic in this context. During the crisis, the CRA started to revise their ratings of CDO, MBS, ABS and the like downwards. Consequentially banks adjusted their risk upwards. The already highly leveraged financial institutions and the banking system were in worse trouble than before. They tried to raise fresh capitals by looking for funding from sovereign funds and state intervention as they now faced serious solvency and liquidity problems. Now, not only individuals (borrowers, mortgage owners) but also banks started to declare default. In the UK, the Northern Rock Bank default was clearly the symptom of a liquidity problem. In the US, the unexpected default of the Lehman Brothers in September 2008 indicated that the crisis would be very big and could extend to the real market, since Lehman's shares were spread widely throughout the financial world and investor confidence would now be close to zero.

Western central banks, the Fed, the Bank of England, and the European Central Bank (ECB) in particular, acted immediately, providing liquidity and lowering the interest rate in stages. The Fed provided $200 billion in the first quarter of 2008 and another $700 billion in the second quarter of 2009. During the same period the interest rate was lowered from 5 per cent to 0.25 per cent. The ECB, although traditionally more prudent with money supply and more focused on targeting low inflation and price stability than the Fed, followed the same line, although with some delay and at lower paces, by providing massive liquidity and lowering interest rates.

The crisis showed what was already known: securitization, i.e. the process of spreading the individual risk of sub-prime mortgage in many tranches, posed a danger to the market. Faulty guarantees by credit rating agencies such as Moody's showed that the financial system was entirely built upon a conflict of interests between controller and controlled societies. CRAs make profits advising firms whose products they are going to assess. Moody's has been awarding improper Triple-A ratings to many of the investment banks and insurance societies which went bankrupt in the fall of 2008, such as Lehman Bros, or were bailed out or saved by the government, such as Fannie Mae, Freddie Mac, Bear-Stearns, Merrill Lynch, AIG, Goldman Sachs, Morgan Stanley, and Washington Mutual. Trust collapsed immediately, matching the rate at which big financial colossuses were going into bankruptcy. The lack of transparency in the financial market and mystery surrounding complex financial tools, combined with corruption and manager greed completed this recipe for disaster. Similar stories, although on a smaller scale, can be told regarding European banks and financial institutions, saved by their governments as the market fell (Frangakis, 2010).

The failure and corruption of the very guarantors of the market economy, the CRAs, is just an example of how little real competition and transparency there is in the capital markets. There is a troupe of 150 rating and vigilante enterprises in the world. However, the majority of securities analyses are made by just two CRAs: Moody's and Standard and Poor's, which account for 80 per cent of the market. Thirteen per cent is controlled by Fitch. The remaining market share, approximately 7 per cent, is split amongst the rest (147 enterprises).

The root of the crisis

The saving glut in the US and in other European and advanced economies along with the financial meltdown, are, however, only the background in which the current crisis emerged. The labour market is in fact a complementary pillar of this systemic crisis. The argument that emerges in the book is that the institutional and structural changes which occurred in the labour market and in the economy over the last 15 years in Europe, and over the past 30 years in US, were functional to the financialization process and have culminated in the current economic crisis. These changes allowed for labour flexibility, wage moderation, and ultimately inequality and profit soar. All this occurred with the demise of the Keynesian policies.

First, the neoliberal approach requires a higher degree of labour flexibility because, in the current post-Fordist era, with the massive shift from the industrial sector to the service sector, technology and innovation bring about rapid structural changes, which demand quick responses from firms. Therefore, labour should adjust to the firms' need. The financial sector in particular, because of its peculiarities, requires a very flexible workforce and fast adjustments. The financial sector has been an early and eager promoter of deregulation in the early 1980s both in the UK and in USA, under the Thatcher and Reagan administrations. This has brought about more labour flexibility (Petit, 2009; Boyer, 2000). Moreover, after the fall of the Soviet Union, Alan Greenspan, who rose to oversee the Fed during the Reagan administration, believed that the world economy could expand greatly through the globalization of the financial sector (Greenspan, 2007; Semmler and Young, 2010). The rest of the economy then followed the financial-led regime of accumulation, with flexible labour and compressed wages. Shareholders want higher dividends because they invested their own capital in firms, taking on a higher level of risk. Since the economic growth and productivity of advanced economies in the post-Fordist market has not been much higher than in the Fordist market, it follows that wages should be compressed in order for shareholders to obtain higher dividends. Labour flexibility and wage contraction is a means to obtain this result.

Financialization, during post-Fordism times, is coupled with globalization and the attempt, in particular among advanced economies, to adopt a stronger export-led model. In fact, since the oil crises of the 1970s firms were pushed to look abroad in order to recover profitability. Exports were one way to avoid the internal crisis and paying more expensive oil prices. National companies became *multinational* in the sense that they transferred their productive segments abroad in order to avoid the internal crisis, recover profitability, and gain prime positions in areas with more robust internal demand. The Fordist compromise of distributing productivity gains and increasing internal demand through high wages had lost its very *raison d'être*, since the demand of foreign markets diminished the importance of sustaining internal purchasing power, from the view of the firms. On the contrary, the export-led economy imposed a more competitive atmosphere; since resource costs were increasing rapidly and mark-up was decided by monopolistic and oligopolistic firms, price advantage was gained by decreasing production and labour costs. The trend was international, all firms in advanced economies adopted the same strategy, to varying degrees. That shift drove a decline in real wages (which were either frozen, or increased less relative to the productivity gains), exerted a pressure on purchasing power, and, therefore, caused a crisis of international demand (Dowd, 2000). As Lipietz

(1992) noticed, at the international level there are no institutional forms of the Fordist–Keynesian type; no mechanisms to increase international demand, no collective agreements, no supranational Welfare State, etc. In summary, the causes of the Fordist type of accumulation are: a decrease in productivity, poor labour organization, the internationalization of problems through pressure on labour costs, and the resulting decrease in the demand. These are supply-side causes, or, as in most of the cases, exogenous to the core of Fordist economic doctrine.

Stopping short of suggesting causality, there is a positive correlation between the level of market financialization and wealth inequality. Typically, the US and other Anglo-Saxon countries have traditionally higher levels of financialization and higher wealth inequality (Gini coefficient). In contrast, the Scandinavian and Germanic nations are typically more equitable regarding wealth distribution.[1] The most interesting case is the US when compared with Denmark, which seem poles apart. However, in general all Anglo-Saxon countries have higher inequality and financialization than the Continental and Scandinavian European countries representing typically a European Social Model.

More in general high financialization is associated with high Gini coefficients and higher labour flexibility. More interesting, however, is the parallel trends of these variables: when financialization increases, one notices both increased flexibility and inequality (Tridico, 2012). A flexible labour market with compressed wages needs to be supplemented by available financing. Hence, to have developed financial tools to sustain consumption, which otherwise were compressed by low and unstable wages. A large number of financial tools were invented to finance consumption, to postpone payments, to extend credit, and to create extra-consumption. Interestingly enough, while income inequality increased in the US dramatically in the last 30 years, consumption inequality did not increase, because borrowing opportunities allowed for workers to consume using credit channels. On the other hand, this consumption was needed by the economy because otherwise the saving glut in Asia and the low income capacity of domestic workers would leave firms with un-bought goods and services and this would create aggregate demand unbalances. Thanks to financial innovation and cheap money workers could now afford to buy cheap goods from China, as well as expensive houses, luxury cars, and other durable goods at home. Such a model of consumption is however unstable, as the financial crash of 2007 showed.

Moreover, at the political level, the transition to post-Fordism seems to be assisted by a neo-conservative ruling class. Hence, a comparison with the previous pre-1920s Fordist era seems legitimate, when the liberist model of development was based on an extensive accumulation regime (Aglietta, 1979) with a pressure on labour costs, without government playing a significant role in the economy, without a productivity sharing compromise, and without the Keynesian Welfare State (Basso, 1998). Such a process of financialization was coupled with both an increase of inequality and a decline in the wage shares over the GDP in the US and in most advanced economies. Biased income distribution and inequality is one of the main factors which gives instability to the current financial-led growth regime, since aggregate demand is weak, and economic growth remain under its real and stable potential path. In general financialization represents a most incoherent set of experiments that cannot be considered a growth regime at all, and its literature tries to impose a coherence to a model that is absent in reality (Engelen *et al.*, 2008; Wolfson, 2003).

The current crisis which followed the meltdown of the 2007–8 in the United States is today a global crisis which involves almost all sectors and labour markets (Posner, 2009; Stiglitz, 2010; OECD, 2010). Mass unemployment emerged in the US and in Europe (Krugman, 2008; Wolff, 2010). After a recession of the GDP in the European Union (EU) with an average of –4.2 per cent in 2009, many EU member states have yet to recover. GDP is stagnating yet the unemployment level is not declining (Fitoussi and Stiglitz, 2009; Barba and Pivetti, 2009). Besides that, there are other problems such as low level of consumption, bank liquidity problems, low levels of private investment, lack of trust, and negative expectations in the financial market and between banks and investors, as well as high public deficits and debts. Despite the varieties of problems, national governments in advanced economies and in particular in the EU seem to focus mostly on a single problem: sovereign debt (Fitoussi and Saraceno, 2010).

EU malaises

In Europe, the Greek crisis, which emerged in May 2010, showed how the European Union member states are much more concerned with national issues than EU integration, in particular during times of crisis (Frangakis, 2010).[2] The lack of coordination and financial solidarity emerged dramatically, and the issue of European imbalances are wrongly regarded as a problem of laziness against effort, virtuous balance against bad discipline, Mediterranean corruption against Northern European integrity (Cesaratto, 2011). This does not help us to look at the real problem behind the deficit-surplus issue within the EU, which is having a single market. A single market (with many imperfections) and a common currency within a non-Optimal Currency Area (OCA) at the very least needs labour coordination, budget centralization, and fiscal policy harmonization (Wray and Randall, 2010). In addition, the "internal devaluation" (i.e. wage moderation) that Germany carried out at least at the beginning of the 2000s, along with other mercantilist policies and the cooperation of the European Central Bank (ECB) monetary policies, allowed German exports to increase dramatically (Cesaratto, 2011). Beside that, however, Germany put forward a strong agenda to boost labour productivity, improve internal competitiveness, and increase exports, in particular towards the less competitive south of Europe.

Such policies were not really in the spirit of EU integration and solidarity. Consequentially the EU situation today looks fragmented. On one side, Greece and the other Mediterranean countries suffer from the efficiency of Northern European firms. Free competition and single market affected the domestic markets in those countries, which were lagging behind in terms of competitiveness and technology at the creation of the Eurozone and the single market. Moreover, Maastricht criteria and stability pacts appreciated the euro and contributed to the declining foreign competitiveness of Southern European economies. On another side, the poorer economies in the EU cannot use monetary policies and exchange rate manipulation to gain competitiveness. They are unable to use state aids and firm subsides, nor fiscal policies which are constrained by Maastricht criteria. Hence, markets have to regulate imbalances despite the fact that labour mobility, single markets, and budget centralization are strongly limited in the EU. It follows that surplus and deficit are two results of the same problem: an imperfect single market and an imperfect currency union. In the EU, Germany's surplus could not exist without Greece's deficit (and similar). Greece should accept, within the EU rules, the German market super-competition, which is historically rooted and state supported, despite the fact that they cannot use policies to enhance their firms' competitive advantage. Unless these imbalances are covered by a central EU plan, it would not be convenient for Greece to accept European monetary union constraints.

At the same time, the solution cannot lie in the suggested wage moderation for Greece and similar countries in difficulties. Wage cuts would lower national income levels and further depress demand with negative effects on capital-saving investments and productivity. On the contrary capital intensive investments are needed, fiscal distribution, at least at Eurozone level, is necessary along with distributional policies inside the national state.

US crisis issues

Since the 1990s, the size of the US government's debt has grown impressively, reaching, on the eve of the crisis in 2006, more than five trillion dollars (United States Treasury, 2010). Long-term data sets show that this public debt started to increase in the 1980s, increased dramatically during the 1990s, and was subject only to a small reduction in 2001; a drop which was not sufficient to offset the increasing trend. Today the gross public debt is around 93 per cent of US GDP, and it is still increasing towards the record peak of the Second World War period, with a public debt in 2010 of almost $9 trillion. The international power of the US dollar favoured such indebtedness, which allows the US to consume and live above its production possibilities (Ivanova, 2010).

In 2010, the US economy was affected by a three separate $9 trillion debts, the national debt, the (non-bank) corporate debt, and the private mortgage debt. The financial institution's debt was even higher, at $12 trillion. Paralleling these trends, both the unfunded Medicare liability and the unfunded Social Security liability were very high ($30 trillion and $12 trillion, respectively). Worse than that, America's net investment position with respect to the rest of the world deteriorated dramatically to –$2.5 trillion (this is around 20 per cent of US GDP) and the Current Account (CA) deficit reached the peak of $800 billion (over 6 per cent of GDP) on the eve of the financial crisis. This seems to be the most troubling data, since it speaks to the big issues of a saving glut and global imbalances, in particular with

China (Tridico, 2011). Trade with China in particular is the Achilles' heel. China's share of the US non-oil goods trade deficit has tripled since 2000. Even during the crisis, although the American CA deficit decreased from the peak of $800 billion in 2006, the trade deficit with China has increased. China's share of the US non-oil goods trade deficit jumped from 68.6 per cent in 2008 to 80.2 per cent in 2009.

How all this debt, deficit, and global imbalances are connected with the financial crisis is then simple to explain. During the process of financialization, since the 1980s, wages in advanced economies and particularly in the US almost stagnated, and profits soared dramatically (Wolff, 2010; EuroMemorandum, 2010). Simultaneously inequality increased sharply (OECD, 2010). In order to keep consumption up, the US manoeuvred economic policies: used cheap money which allowed bubbles in the housing sector and private debt soaring; and allowed huge amount of cheap imports from China. This eventually ended up with huge CA deficit (IMF 2009). US financed the CA debt issuing US bonds which were bought in turn by Chinese, whose low level of consumption far compensates the American saving shortage. This scenario suggests a declining hegemony of the US economy, because policy options seem to be restricted and the supremacy of the US dollar as the main international currency started to be questioned (Zhou Xiaochuan, 2009). It underlines also new weakness of the financial system on the basis of which the US economy nowadays seems to rotate (Clelland and Dunaway, 2010). When the bubbles burst, mortgage companies and lenders fell down and mortgage default correlations followed, since the securitazion of mortgages and loans was an international, and opaque, issue. Credit markets seized up as risk increased and expectations worsened. Consequentially, the financial crisis floated in the real markets now also squeezing productive investments, economic activity, and employment.

If in the East (China and South-East Asia), where there are emerging economies and growing middle classes with theoretically high consumption potential, people save too much, in the West (mainly the US and UK), advanced economies have to stimulate extra-consumption, and therefore monetary policies are enacted which authorities hope will encourage spending. At least that is what the monetarists argue (Cooper, 2007; Caballero *et al.*, 2008). In this way, the claimed money glut is just a consequence of the saving glut. A more appropriate fiscal stimulus would be one based on increasing public investment. In the West (mainly in the US and UK), a well-developed financial system allows for extra-consumption, mechanisms of future repayment, and sophisticated forms of saving with high risk. In the East, safe and ordinary saving tools guarantee low returns and low risks within the framework of an underdeveloped financial system. Unfortunately, high levels of saving in the East do not manifest in the West as high levels of investment that could compensate the lack of aggregate demand. The lack of demand cannot be absorbed by the insufficient domestic investments. Simultaneously net capital inflow to the US increased, but this did not help productive investments, but rather fed financial speculation and extra-consumption.

In the West, one can observe the increase in demand for finance from those goods and services which go un-bought because of high global saving

(Lowenstein, 2009). Consequently, financing for consumption and portfolio movement has increased massively since 2001.

Global issues

At an international level, global imbalances and the saving glut theory call into question the role of the US dollar as a global currency and raise the issue of a possible new global currency and/or governance. Clearly, there can be a conflict between international and domestic objectives. As argued by Zhou Xiaochuan (2009), national monetary authorities may fail to meet growing global demand for money when they try to keep inflation low at home, and conversely, they may create an excess of liquidity at the global level when they try to overstimulate domestic demand. The current crisis, Zhou Xiaochuan says, is an inevitable outcome of the current institutional flaws which have the US dollar acting as a global currency for debts and international transactions.

Many scholars, notably in the World System field, recognize the unique position of the US as a hegemonic borrower (Frasnk, 2005; Clelland and Dunaway, 2010). The US has the unique and indefinite capacity to sell Treasury notes for dollars, in massive quantities and practically without constraints, and became the key source of global liquidity. Obviously it has also the capacity to manufacture dollars indefinitely, in the last instance. The US current account has been in massive deficit for the past 30 years. Therefore, every year, billions of dollars have been transferred from foreigners to the US balance (Clelland and Dunaway, 2010). Debt could rise to finance practically everything: government expenditures, military operations, private debts, because the unique status of the US currency ensured an international stable demand of its debt. At the same time private finance created tools which allowed for the recycling of capital inflows and for the mitigation of the US trade deficits. In this way, over-consumption in the US was guaranteed, even with stagnant wages (and profit soar) since the end of the 1970s (Wolff, 2010). The opacity of interconnection of massive transnational securitization and speculation eventually brought the financial implosion of 2007–8, which, however, was a natural outcome of such an institutional framework (Ivanova, 2010). Very interestingly in 1965, when General De Gaulle had already denounced the "exorbitant privilege" of the international seigniorage of US dollars, Rueff and Hirsch (1965: 3) wrote:

> ...when a country with a key currency has a deficit in its balance of payments – that is to say the United States, for example – it pays the creditor country dollars which end up with its central bank. But the dollars are of no use in Bonn, or in Tokyo, or in Paris. The very same day, they are re-lent to the New York money market, so that they return to the place of origin. Thus the debtor country does not lose what the creditor country has gained. So the key-currency country never feels the effect of a deficit in the balance of payments. And the main reason is that there is no reason whatever for the deficit to disappear, because it does not appear. Let me be more positive: if I had an agreement with

my tailor (CHINA) that whatever money (IMPORTS) I pay him he returns to me the very same day as a loan, I (USA) would have no objection at all to ordering more suits from him (MORE IMPORTS).[3]

The solution, according to Zhou Xiaochuan, has to be found in an international currency disconnected from any single nation. In this international currency project, the international monetary authorities should come from a wide consensus which exercises control and lends prestige to the new international system. Moreover, the issue of democratic deficit and of under-representation of emerging and developing countries should be solved. The new project should go beyond the current IMF framework, which is based on institutions designed in North America and Western Europe, with big countries (mainly G7), having more power, more vetoes, and more right to votes than others. A good starting point could be the G20 or any other wider organization (see Stiglitz, 2010).

In regards to global imbalances, China would not volunteer, in the current institutional framework, to change from a quickly growing country to a slowly developing one in order to save international capitalism and eliminate global imbalances. China will not allow for an appreciation of the exchange rate and tight monetary and fiscal polices at the expense of low employment. Moreover, China knows very well the causes of the Asian crisis in 1997, and with a population of almost 1.5 billion people, and a delicate political situation, she prefers to stay on the safe side. International responsibilities should be passed to the richer countries, the ones which have already reached high living standards, unlike China. On this line, world systems scholars have already opened a debate (Wallerstein, 2008; Wallerstein, 2009; Clelland and Dunaway, 2010).

The crisis itself proves that a Coordinated Market Economy (CME) may do more to shape a new global governance and may be more appropriate to help prevent further crises (Pontusson, 2005). The CME would guarantee a more stable path of development and of accumulation, mitigating the risk of boom and bust cycles illustrated by Minsky (1986). Examples of CME can be found in the EU and in particular among continental and Scandinavian economies (the socalled European Social Model), which combine interesting and functional elements of competitive markets economies such as competition and private investments, with useful market coordination systems such as financial regulation, public strategies of investments and Welfare and important public goods (Pontusson, 2005). However, when a new global governance needs to be put in place, global politics and power relations come into play, and this reveals that the EU's political position is weaker and less reliable than the US position, which may appear, to the rest of the world at least, more convincing and backed by the voice of a unique and powerful government.

The structure of the book

The book is divided into two parts. Part one is more theoretical and poses the main criticism to the financial-led regime of growth in which the current economic crisis emerged. The second part deals with empirical data, models, and statistics which confirm the assumptions of unsustainable growth made in the first part. They analyse both labour markets and financial markets and consider alternative and more stable paths of growth regime useful for policy makers. The neoclassical framework from which policy makers implemented the neoliberal policies is considered the main source which boosts the crisis. Hence, it is suggested, the way out from the crisis needs a radical policy change and a different analytical framework.

The first part starts with the contribution of Richard Wolff. Wolff argues that the economic crisis which has centered on Europe and North America since 2007 is a systemic crisis of the capitalist system and especially US capitalism. There, since the mid-1970s, stagnating real wages combined with rising productivity to yield (1) an increasingly indebted working class and (2) a class of employers, share-holders, and top professional employees that appropriated all the fruits of rising productivity. Increased inequality of wealth, income, and political power distributions resulted. When their stagnant wages precluded workers from further borrowing, they increasingly defaulted on their debts. Then the proliferating securities based on workers' mortgage and other debts (asset-backed securities, credit default swaps, etc.) could not be paid off. The speculations in those financial securities consequently collapsed. A credit freeze ensued among banks, insurance companies, large corporations, and wealthy individuals most heavily invested in those speculations. The crisis hit. Meanwhile, rising economic inequality realigned US politics after the 1970s, substituting neo-liberalism for the welfare state inherited from the 1930s New Deal. To overcome crisis, neo-liberal regimes borrowed heavily to unfreeze credit by bailing out banks, etc. That shifted private sector debt onto governments' balance sheets. Next, "austerity" transferred the burden of government deficits and debts onto the working class (reduced government jobs and services freed monies to reduce deficits and national debts). The burdens accumulating on the working classes – unemployment, home foreclosures, real wage cuts, government service reductions – are provoking intense debates, renewed mass actions, and a growing rage that promises to shake and challenge contemporary capitalism in ways not seen for at least half a century.

The contribution of Bob Jessop, in Chapter 2, poses four questions. First, what kind of evolutionary and institutional political economy is appropriate to explain normal and crisis periods, their alternation, forms of crisis-management, and failures of crisis-management? Second, it considers whether different varieties of capitalism are more or less crisis-prone and whether the global financial crisis can be attributed to one or another variety more than others. It argues that each variety of capitalism has its own specific crisis-tendencies, that the global financial crisis is grounded in a neo-liberal variant of the liberal market economy (compounded by speculation and open criminality), and that the uneven global character of the crisis is related to the current forms of integration of the world market. Third, it questions whether the crisis can be explained in terms of the dynamic of the real economy apart from the crucial role of money and credit not only as a mediating factor but also as an autonomous factor in crisis dynamics. It refers here to the work of Minsky and his followers but also shows the limits of Minsky's approach to the current crisis. In this context, as a fourth point, Jessop's contribution suggests that there are some neglected theoretical resources in Marx's critique of capitalism and shows how they can be reworked to explain some otherwise problematic features of the current crisis.

Drawing on the work of Hyman Minsky, Anastasia Nesvetailova's contribution, in Chapter 3, addresses the conceptual dilemma of the relationship between first, financial innovation and liquidity, and second, between the official and shadow banking system, in light of the lessons of the global credit crunch. Nesvetailova argues that the notion of Ponzi finance captures only one of the many disturbing elements in the complex set of the causes of the crisis. Engaging with the emergent theories of the credit crunch, she argues that the main controversy raised by the crisis and its consequences centres on the role of financial innovation in the economic system. More specifically, it concerns the problems of liquidity, risk, and liquidity arbitrage and its metamorphoses in the financial system, a large part of which constitutes what has been named a "shadow banking system".

Malcolm Sawyer, in Chapter 4, argues that the crisis of the Eurozone is calling its continued existence into doubt, and is raising questions on whether it can function effectively. The policy remedies (in the form of the "fiscal compact") which are being put into place, Sawyer argues, will not work on their own terms and will make the economic performance of the Eurozone countries worse. He outlines some Keynesian remedies for the crisis in terms of alternative policy proposals for the operation of the Economic and Monetary Union.

Engelbert Stockhammer's contribution, in Chapter 5, argues that the process of financialization has profoundly changed how capitalist economies operate. The crisis is the outcome of a bad interaction between financialization and changes in income distribution. The financial sector has grown relative to the real economy and become more fragile. Non-financial businesses have adopted shareholder value orientation, which had negative effects on investment. Working class households became squeezed because of rising inequality and have become more indebted, in particular in countries with real estate bubbles. Financial globalization has given rise to growing international imbalances, which have allowed two growth models to emerge: a debt-led consumption growth model and an export-led growth model. Both should be understood as reactions to the lack of effective demand due to the polarization of income distribution. The resulting finance-dominated accumulation regime is characterized by slow and fragile growth.

The second part starts with the contribution of Sebastiano Fadda (Chapter 6). Fadda's chapter, after removing what he considers a fundamental misunderstanding concerning institutions and refusing to assume that institutions are *per se* detrimental to the workings of market forces, focuses on the role played by labour market institutions at the origin and after the crisis. He questions the soundness of the "labour market reforms" suggested by the well known "Jobs study" and argues, both on theoretical and on empirical grounds, that they have greatly contributed to build up the crisis. A decline in labour productivity, a reduction of the labour share and a contraction in aggregate demand have been their major perverse effects. Finally, the chapter provides some suggestions about the directions in which labour market policies should evolve in order to enhance the chances of success in overcoming the crisis.

Pasquale Tridico's contribution, in Chapter 7, shows how the European Union, which employs different varieties of capitalism, and the United States, which operates based on a competitive capitalist model, are coping with the current economic crisis. He argues that although the EU is fragmented and needs to work towards better and deeper integration among member states, the main features of the European Social Model (ESM) allow for a more sustainable recovery and lessens the social costs. He proposes a new index (the Synthetic Vulnerability Index) which shows that the US position is worse than the Eurozone position in terms of social costs, recovery from the current crisis and of exposure to further crises. Nevertheless, he concludes that current financial reforms, both in the US and EU seem to be insufficient and the recent fiscal austerity measures seem to be moving the economies in the wrong direction.

The contribution of Kleinknecht *et al.*, in Chapter 8, question, first of all, the neoclassical assumption of a positive relation between labour productivity and economic growth and discuss several arguments why more rigid and long-lasting labour relations can be favourable to labour productivity and innovation. Among these are the argument that long-lasting contracts and fair HRM practices can be considered as an investment in loyalty and trust that prevent leaking of (technological) knowledge to competitors and reduce the need for monitoring and control. The need for monitoring and control of a flexible work force causes bigger management bureaucracies in "flexible" Anglo-Saxon countries. Rigid labour relations also favour (firm-specific) training, the accumulation of (tacit) knowledge and they strengthen the historical memory of a learning organization. Protected insiders in internal labour markets will also be more willing to reveal their "tacit" knowledge that is needed for the implementation of labour-saving technology. Good protection of insiders appears to be an institution that fits particularly well to the requirements of a Schumpeter II ("routinized") innovation regime. In general, the authors observe that flexible labour markets in Anglo-Saxon countries tend towards a more labour-intensive growth path but it is doubtful whether this results in lower unemployment rates.

Enrico Marelli and Marcello Signorelli, in Chapter 9, argue that a feature of financial crises is that they cause larger effects (compared to normal recessions), since the falls in production are accompanied by an increase in "systemic" uncertainty. They propose a model to detect this additional impact compared to that passing through GDP changes (Okun's law). The model is applied to data concerning a large panel of countries (period 1980–2005). It is able to distinguish the specific impact of particular types of financial crises. The empirical results are presented considering different scenarios of GDP change.

Notes

1 See Tridico (2012) for more details.
2 Media pointed out how an election in the small Lander of Lower Saxony in Germany during the Greek crisis in Spring 2010 was enough to keep German chancellor Angela Merkel far away from the idea of integration and financial solidarity, to which populists in Germany objected.
3 Capitalized words in brackets are added to the authors' metaphor of the tailor, to emphasize the interesting parallel with today's situation between China and the USA.

References

Aglietta, M. 1979. *A Theory of Capitalist Regulation: The US Experience*, London, Verso Classics.
Barba, A. and Pivetti, M. 2009. Rising household debt: its causes and macroeconomic implications – a long-period analysis, *Cambridge Journal of Economics*, vol. 33, no. 1, 113–37.
Basso, P. 1998, *Tempi moderni, orari antichi. Il tempo di lavoro a fine secolo*, FrancoAngeli, Milano.
Boyer, R. 2000. Is a finance-led growth regime a viable alternative to Fordism? A preliminary analysis, *Economy and Society*, vol. 29, no. 1, 111–45.
Caballero, R., Farhi, E. and Gourinchas, P.-O. 2008. An equilibrium model of "global imbalances" and low interest rates, *American Economic Review*, vol. 98, March, 358–93.
Cesaratto, S. 2011. Europe, German mercantilism and the current crisis, in Brancaccio, E., Fontana, G. (eds), *The Global Economic Crisis. New Perspectives on the Critique of Economic Theory and Policy*, Routledge, London.
Clelland, D.A. and Dunaway, W.A. 2010. The current economic crisis: What insights does the world system perspective offer? Paper presented at the Annual Meeting of the American Sociological Association, August 2010.
Cooper, R.N. 2007. Living with global imbalances, Brookings Papers on Economic Activity no. 2, 91–110.
Dowd, D. 2000. *Capitalism and its Economics: A Critical History*, Pluto Press.
Engelen, E. 2008. The case for financialization, *Competition and Change*, vol. 12, no. 2, 111–19.
EuroMemorandum. 2010. Confronting the crisis: austerity or solidarity, European Economists for an Alternative Economic Policy in Europe – EuroMemo Group, www.euromemo.eu.
Fitoussi, J.P. and Saraceno, F. 2010. *Inequality and Macroeconomic Performance*, Paris, OFCE, p. 13.
Frangakis, M. 2010. Rising sovereign debt in the EU – Implications for economic policy, Athens, Nicos Poulantzas Institute, www2.euromemorandum.eu/uploads/wg1_frangakis_rising_public_debt_in_the_eu_implications_for_economic_policy.pdf (accessed 1 December 2011).
Frank, A.G. 2005. The naked hegemon: why the emperor has no clothes? *Asia Time* (11 January) www.asiatime.com.
Greenspan, A. 2007. *The Age of Turbulence: Adventures in a New World*, London, Allen Lane.
Ivanova, M.N. 2010. Hegemony and seigniorage. The planned spontaneity of the U.S. current account deficit, *International Journal of Political Economy*, vol. 39, no. 1, 93–130.

Kindleberger, C. 2005. *Manias, Panics, and Crashes*, New York, Wiley & Son.

Krugman, P. 2008. *The Return of Depression Economics and the Crisis of 2008*, New York, Norton & Co.

Lipietz A. 1992. *Towards a New Economic Order. Postfordism, Ecology and Democracy*, Polity Press.

Lowenstein, R. 2010. *The End of Wall Street*, London, Penguin Press

Minsky, H.P. 1986. *Stabilizing an Unstable Economy*, New Haven, Yale University Press.

OECD 2010. Economic Outlook, www.oecd.org/document/18/0,3746,en_2649_34109_20347538_1_1_1_1,00.html (accessed 30 November 2011).

Petit, P. 2009. Financial globalisation and innovation: Lessons of a lost decade for the OECD economies, CNRS Working Paper No.: 2009–14.

Pontusson, J. 2005. *Inequality and Prosperity. Social Europe vs. Liberal America*, Ithaca and London, Cornell University Press.

Posner, R.A. 2009. *A failure of capitalism*. Cambridge, Harvard University Press.

Rueff, J., and Hirsch, F. 1965. The role and rule of gold: An argument, Princeton Essays in International Finance, no 47, Princeton University International Finance Section.

Semmler, W. and Young, B. 2010. Lost in temptation of risk: Financial market liberalization, financial market meltdown and regulatory reforms, *Comparative European Politics*, vol. 3, no. 3, 327–53.

Stiglitz, J. 2010. Recommendations by the Commission of Experts of the President of the General Assembly of United Nations on reforms of the international monetary and financial system. New York.

Tridico, P. 2012. Financial crisis and global imbalance: its labor market origins and the aftermath, *Cambridge Journal of Economics*, 36, 17–42.

Wallerstein, I. 2008. The Depression: A long-term view. Commentary No. 243, Fernand Braudel Center, Binghamton University.

Wallerstein, I. 2009. Crisis of the capitalist system: Where do we go from here? Harold Wolpe Lecture, University of Kwa Zulu-Natal, 5 November 2009. Online at Fernand Braudel Center, Binghamton University.

Wolff, R. 2010. *Capitalism Hits the Fan. The Global Economic Meltdown and What to Do About It*, New York, Pluto Press.

Wolfson, W. 2003. Neoliberalism and the social structure of accumulation, *Review of Radical Political Economics*, 35, 3, 255–62.

Wolfson, M. 1994. *Financial Crises. Understanding the Postwar US Experience*, Armonk, M. E. Sharpe.

Wray, L. Randall, 2000. *The Neo-Chartalist Approach to Money*. Center for Full Employment and Price Stability. URL: www.cfeps.org/pubs/wp/wp10.html.

Zhou, Xiaochuan, 2009. Reform the international monetary system. Essay by Dr Zhou Xiaochuan, Governor of the People's Bank of China, 23 March 2009. *BIS Review* 41/2009.

Part I
Capitalism in crisis
Nature and origins

1 Capitalism in deep trouble[1]

Richard Wolff

1 Capitalism and crises

Capitalism has had an extraordinary run in the world and nowhere more so than in the United States. Its celebrants demand and capitalism as a system deserves much credit for catapulting Britain's former secondary colony into a global economic, political and cultural super-power in 200 years. The costs of the ride were huge and widely distributed; the gains were also huge, but less widely distributed. Therein lay a first seed of trouble to come. Moreover, the long-term rise in real wages bred conditions and expectations that eventually outran capitalism's capacities to sustain them. Therein lay another seed. The former colony turned to immigration and to imperialism as key means of its ascendancy. Yet they also contributed to dependencies upon an evolving globalization of capitalism: another seed.

Underlying and amplifying all of these seeds of trouble was the basic structural soil of the capitalist system. Its internal contradictions, tensions and conflicts – ceaseless and unevenly developing antagonisms of labor and capital interwoven with the competitive struggles among capitalists – periodically generated downturns, crises, panics, cyclical booms and busts. Those were often moments of harsh but clear insights into the system's darker dimensions. Slowly they accumulated not only appreciation of its profound social costs and many victims, but also increasingly powerful anticipations of economic and social systems better than capitalism. Today yet again, in the wake of one of capitalism's deepest and longest crises, critical insight has been revived and sharpened. It builds on capitalism's history, its present dilemmas, and its critics' accumulated understanding.

Perhaps most importantly, the criticism of capitalism we can articulate today – as presented in Part I of this book – allows us more clearly than ever to envision a genuinely new solution. That solution not only overcomes many of capitalism's flaws and failures. It also learns from earlier efforts to go beyond capitalism which of its misunderstandings and resultant missteps to avoid. Together, the critique and the solution offer more hope for a breakthrough beyond a system in deep trouble than we have had for the last half-century.

Like all important topics, capitalism has been defined and understood quite differently by different people and groups throughout its history. That fact requires each user of the term to be clear and explicit about the particular definition being used. No one should proceed as if any one definition were either the only one or was a definition on which everyone agreed.

For example, many contemporary usages of "capitalism" – in the media, among politicians, and in academic treatments – focus on two key dimensions. The first is private property: capitalism is a system in which the means of production (land, tools, equipment, raw materials, etc.) and products (goods and services) are privately owned by individuals and enterprises. They are *not* owned collectively by society as a whole or by the state apparatus (representing, for example, society as a whole). The second dimension is the market: capitalism is a system in which productive resources and produced outputs are distributed by means of freely negotiated exchanges between their private owners. Distribution is not accomplished by means of the state's or any other collective agency's planned decisions. Thus, the twentieth century's great confrontation between "capitalism" and "socialism" was widely defined to be a struggle between private property and markets, on the one hand, and socialized property and government planning, on the other.

We do not use that popular definition in this chapter. A full discussion of the different definitions and of the arguments and disagreements among them would take us far afield. Instead, we will underscore some problems with the popular definition as an introduction to the different definition we use.

Private property is indeed a frequently encountered feature of capitalism. However, what most call capitalist economies also typically contain significant amounts of productive property and products owned by state apparatuses in the name of the society as a whole. In the US, for example, large tracts of land, harbors, air space, transportation facilities, military equipment, and educational institutions are publicly owned.

Likewise, markets are widely used mechanisms of distribution, yet what many call capitalist economies also include the distribution of goods and services in non-market ways. In the US, for example, food is distributed via food stamps issued to certain parts of the population, and many communities distribute park, fire, police and school services to citizens based not on market exchanges, but rather on local notions of citizens' needs. Inside most households, members produce all sorts of goods and services (cooked meals, cleaned clothes and rooms, repaired furniture, and so on) distributed to other household members according to traditional plans and procedures and not by means of market exchanges.

Private property and markets are also not features that distinguish capitalist from other types of economic system in human history. For example, the slaves in the non-capitalist economic system of the US south before the civil war were private property. Similarly, in many parts and periods of medieval Europe, the land, horses, plows and mills were often privately owned means of production, yet we refer to the economic system of that time as feudalism, not capitalism. Markets were also often features of slavery and feudalism as well as capitalism. For example, feudal lords often sold the produce of their serfs' labor in markets;

feudalism thus worked with a market system of distribution. Similarly, the cotton produced by slaves in the US south was regularly sold in world markets by means of exchange for money.

In short, private property and markets do not provide us with a clear demarcation between capitalism and, for example, slavery and feudalism as economic systems. Nor do we get much further if we try to deal with this problem by invoking individual "freedom." The idea here is that slaves lack freedom because they are property and serfs lack freedom because they are tied to their feudal manors, but workers in capitalism suffer neither of those lacks. Among problems with this definition is the widely noted fact that in capitalism wage workers are not free (other than formally, legalistically) because to live even minimally, they must work for others.

Because of these and many other difficulties, we define capitalism differently. Our distinctive focus will not be on property or distribution mechanisms or freedom. Rather we highlight the internal organization of production and distribution: how the social sites where goods and services are produced and distributed *organize those processes*.

A capitalist system is then one in which production and distribution are organized as follows: a mass of people – to be called productive workers – interact with nature to fashion both means of production (tools, equipment and raw materials) and final products for human consumption. They produce a total output larger than the portion (wages) given back to them. The wage portion sustains the productive workers: it provides their consumption and secures their continued productive labor. The difference between their total output and their wage portion is called the "surplus," and it accrues to a different group of people, the employers of productive laborers. We define the latter as capitalists.

The capitalists receive the surplus from the productive laborers by virtue of a wage labor contract entered into between capitalist and worker. This wage labor contract specifies a particular commodity exchange. The capitalist agrees to buy – pay the worker regularly for – his/her capacity to labor or labor power. The worker agrees to sell his/her labor power to the capitalist. The worker further typically agrees to use the tools, equipment, raw materials and space provided by the capitalist. Finally, the worker agrees that the total output emerging from his/her labor is immediately and totally the private property of the capitalist.

The productive laborers – those who produce the surplus – use the wages paid to them by the capitalists to buy the goods and services they consume and to pay personal taxes. The capitalists use the surplus they obtain from their productive employees to reproduce the conditions which allow them to keep obtaining surpluses from their productive employees. For example, they use portions of their surpluses to hire supervisors to make sure the productive laborers work effectively. They use another portion to pay taxes to a state apparatus that will enforce the contracts they have with their workers. They use yet another portion of the surplus to sustain institutions (churches, schools, think tanks, advertising enterprises) that persuade workers and their families that this capitalist system is good, unalterable, etc. so that it is accepted and perpetuated.

The workers who sign contracts with capitalist employers thus fall into two kinds. Productive laborers are those directly engaged in the production of the goods and services that their employers sell; their labor yields the surplus that employers receive and distribute to reproduce their positions as capitalists. The term "unproductive laborers" refers to all those engaged in providing the needed context or "conditions of existence" for productive workers to generate surpluses. The unproductive laborers have their wages paid and their means of work provided by capitalists. The latter distribute portions of the surpluses they get from productive laborers to pay and provision the unproductive laborers. The terms "productive" and "unproductive" differentiate wage workers into two groups: one that produces the surplus directly and one that provides the conditions for surplus production.

In short, the capitalist economic system divides people into three basic economic groups: productive laborers, capitalists and unproductive laborers. Just as the social context for the economic system – the politics and culture – shape and influence the economy, so the reverse also holds. To focus on a society's economic system – as this chapter does – does not mean that economics is any more important than politics, culture or nature in the interaction among them all that comprises each and every society. Our focus on the capitalist economic system is driven chiefly by the widespread neglect of that dimension of today's social problems and crises and our aim to rectify that neglect.

For the last half-century, the capitalist economic system in the US and indeed in many other parts of the world has gotten a free pass in terms of criticism and debate. Intense debates have swirled around *other* basic institutions or systems (marriage, schools, health care delivery, transportation, urban structure and so on). Criticisms about their current conditions and problems have informed proposals for changes ranging from the relatively minor to the fundamental. However, our economic system – capitalism – was almost entirely exempted as if some taboo precluded criticism. About the capitalist system, business and political leaders, mainstream mass media, and the bulk of the academic community substituted celebration and cheer-leading for serious criticism and debate. This was their response to the Cold War and even more an intrinsic part of the conservative resurgence after the Great Depression, New Deal and wartime US alliance with the USSR which frightened and galvanized them into reaction. They insistently treated capitalism as beyond criticism, debate, or basic change and demanded no less of others.

Critics of capitalism were marginalized. Laws were passed and conventions established that linked such criticism to disloyalty. Colleges and universities discriminated against such critics. Politicians competed in their adulations of capitalism and condemnations of all alternatives. Culture wars yielded purges of journalists, film-makers, playwrights and others suspected of sympathies with criticism of capitalism as a system. The post-1940s history of the US labor union movement shows the stark social consequences of punishing criticisms of capitalism. First, the state apparatus pressed successfully for the systematic rooting out of those union leaders and activists who dared to include criticisms of capitalism in their work. They were excoriated for "subversive" and "ideological" politics rather than doing their proper jobs of "serving their members." Yet, as most unions fell into line, they also declined in part because of repeated attacks on unions as a "special interest serving only its members" at the expense of the broader social good.

Criticism of particular capitalist enterprises or their particular practices did sometimes surface over the last half-century. Their monopolistic activities could be targeted, so too their racial and gender discriminations, environmental degradations, and even their corruption of political institutions. However, critics learned quickly to focus only on specific misbehaviors but not the economic system that induced, rewarded and thereby reproduced them. Many of the critical movements foundered or collapsed because their members who dared venture some criticism of capitalism as a system could not be tolerated by those determined to avoid such criticism at all costs. In contrast, the 2011 Occupy Wall Street movement broke with the traditional taboo as it clearly and consistently affirmed the legitimacy of criticizing capitalism as a system.

Like any social system long exempted from criticism and debate, the capitalist system deteriorated behind its protective wall of celebration. Big business subordinated the small when it did not eat them. Laws protecting labor and labor unions were amended, repealed or simply unenforced. Freedom came to be redefined as first and foremost the freedom of businesses to decide what, where, and how to produce *without interference from other parts of society.* The results of so long-lasting a pass on serious criticism and debate of the capitalist system are many and sobering. These include returns to levels of inequalities of wealth and income typical a century ago, consequent inequalities in the distributions of political power and access to culture, atrophy of government-provided social services and supports, multi-dimensional ecological crises and so on. Indeed, two central objectives of this book are (1) to show how the severe crisis since 2007 is partly another result of capitalism and (2) to help reopen the space for criticism of capitalism as a key step towards fundamental social change.

The capitalist economic system persists so long as labor contracts between capitalists and both productive and unproductive laborers provide acceptable quantities of surpluses to capitalists and employment and incomes to workers. Developments within the capitalist economic system and/or in its social and natural environment can disrupt – suddenly or gradually – the system's reproduction. Then unemployed workers, unutilized means of production and the resulting loss of output coexist – often for years – in a stunning reproach to capitalism's pretensions to efficiency, equity and progress.

Such disruptions are viewed by the masses of people in capitalist economies as "hard times" to be prepared for and endured. Capitalism's defenders fear disruptions as threats to the system. Capitalism's enemies treat them as opportunities for organizing workers to change or supersede the system. No wonder then that capitalism has evolved mechanisms to avoid, evade and respond to such disruptions.

Among these mechanisms have been government interventions that mix (1) rescue of capitalists by direct subsidies (direct investments, loans, loan guarantees, below-market exchanges and so forth), (2) moderation of mass suffering by provision of state support to the unemployed and others, and (3) regulations to reduce the most egregious of economic practices that aggravated the economy's development into the crisis. Simultaneously there are the ideological rationalizations of economic crises expressed in claims that they weed out the inefficient enterprises and thereby strengthen the economic system. Finally, there are the bold assertions by politicians that newly enacted reforms and regulations will not only extricate the society from a crisis but also prevent any recurrence of them.

2 Capitalism's instability and unevenness

Capitalism is a notoriously unstable economic system. Times of growth oscillate, often in extreme ways, with times of decline. It has always been so since capitalism replaced feudalism in Europe and expanded globally from there. Its oscillations took many names, from downturns, busts, deflations, contractions, recessions and depressions to upturns, booms, inflations, expansions and prosperities. Professional economists had to admit that capitalism displayed endemic "business cycles" but kept hoping that something might be done to prevent them or at least to keep them from undermining the system. Many economists built on the work of John Maynard Keynes' work to assert that the proper exercise of monetary and fiscal policies by government could realize that hope. Politicians took that assertion another step. In the US, every President who presided over a cyclical downturn promised that his economic interventions (his mix of monetary and fiscal policies) would not only end that downturn "but make sure we don't have another in the future." No politician and no policy mix in the history of capitalism has yet delivered on that promise.

Capitalism also develops unevenly across space and always has. Thus, the growth of wealth in some parts of the world entailed its opposite elsewhere. Every particular economic development path chosen has its winners and its losers. Over the same period of time, employers are often gaining while (and often because) employees are losing. This particular unevenness was a crucial contributor to the global capitalist crisis that erupted in 2007, as we shall show below. Merchants and manufacturers developing in urban areas often produced simultaneous devastation in rural agricultural areas. Competitive success of one company in one town devastated its rival companies and their towns. British capitalism's success was Indian civilization's crises and decline. Capitalist enterprises' recent explosive growth in China finds its counterparts in devastated former manufacturing zones of the US, much as earlier Europe's industrial revolution worked then to undo production systems in Asia.

Capitalism's uneven oscillations across time and space have always provoked complaints from those who suffered their results. The complaints could and often did evolve into criticisms of capitalism as a system and from there often to demands for change toward non-capitalist systems. The defenders and champions of capitalism sometimes responded with arguments that the causes of decline and underdevelopment were external to capitalism, not its fault. They blamed natural conditions (e.g., floods and droughts), political disruptions (e.g., wars and government interventions), or cultural patterns (e.g., inadequate entrepreneurship or savings behaviors).

The favorite and most enduring of such defensive arguments focus on state economic intervention as the key external cause of capitalism's problems. Thus, for nearly a century now, the dominant argument blamed capitalism's instability and unevenness on the government. Its economic interventions – taxation, expenditures and regulations of markets – were seen to be the culprits. The major counterargument – associated since the 1930s with Keynes, who focused on instability – sees the causes of capitalism's oscillations in culture (how individuals cope with uncertainty about the future and their "propensities" to consume and save) and how culture and economy interact. Thus Keynes and those influenced by him see government economic interventions as useful and necessary offsets to or cures for the capitalism-destabilizing interaction between culture and economics.

Yet since capitalism's instability and unevenness were continually reproduced across every variation of external natural, political, and cultural conditions, some of those defending the system felt compelled to find better arguments that did not rely on external causes. They sought to justify capitalism by insisting that its negative dimensions (e.g., cyclical downturns and underdeveloped areas) were simply the necessary prices to be paid for economic and social progress. They claimed that the gains of capitalism's winners were greater than what its losers lost and that therefore instability and unevenness were ultimately – in terms of their net social effects – *progressive*. Capitalism was thus an efficient system, notwithstanding its instability and unevenness.

Yet this notion of efficiency, much beloved by the celebrators of capitalism (and others too), is actually quite elusive. To know whether an economic system is efficient requires identifying and measuring all its effects, the positive that accrue to the winners, and the negative experienced by its losers. Yet no person or group can do or ever has actually done such a complete identification and measurement. The problem is quite simply that the costs and benefits of capitalism at any time are infinite in number and project long into a future we can never know in advance. Besides the unsolvable problem of identifying and measuring *all* of capitalism's direct and indirect effects, there is an additional and insurmountable problem. Whatever effects are identified and measured by an efficiency calculus are never the results only of capitalism as an economic system (that would be a grossly economistic or economic determinist claim). Those effects also have other causes (political, cultural and natural) too numerous to identify or measure. In short, the notion of measuring the efficiency of economic events or processes or of an economic system is a mirage. It is not possible to identify or measure all the effects of anything, nor is it possible to separate and weigh all the influences that combine to produce each effect. The very concept of efficiency would have been banished from discourse, let alone science, long ago but for its proven ideological usefulness. In that, efficiency resembles the medieval doctrines and debates concerning how many angels can dance on the head of a pin. Efficiency notions will also one day strike people looking back as comparably bizarre and absurd.

Capitalism's winners often face its losers' demands for compensation or for change to a system with a different pattern of winners and losers. To undermine or overwhelm those demands, the winners undertook "efficiency" studies, otherwise known as "cost–benefit analyses." These claimed to compare the total of benefits to the total of costs of the system and to then declare the system efficient if the total benefits exceeded the total costs. By undermining the losers' confidence in their own position or persuading those outside the immediate struggle between winners and losers, such efficiency arguments proved very useful to the winners. It has become common across the history of capitalism for such efficiency calculations to serve those campaigning for nearly everything imaginable: a change in interest or tariff or tax rates, allowance to build a highway, housing development, or mall on what was forest, regulation or deregulation of markets, and so on.

Of course, the unsolvable logical problems of these calculations required every calculator to select from among the infinite effects which subset would be identified and measured. No person or group could ever count the infinity of effects of any economic event, plan or system chosen for such efficiency studies. No one could ever know which are the most important effects to count without knowing that all those ignored are less important, and that is precisely what cannot be known. Efficiency studies proliferated as all sides in struggles over economic events, processes and systems resorted to them: each side commissioned its efficiency calculators to identify and measure its preferred subset of "most important effects" to reach the conclusion each side preferred. Each side's goal was to win over public opinion by claiming that what it preferred just happened also to be *objectively* the "most efficient" course to take. Each side insisted that what it wanted was the best in the sense that its social benefits maximally exceeded its costs. Elaborate calculations of costs and benefits suitably dressed in charts and graphs were the key props in the efficiency theater that provided ideological cover for the endless struggles attending capitalism's uneven development.

The usual winners in these struggles not only determined what economic event, plan or system would prevail and its actual development path, they also wrapped that path in the ideological mantle of "the most efficient" or "progress." Winning became a matter of overwhelming one's opponents' contradictory efficiency calculi. Absent strong social forces pushing the other way, winning usually resulted from devoting more resources to advertise, promote and purchase support for your efficiency calculus than your opponents did. However, strong social forces were not always absent. Capitalism's recurrent crises – and especially those that cut deep and endured for years – could and repeatedly did undermine the capitalist efficiency narratives of their times.

The efficiency argument for capitalism rings hollow when confronted by high and enduring unemployment affecting jobless millions and their relatives, friends and neighbors. Watching the growing absurdity of foreclosures creating both homeless people and empty homes is not conducive to an appreciation of capitalist efficiency. Nor is efficiency what springs to mind in the face of US government statistics that document the lasting co-existence since 2007 of unemployed people, underutilized productive capacity (tools, equipment, raw materials and buildings), and a society's urgent needs for new output (to rebuild neglected infrastructure and inner cities, to recover from capitalism's tragic – and hardly efficient – history of environmental degradation, to overcome endemic poverty and so on).

So powerful was the tradition of efficiency arguments for capitalism that even when capitalist crises undermined them, those arguments often resurfaced in the claims of capitalism's enemies. Socialists and communists often simply inverted the argument by insisting that it was socialism or communism that was efficient (or more efficient than capitalism) and thus represented progress. They too could and often did ignore the impossibilities of identifying and measuring all costs and benefits and of separating and evaluating each of the myriad influences that produced them. Such socialists and communists also discovered that when social forces pushed against them strongly enough, their efficiency arguments stopped succeeding. People became skeptical and eventually dismissive of those system's claims to efficiency much as happened to capitalism in its crises. The late twentieth-century end of the communist governments in eastern Europe followed a mass loss of confidence in claims for socialism's greater efficiency as compared to capitalism.

3 Welfare state capitalism, 1945–1970s

In the wake of the Great Depression of the 1930s and World War II, both the US and Europe turned dramatically from relatively laissez-faire to relatively state-interventionist sorts of capitalism. State authorities in most countries limited the powers and wealth of corporations and enhanced the wages and state support for people. State-interventionist capitalism "with a human face" replaced the more laissez-faire, harsher capitalism that had built up since the late nineteenth century.

From 1945 to the 1970s, state-interventionist capitalism was the norm with Keynesian economics its dominant theoretical frame of reference. Thereafter, until the crisis that broke in 2007, laissez-faire capitalism was the norm within a neoliberal ideological framework. The last half of the twentieth century was thus a paradigm example of the ceaseless oscillations within capitalism between more and less state-interventionist phases. In capitalism's current crisis, an ongoing struggle concerns the pace and form of the next possible oscillation. This time, however, the possibility of a break from capitalism's repeated oscillations to an altogether *other* economic system – different from both basic forms of capitalism – is stronger than it has been since at least the 1930s. This chapter is in part a response to that possibility.

The extremes of wealth and poverty produced in the 50 years before 1929 generated a critical response. So too did the wrenching transformation of rural and agricultural people into urban, industrial proletariats. Organized and militant trade unionism developed. So too did large and equally militant socialist and then communist political parties. While their developments were uneven (with reverses), they were large, strong, and unified enough to quickly become an important political force as the 1929 capitalist economic crisis deepened into a broader social crisis in many countries.

Thus, in the US, for example, that force transformed a rather conventional, centrist new democratic President, Franklin D. Roosevelt, into an active promoter of massive state-interventionist capitalism. In the depths of the Great Depression he found himself caught politically between the conservative, largely anti-state-interventionist business leaders and the de facto alliance of the Congress of Industrial Organizations (CIO), various Socialist and Communist Parties. That alliance demanded immediate and massive government relief for the depression-induced sufferings of average Americans. Militants within that alliance criticized capitalism as the dispensable cause of those sufferings as well as the 50 years of unequal and thus unjust development leading to the crisis.

Roosevelt's strategy took shape, he maneuvered deftly toward his "New Deal," and the result was a welfare state capitalism in the US from 1945 into the 1970s. To the masses and the union-leftist alliance he offered the following: give up your anti-capitalist, revolutionary politics and I will provide legal protections for unions, political legitimacy for leftist parties, and mass social welfare expenditures. Chief among the latter were the establishment of the Social Security System, the unemployment insurance program, and the direct hiring of over 12 million new federal employees between 1934 and 1941. To the capitalists he offered the following: give up significant portions of your personal and corporate incomes (in the form of increased federal taxes) to help pay for the federal government's new social welfare spending and accept the new legal protections for unions and legitimacy of left political parties. In exchange, Roosevelt promised to provide labor peace and a left political alliance committed to reforms and collaboration with the government and turned away from revolutionary anti-capitalism. Roosevelt also warned the capitalists that failure to accept the deal he offered would risk their having to cut a far less advantageous deal with the a CIO-Socialist-Communist alliance rising quickly across the country.

Roosevelt's strategy succeeded. The struggle within the alliance between revolutionary, anti-capitalists and reformers was decided for the latter. Coalition with Roosevelt and the Democratic Party around a reform agenda became the dominant politics of almost all parts of the CIO-Socialist-Communist alliance (although other parts maintained, with much difficulty, revolutionary attitudes and goals). The capitalists were split. One portion, supporting Roosevelt and his strategy, was sufficient to win over the political support needed to carry through Roosevelt's major commitments to establish a welfare-state capitalism. The other portion remained steadfastly opposed and immediately began a massive agitation against Roosevelt's New Deal. When the capitalists opposed to welfare-state capitalism lost, they commenced their version of a long march to undermine and then undo the New Deal in the decades after 1945.

Capitalism in deep trouble 29

Roosevelt's reward for crafting the broad coalition was to become the most popular president in US history. He won four consecutive elections, prompting the Republicans to pass a law limiting all future presidents to two consecutive terms. He overcame the limits to his federal employment program when World War II enabled him to provide jobs to the remaining unemployed millions either as military personnel or in private enterprises producing for the military. The war, like the New Deal, provided some immediate benefits to employers and workers alike.

The cumulative traumas of depression and war, from 1929 to 1945, profoundly shaped US history thereafter. The political, ideological and psychological commitments to a welfare-state capitalism were so vast and deep that it could not be questioned, let alone overturned. However, its opponents became more, not less, determined to do exactly that. On the one hand, they were deeply troubled by the growth of socialist, Marxist and communist thinking and organizations across US society under the benevolent allowance of the FDR administration. The war-time alliance with the USSR only deepened their concerns and fanned their paranoias. On the other hand, as fears receded that the end of the war might return the US economy into economic depression, ever more capitalists saw less need to support the welfare state form of capitalism. They allowed themselves more demands to re-establish the tax rates, anti-union laws and conditions, and anti-left ideological biases of the decades before 1929.

What became the prevailing theme of the post-war period was the capitalist strategy of destroying the New Deal coalition as prelude to rolling back (undoing) the welfare state it had achieved. The first major step was to break up the coalition by focusing attacks on the unions and the left political parties. The Taft–Hartley Act and the anti-communist witch hunts (of which McCarthyism was a part) were chief components of that first major step in the later 1940s and 1950s. An old political coalition was reformed among capitalists, the Republican Party leadership, and various conservative religious, racist, regional, media and patriotic organizations. This new right wing coalition led the way to break up the war-time alliance with the USSR as a key means to break-up the New Deal coalition and thereby undo the New Deal's achievements.

The new right did not always win. It suffered some divisions and splits in the face of the civil rights movement of African-Americans and the feminist movement thereafter. It also faced a broad cultural and political counterattack during the 1960s. Changing family conditions, attitudes and sexual mores have repeatedly produced other splits. Yet, the new right found a substantial glue to hold itself together in a revival of the peculiar American tendency to demonize government as the ultimate cause of all social evils. By insisting that the cure for those evils requires only the removal or elimination of government's intrusions on individual freedom, all components of the new right could agree on attacking the government.

For capitalists, this worked beautifully to focus animosity and opposition on the welfare state bequeathed by the New Deal to post-war generations. It allowed the summary demonization of unionists, socialists, communists, and a vast array of liberal reformers as undifferentiated proponents of state power, state-intervention, bureaucracy, state social engineering and state oppression. Each component of the new right coalition could and did define its goals in terms of opposing one or another state policy blamed for whatever problem it addressed.

Capitalists after 1945 were generally much more successful than other members of the new right coalition in achieving their goals. New Deal laws and regulations were increasingly evaded, weakened or repealed. The pre-1929 conditions of race, sexual, ethnic, religious and cultural relations generally were never comparably reconstituted; some were significantly altered in directions opposed by much of the rightist coalition. This has continually reproduced serious differences and tensions within that coalition.

From 1945 to the 1970s, the rightist attacks took their tolls. The rightist coalition grew, winning more adherents especially among business and upper income groups. They came in response to such victories as obtaining the Taft-Hartley restrictions on labor unions and shifting the burden of federal taxation from corporations to individuals and from upper-income individuals to middle income groups. Meanwhile, defeats of and defections – especially in the South – from the Democratic Party made it incapable or unwilling to defend the New Deal legacies. Tensions between a centrist and a progressive wing hardened into conflicts and splits. The New Left that arose in the 1960s was deeply critical of the Democrats as well as the Republicans.

The leftist surge across the later 1960s marked a major milestone in the demise of the New Deal legacy. On the one hand, it represented the protest – especially of younger Americans – against the long ideological and practical decline of that legacy across the later 1940s, 1950s and 1960s. On the other hand, that protest intensified its object. During the 1970s, the right reacted and over-reacted to the 1960s resurgence of struggles for just what the rightist coalition had been working to eliminate from US society. The culminating election of Reagan revealed shrinking working class support for a Democratic Party incapable of inspiring much hope because it could not even protect, let alone advance, New Deal gains. Reagan's election also represented the right's renewed confidence and determination to govern the next phase of US history.

The right coalition's agenda largely governed the US from the later 1970s to the Great Recession's beginning in 2007. The Republican Party led the way and the dominant center of the Democratic Party followed, albeit less harshly and more slowly. Thus, the more progressive wing of the Party (active within its labor union, African-American, student, and social-movement allies) became increasingly isolated and ineffective in terms of shaping policies. Civil rights and civil liberties were compromised, already existing anti-Soviet and anti-communist foreign policies were sharpened, and neoliberal economic policies imposed.

Much of the New Deal was systematically undone. Capitalism's previous oscillation, in the wake of the Great Depression, toward the rule of Keynesian economics, welfare states and social democracy, gave way in Reagan's election to a rapid, sustained oscillation in the opposite direction. Reagan and Thatcher rode that oscillation of capitalism back toward an Anglo-American, relatively more laissez-faire version of capitalism that came to acquire the name "neo-liberalism." The US and UK leaderships effectively reversed the post-1929 movement toward the more state-interventionist, social democratic version championed by the major continental European economies. Much as the Democratic Party in the US hesitantly followed the Republican Party's rightward lurches, so European social democracy moved slowly in the direction of the US–UK model of capitalism. Indeed, in both cases the shifts continued even when loud rhetoric proclaimed otherwise. In much of the rest of the world, too, parallel shifts were also under way.

These political shifts coincided with certain economic changes that had been building for quite a while: parallel surges in economic growth, the share of profits in national income, employers' profitability, and income and wealth gains disproportionately appropriated by the upper income groups. Much as the processes of laissez-faire capitalism had built to a crisis in 1929, so the processes of welfare state capitalism built to its crisis in the 1970s. We turn next to how the neoliberal capitalism from the 1970s to 2007 worked its way to its crisis.

4 Capitalism, 1970s–2007: the crisis building from below

The 1970s brought to an end over a century of rising average real wages in the US. It had been a remarkable run for workers unmatched by workers' experiences in any other capitalist country. So profitable had been US capitalism, so steady its workers' rising productivity, that capitalists could keep raising real wages to solve the US economy's major problem and thereby sustain capitalist growth. That problem was a labor shortage. From the beginning, as arriving Europeans ethnically cleansed the native population, the profit-possibilities of vast, fertile lands, good harbors, welcoming European markets and a conducive climate were endangered only by the problem of finding enough labor. Part of that problem was solved by the slave trade for the southern states. But the major part of the solution was immigration in wave after wave.

Real wages higher than workers got or could anticipate in many parts of Europe and rising real wages were key to inducing European immigrants. Not only were rising wages needed to get the immigrants, they were also needed to keep them as wage-earners lest they soon decamp from the eastern seaboard to the ample, nearly free lands of the US interior. There they might resume lives not so different from their European origins. For over a century before the 1970s, labor shortages were recurring problems and real wage increases recurring responses.

The profitability of US capitalism enabled it to pay rising real wages as well as sustain the costs of labor productivity growing even faster than wages. So profits rose too and the result was the century of dramatic US economic growth to the 1970s.

But in the 1970s, a set of broad economic changes coincided with the oscillation of US capitalism back from a relatively less to a relatively more laissez-faire phase to finally end the endemic US labor shortage. The key result was an end to rising real wages in the US. They have never had a sustained rise since. The impacts of the end of rising wages on the US economy were profound and contributed greatly to the crisis that began in 2007.

Real wages stopped rising because of changes on both sides of the labor market. Demand for workers declined in two major ways, while the supply of workers rose in two major ways. That combination of declining demand for workers and rising supplies of them ended the labor shortages, allowing capitalist employers everywhere to stop raising real wages. It was simply no longer necessary for them to do so.

The demand for labor in the US fell because the introduction of computers across the manufacturing and service industries in the 1970s and 1980s represented a sharp moment of automation in the US. The demand for labor also fell because of the simultaneous movement of manufacturing jobs out of the US to locations where workers could be hired for far less. The export of US manufacturing jobs took off in the 1970s and 1980s, followed by the export of service sector jobs (that took the name "outsourcing") that continues into the present.

Both of these economic developments were partly responses of US capitalism to a long period of rising real wages and partly to the post-war revival, by the 1970s, of real competitors for US capitalism especially in Europe and Japan. Real wage increases that had been affordable became competitive liabilities pushing US capitalists to seek profits as well as competitive advantages by substituting cheaper foreign workers for higher-wage Americans.

Just as these decreases in labor demands hit the US economy, two new groups of people were massively moving into the US labor market looking for jobs. First were millions of adult women who were changing their self-definition and their lives. Often this happened through participation in or response to the women's liberation movement that became socially powerful and influential in the 1970s. No longer satisfied with only traditional wives' roles, childcare and other unpaid household labor, many women sought and took part and full-time paid employment. The supply of labor surged as women by the millions entered it. Much the same happened as a new wave of immigration flooded into the US, this time mostly from Latin America (especially from Mexico and central America). Once again, capitalism's uneven development forced mass worker emigration from those area and the US was the most attractive destination.

The North American Free Trade Agreement that came into force in 1994 facilitated the entry of multinational US capitalists' exports into and investments in Mexico. This destroyed the livelihoods of millions of Mexicans, especially farmers and small shopkeepers. They faced unspeakable economic hardship unless they emigrated and that was facilitated by NAFTA. Mexico not only managed to export millions who no longer had decent job prospects in their native country, it also thereby acquired a massive cash inflow of remittances sent by Mexican workers in the US back to relatives and friends. NAFTA's benefits to Mexico accrued to a tiny top portion of Mexican employers, whereas its huge costs were more democratically distributed. The large economic disaster that these unequal consequences of NAFTA threatened were postponed for Mexico by the expedient of mass emigration and huge inflows of remittances. When, after the next capitalist crisis hit in 2007, the US housing industry dragged the whole economy into a long, deep downturn, millions of Mexican and other immigrants lost their jobs in the US and began returning to Mexico while, for the same reasons, the remittance flow to Mexico decreased. What emigration had postponed for Mexico – coping with the disastrous consequences of uneven capitalist development and NAFTA – the 2007 crisis in the US brought crashing back upon an utterly unprepared Mexico. That country quickly descended into a social disintegration documented by spirals of unemployment, drug industry explosion, police and government corruption, and daily news accounts of gruesome, violent social decline.

The combination of computerization, export of jobs, women surging into the labor market and a wave of Latino immigration ended the US history of rising real wages. Capitalists from Main Street to Wall Street quickly realized that when supplies exceed demands in the labor market, employers can slow or stop wage increases. Thus the average real wages of US workers stopped their long historic rise in the US in the later 1970s. Employers never needed to resume them in any sustained way since. Real wages today are roughly what they were over 30 years ago.

The end of the long US history of rising real wages has never been widely enough recognized nor sufficiently understood – in terms of its social significance – to obtain the public discussion and debate it merited. As the end of rising real wages settled as an ongoing feature of American life, it was a trauma for the working classes. For decades, American workers and their families had believed that hard work would yield a rising standard of living for the family, that each generation in this blessed land would live better than the one before. Something called the American Dream was within every working person's reach. An enduring labor shortage had been theorized into an American exceptionalism that focused on everything but that labor shortage. It insisted that America produced a unique capitalism that delivered a permanently rising standard of living to most workers because of reasons like climate, a culture favoring entrepreneurship, God's love, civil freedoms, and so on.

Working class parents promised themselves and their children better diets, clothing, housing, cars, appliances, higher educations, better recreation and vacations, and so on. Until the 1970s, rising wages had enabled workers to afford many of those things, to deliver on those promises. No wonder, then, that when real wages stopped rising no matter where or how hard one worked, workers were unwilling to give up, to default on those promises. Absent any national discussion of the changing labor markets and their social impacts, American workers tended to blame themselves for the end of their rising real wages; they felt individually responsible for what was actually a social problem, an economy-wide set of changes.

Correspondingly they sought and found individual responses ("solutions," they hoped) to what they believed were individual problems. If real wages per hour no longer rose, then American workers would do more hours of work per week, take a second or even a third job, and get other members of the household to do some regular paid work. All these individual responses happened in millions of families. Especially for American women, besides the women's liberation reasons to seek paid employment, new pressures developed to seek paid employment. Since their husband's stagnant wages alone could no longer afford the American Dream, the family needed the addition of wives' paid labor to provide the necessary household income. And across the last 30 years, especially women in middle and upper-income groups moved steadily and massively into the paid labor markets; most lower-income women had already been doing paid labor.

This post-1970 change in the conditions and lives of American women altered their families and households in ways that also altered US capitalism. Briefly, the mass movement of adult women, mostly married and with children, into paid labor, mostly full-time, transformed households and families. Wives and mothers had long had disproportionate responsibilities (relative to those of husbands) for maintaining the emotional integrity of the traditional nuclear family and the physical integrity of the traditional household. Even after those women undertook paid labor, they still performed the major parts of the emotional and physical labors involved in shouldering those responsibilities. Husbands either could not or would not take a significant portion of those responsibilities nor perform the corresponding emotional and physical labors. Women doing the "double shift" of workplace and household jobs simply could no longer devote the same time, energy and attention to maintaining the emotional life of the family and the physical chores of the household as they had before adding paid work outside the household to their job descriptions. Huge strains on families and households accumulated.

Divorce rates rose as tensions and strains within households mounted. Women brought home their job stresses to aggravate and be aggravated by their husbands'. Two incomes had to be conjointly allocated and two sets of job-related expenses covered. Children got less time and attention from parents. On American TV, situation comedies changed from celebrating the happy nuclear and patriarchal family of the 1950s and 1960s to laughing with compassion at the increasingly dysfunctional families of the last two decades. A historically unprecedented and growing proportion of the US population is choosing not to get married.

Flowing from these family and household changes, US consumption of all kinds of psychotropic drugs, legal and illegal, has soared. We became, in one revealing phrase, a "Prozac nation." Millions of family and household members felt acutely troubled that the support provided for them by these traditional institutions seemed to be dissolving. Churches, synagogues and mosques, and the Republican Party, sometimes separately and sometimes together, found that by championing a "return to family values" they could very effectively draw new adherents to their respective institutions. Women's former household labor (shopping, cooking, cleaning, and repairing clothes, appliances and furniture) was increasingly replaced by purchasing substitute commodities (prepared meals, cleaning services and disposable goods). Given the poor mass transit systems in the US, when wives and mothers took paid jobs, the family often needed to buy and maintain a second automobile.

The US economy adjusted to all these changes in family and household life that were themselves consequences of earlier economic changes (above all, the end of rising real wages). The prepared food industry zoomed; so too did pharmaceuticals and women's clothes as it was quickly discovered that housewives and mothers who took full-time paid work needed the appropriate wardrobes. The pornography industry grew fastest of all. As the manufacturing sector kept shrinking relative to the service sector, typically male-identified jobs declined relative to female-identified jobs. Males' real wages stagnated, became insufficient to yield the American Dream for their families, and necessitated wives entering paid employment. The stresses and strains of all these changes made many men feel diminished, unmanned and devalued. For many, pornography provided, in voyeuristic fantasy, the control, domination and manly success that their real lives had eroded.

Despite more hours of paid labor by more household members, the financial conditions of millions of households did not improve much. Women's entrance into paid labor had incurred a set of new costs that absorbed a major part of their additional income. Prepared meals cost much more than raw food, a second car sharply increased household expenses as did buying and cleaning women's workplace clothes for service sector jobs. Household maintenance became increasingly a cost covered by cash outlays rather than the product of household members' labors. The higher education of daughters finally became as important a family consideration as that of sons, and that too meant higher household expenses.

US families discovered that doing more hours of paid labor and covering the associated extra costs left too little net income to offset the impact of stagnant real wages. The American Dream threatened to move beyond their reach. Threatened with the prospect by slowing US consumption, advertisers intensified their association of personal worth and success with the extent of one's consumption of commodities. Without rising real wages and unable to earn enough more with extra hours of labor, US households turned en masse to the only remaining way to achieve the American Dream. In the last three decades, US consumers did a massive amount of borrowing and took on vast new household debt.

Mortgage debt soared, partly enabled by rising home prices and partly contributing to those rising home prices. More borrowing to buy homes increased demand for them and thus their prices. As prices rose, home-owners could refinance and borrow more against the increased collateral their rising home values represented. It was a wonderful "virtuous circle" that yielded a housing expansion and the economic upturn that it fueled. When the Federal Reserve, anxious about a recession after September 11, 2001, lowered interest rates far and fast, the housing expansion became a housing boom and bubble. When that broke in 2007, the virtuous circle turned into a vicious circle of falling housing prices reinforcing declines in mortgage credit and home foreclosures that further depressed housing prices. The housing industry's depression from 2008 onwards has been a major cause of the depth and duration of the economic crisis, making it the worst since the Great Depression of the 1930s.

Other forms of personal debt zoomed as well. The credit card was transformed in the 1970s from a non-debt-accumulating convenience for business and elite travellers to a debt-accumulating necessity for nearly everyone. As working families increasingly needed two cars to enable multiple members to do paid work, auto loans became important components of household debt. Finally, higher education for multiple children – deemed a necessity for future job and income prospects – attached mounting levels of debt to students. Unprecedentedly high and rising consumer debt in all these forms became a basic fixture of the US economy in the new millennium. Widely quoted statistics showed that when the Great Depression hit in 1929, the average US family had debts roughly equal to 30 percent of its annual income. In 2007 the comparable number was well over 100 percent.

Across the 1980s, 1990s and to 2007, US families worked and borrowed ever more, while real wages stagnated. Households accumulated physical exhaustion from added paid labor, emotional and psychological stresses from changing labor and gender roles, and mounting anxiety about accumulated levels of debt that could not be sustained. This mix of working class responses to the end of rising real wages had postponed the national reckoning with the significance, implications and social costs of that ending. However, when those households could no longer manage the costs of that postponement, when they began defaulting on their debts, the system crashed. But the crash was not only or mainly caused by a working class that could no longer earn, borrow or spend more.

5 Capitalism, 1970s–2007: the crisis building from above

The crash also resulted from the huge financial speculations that employers, top executives and professionals had built up on the foundation of consumer debt. The mechanism here was straightforward. First, banks packaged consumer debts (mortgages, credit card debt, auto loans and student loans) into a new kind of financial investment: asset backed securities (ABS). Where regular stocks and bonds were investments in and thus claims upon companies that produced goods or services, the ABS were different. The ABS gave those who bought them a claim on the principle or interest payments of consumer loans. Those who invested in ABS got in return a portion of the regular flow of consumers' payments servicing their debts. Successful businesses (especially but not only in the financial industries) and wealthy individuals (often business executives and professionals serving businesses) were the main investors in ABS.

To understand where ABS investors got the money to invest in and thereby fuel the explosion of ABS leading up to the crash of 2007, we need to briefly explore yet another consequence of the stagnation of real wages since the 1970s.

While real wages stayed flat, worker productivity rose steadily over the last 30 years. Workers in the US were better educated, worked with more and better machines (computerization), and were worked harder and faster over those years. They steadily produced more output (in goods and services) per hour year after year. Meanwhile, their employers did NOT pay them higher real wages; those wages stagnated across those years.

As a result, the gap grew between what employers paid workers per hour and what workers produced for their employers per hour. That gap showed up as employer profits. Since real wages stayed flat as productivity kept rising, so too did profits keep climbing. Such a profit scenario in turn prompted an historic peacetime boom of the stock market. The top executives of US corporations, the smaller businesses and professionals who served them, and the owners of stocks in those enterprises became very wealthy. A culture of the rich developed in which they competed in terms of lavish lifestyles but also in terms of finding profitable investments for their accumulating financial wealth. Hedge funds proliferated as businesses focused on helping these new rich find profitable investments to become yet richer. And one major new profitable investment they promoted were ABS.

So now, by following the money, we can grasp the economic interconnections that drove world capitalism into crisis. First, stagnant real wages and rising productivity sharply altered the distribution of income and wealth in favor of profits and the rich. Second, the working class responded by borrowing vast sums to postpone the end of rising consumption that would have happened had they relied on their wages. Third, employers and the rich lent back to the workers (via ABS) a portion of the extra profits they made from real wage stagnation. For 30 years these interconnections generated sufficient satisfactions – rising debt-based consumption for the masses and rising wealth for the employers and the rich – to reproduce itself. But it did so on an unsustainable foundation.

A pyramid of speculations was erected on the ABS – as ever more profit-based incomes piled into them – and on their allied financial instruments such as the peculiar ABS insurance policies called credit default swaps (CDS). Ever greater risks were taken as hedge funds and banks competed for returns with which to lure the investments from those who kept accumulating profits. Alongside rising investor risks of ever more wealth, workers' rising debt levels combined with stagnant real wages to erode their capacity to service those debts. So when that capacity was exhausted, the workers defaulted. So did the major banks and many of those who had issued and owned ABS, CDS and other speculative instruments whose worth was tied, directly or indirectly, to the values of workers' debts. Very quickly, the capital markets, increasingly interconnected across the world by the previous decades of globalization, spread the US credit collapse to everywhere else. Before, they had facilitated marketing toxic ABS, CDS and related investments around the globe; they equally facilitated the globalization of crisis.

6 A digression on what or whom to blame

Capitalism had driven workers and capitalists to play the roles assigned to them by the system that defined their positions. All the players sought to reap the system's rewards and avoid its penalties, to take the necessary risks and pay the necessary costs to enjoy the system's benefits. Capitalism had also assigned the state its roles in supporting and undergirding certain activities, regulating other activities, and preventing certain excesses. State officials performed these functions, just as workers and employers performed theirs.

Did some perform badly, become corrupt or do both in some indecipherable combination? No doubt, but that was true in both capitalism's upswings and downswings. Because of the durability and social influences of anti-statism on the right and left, many have been tempted to attack some or all state institutions or officials (or state-private partnership institutions and officials). Rightists see in the state's activities the roots of most evils including cycles and crises. The Nobel laureate and economist, Milton Friedman, explained and blamed the Great Depression as the result of governmental economic interventions. Republicans often claim that Democrats in Congress or the White House spend and borrow excessively yielding deficits and cycles. Leftists usually prefer to target one or another part of the state and especially state-private institutions. For example, one favorite target of the left (and of the right as well) has been the Federal Reserve System for mismanaging the monetary system in favor of bankers' interests yielding both crises and unjust governmental bailouts. Democrats likewise blame Republicans in Congress or the White House for failing to grasp Keynesian insights, failing to undertake countercyclical deficit spending, and thereby worsening and prolonging economic crises and their massive social costs. The Nobel laureate and economist, Paul Krugman, analyzes the US and European governments' responses to the post-2007 capitalist crisis in just such terms.

These arguments on left and right are peculiar. We are asked to believe that different parts of the state apparatus and different subgroups of state officials work to undermine the capitalist system. Were they not created within and continuously shaped by the capitalist system in ways that celebrated and justified reproducing that system? Somehow, in these arguments, the rest of us were properly socialized into the capitalist system, but they were not. The behavior of state institutions and officials disrupted the smooth, non-cyclical reproduction of capitalism. Otherwise our behavior would have accomplished just that reproduction. Private businesses and individuals respond appropriately and successfully to the signals, risks and rewards of capitalism, whereas the state does not.

State interventions in capitalist economies were crucial to their beginnings and early growth, have been continuous ever since, and, over the longer historical span, have mostly grown absolutely and relatively. Over the same time, the focus on the state as the rogue, disruptive part of the entire system has long attracted those who, for various reasons, cannot bear to question, criticize or even debate changing the capitalist system as a whole.

Another rogue actor within the capitalist system blamed for its cycles has been "the criminals." Those illegally gaming the system are depicted daily in capitalism's mass media and denounced by the appropriate authorities. They range from the insider trader near the top to the underpaid secretary who embezzles to the syndicate that runs whole industries or cities. Their illegal economic activities happen all the time, and if they happen more during crises, it is likely that the pressures on people then exceed those when prosperity reigns. Criminal activities are thus more effects than causes of capitalism's cycles. Yet historical and contemporary records overflow with blame variously heaped on illegal acts of financiers, corporate executives, corrupt state officials, union leaders and "organized crime" for causing capitalism's cycles and crises.

The focus on misbehavior by the state or by criminals is rather the attempt, conscious or not, to avoid blaming the system and its rules and regulations, its structure of rewards and penalties. Pinpointing the bad guys revives the ancient art of scapegoating. Our perspective is rather that the system is the problem. It offers mixes of risks and rewards that explain and drive most of the behaviors of workers, consumers, entrepreneurs, capitalists, state officials and criminals.

Every individual and business ever blamed for contributing to capitalism's recurring crises has defended their actions by explaining how they were just participating in the economic system, responding to its signals and trying to succeed. For centuries and in every capitalist country, some individual economic actors (workers, employers, etc.) have been charged, convicted and imprisoned for violating some law, and businesses have been terminated for parallel reasons. Those who replaced them sooner or later replicated their behaviors. For example, long before Charles Dickens' 1857 novel *Little Dorrit* and through the later escapades of its namesake to the stunning multi-billion dollar Bernard Madoff enterprise exposed a few years ago, Ponzi schemes kept happening across capitalism's history. Their sizes enlarged in step with capitalism's growth. Capitalism produced those Ponzi schemes. It likewise produced the laws and prosecutions aimed to stop them. But perhaps most tellingly, capitalism also proved incapable of preventing the recurrence of Ponzi schemes in economic upswings and downswings

The slave and feudal systems that preceded capitalism no doubt contained and fostered their sorts of crimes and criminals responding to their mixes of risks and rewards for economic behaviors. Those systems likewise often displayed powerful states that actively intervened in their economies. However, those systems never displayed the recurring cycles common to all capitalisms.

Those cycles are thus products of capitalism. They ought not to be blamed on this or that group (the state, criminals, others) functioning within and in response to that system during its upswings and downswings. Capitalist societies can continue to monitor, identify and prosecute economic misbehaviors, but doing so never will prevent cycles and crises; it never has. To overcome the systemic roots and nature of capitalist crises requires system change.

Note

1 This chapter appeared first in the book of Richard Wolff, *Democracy at Work. A Cure for Capitalism* (Part 1, Chapter 2). Published by Haymarket Books, September, 2012.

2 The North Atlantic financial crisis and varieties of capitalism

A Minsky and/or Marx moment? And perhaps Max Weber too?

Bob Jessop

1 Introduction

This chapter poses four sets of questions that bear more or less directly on the North Atlantic financial crisis and its wider economic, political, and social repercussions.[1] First, what kind of evolutionary and institutional political economy is best suited to explain normal and crisis periods in economic development, their alternation, forms of crisis-management, and failures of crisis-management? I argue for a heterodox approach that recognizes the improbability of stable capital accumulation, identifies crisis-tendencies and the challenges of crisis-management, and analyses why crisis-management tends to fail. Second, are different varieties of capitalism (hereafter VoC) more or less crisis-prone and is one variety more responsible for the North Atlantic crisis with its global repercussions than others? Here, while noting that each variety has its own crisis-tendencies, I argue that this crisis is rooted in a neo-liberal variant of the liberal market economy – compounded by speculation, control fraud, financial 'criminnovation',[2] and other forms of predatory and/or political capitalism. Yet I also note that the uneven global impact of the crisis is linked to the current forms of integration of varieties of capitalism into the world market.

Third, can the financial crisis be explained through the autonomous role of money and credit relations in crisis dynamics without regard to the circuits of productive capital? Here, noting that the outbreak of the crisis has often been described as a 'Minsky moment', I affirm the relevance of his approach but seek to show its limits, both in general and for the current crisis. Fourth, can the crisis be explained in middle-range institutional terms or is it linked to the abstract possibilities of crisis inherent in foundational contradictions and dilemmas of the capitalist world market? Here, whilst affirming that institutions matter and merit a critical institutional analysis, I suggest that some neglected theoretical resources in Marx's critique of political economy can be reworked to explain some key features of the current crisis. In this sense, the North Atlantic crisis can also be seen, and more significantly so, as a Marx moment. But I also preserve a special place for Max Weber in this account.

2 On evolutionary and institutional political economy

It is a commonplace among heterodox scholars that 'mainstream economics, an organized bulwark against radicalism, filters out all theories that do not meet two requirements: that they must view capitalism as eternal, and crisis as external' (Freeman 2010: 89; cf. Dymski 2009: 66; Moseley 2009: 15; Shaikh 1978). An evolutionary political economy that takes seriously the historical specificity of the capitalist mode of production would reject the universalizing, transhistorical, and, consequently, ahistorical categories and assumptions deployed in mainstream economics. Moreover, by moving from the initial abstract-simple categories of a critique of political economy through to more concrete-complex categories, it can locate the abstract possibilities of crisis in the basic forms of the capital relation (form analysis) and move to more institutionalist accounts of how crisis-tendencies are actualized in specific periods and/or types of capitalism in the world market. Such an analysis is more likely to produce a multi-dimensional, multicausal approach to crisis tendencies and so provide better grounds for periodization and conjunctural analysis. This has implications not only for explaining the crisis-tendencies of capitalism even when it appears crisis-free but also for the resulting problems of crisis-management.

Various forms of heterodox economics (but not all) adopt such an evolutionary and institutional approach. This chapter develops an approach that combines critical political economy and critical semiotic analysis to facilitate: (1) an ideological critique of dominant economic and political categories, including their emergence, naturalization, reification, vulgarization, and penetration as 'common sense' into everyday life; (2) an analysis of differential accumulation, its crisis-tendencies and counter-tendencies, the alternation between capitalism *en régulation* and more or less chronic states of crisis and economic emergency; and (3) a critique of domination (*Herrschaftskritik*) concerning the power dimensions of differential accumulation, their articulation to political and ideological domination, and the extent to which other societal spheres are penetrated by the capital relation. Combining these interests involves moving from critical form analysis through critical institutionalism to the specific forms of appearance of structural contradictions and strategic dilemmas and, then, to the ways in which economic (and other) forces handle these dilemmas in specific conjunctures. Regarding crisis-management, this means studying: (a) how crises emerge when established patterns of dealing with structural contradictions, their crisis-tendencies, and strategic dilemmas no longer work as expected and, indeed, when reliance thereon may aggravate matters; and (b) how contestation over the nature of the crisis shapes actors' responses through processes of variation, selection, and retention that are mediated through a changing mix of semiotic and extra-semiotic mechanisms.

An ideal approach, which is admittedly hard to implement, would follow Marx's six-book plan for his eventual critique of political economy. The plan started with capital and moved, successively, to labour, landed property, the state, foreign trade, and the world market and crises. Like much of his work, this outline regards the world market both as the presupposition and posit (result) of differential accumulation. One implication is that, while the analysis would begin with the *abstract possibilities of crisis* inherent in the capital relation, a comprehensive account of *actual crises on a world scale* would depend on satisfactory treatment of the topics intended for other books. This would involve moving from basic forms of the capital relation, their contradictions, crisis-tendencies, and dilemmas to historically and institutionally specific mediations and, equally importantly, to the changing balance of forces up to a world scale. It should move beyond 'pure economics' to cover economic and extra-economic relations. For Marx also showed how capital accumulation depends on various non-market mechanisms within and beyond the profit-oriented, market-mediated economy. But these mechanisms cannot prevent 'market failures' or correct them automatically and without repercussions. Indeed, the mixes of economic and extra-economic conditions conducive to accumulation are opaque, indeterminate, and variable. This sets important cognitive and institutional limits to solving coordination problems and helps to explain the trial-and-error nature of efforts to regularize and govern differential accumulation. I return to this topic below.

2 Varieties of capitalism

It is widely recognized that there are many forms of capitalism. Indeed, as Minsky observed: 'The Heinz Company ... used to have a slogan "57 varieties" [and] I used to say that there are as many varieties of capitalism as Heinz has pickles' (1991: 10). There are also many ways to explore these multiple forms and their interaction. This is reflected in the range of taxonomies, sets of ideal-types, empirically-based cluster analyses, and logical-historical analyses that have been developed over 150+ years. One typology that is rarely cited by economists was developed by Max Weber, who distinguished six modes of capitalist orientation to profit (Weber 1961; cf. Swedberg 1996). They are: (1) traditional commercial capitalism, based on traditional types of trade or money deals; three modes of political capitalism, based respectively on (2) predatory political profits, (3) profit on the market from force and domination, and (4) profit from unusual deals with political authority; and two modes of rational capitalism, based on (5) rational calculation of opportunities for profit in the market from trade in free markets and capitalist production, with the basis of calculation being the likely impact on balance-sheets; or on (6) trade and speculation in money and credit instruments. Rational capitalism is, remarkably, the analytical focus of Marx and mainstream economics alike. However, whereas Marx focused his form-analytical critique on the historically specific, antagonistic, and contradictory nature of rational capitalism, mainstream economics proposes formal models on the assumption that rational capitalism is universal, harmonious, and self-equilibrating. Whilst broadly accepting Marx's approach as the starting point for an analysis that does not presume that capitalism is eternal and crises are external, I suggest that all of Weber's six modes belong in an inclusive analysis of the world market and crises.

Much recent heterodox evolutionary and institutional political economy has explored the varieties and/or diversity of capitalism – with those interested in varieties inclining towards parsimony (with their numbers in single figures rather than reaching 57 or more!) and those interested in diversity emphasizing plurality, heterogeneity, and hybridity. While these approaches (plus cluster analysis) have their uses, the following analysis relies on a logical-historical approach that moves between conceptual elaboration and historical investigation to show how abstract possibilities are translated into actual dynamics. And, given its eventual concern with the world market and crises, it introduces the idea of 'variegated capitalism' to capture the interaction of forms of capitalism in the world market viewed as the ultimate horizon of economic and political calculation about differential accumulation.

Indeed, its increasing integration makes it especially inappropriate to study the world market in terms of a mechanical juxtaposition and interaction of 'varieties of capitalism'. There are four main grounds for this. First, this approach is overly concerned with distinct (families of) national models of capitalism, treating them as rivals competing on the same terrain for the same stakes. This is especially problematic given the long-term trend towards greater world market integration. For capital accumulation on a world scale depends on reproducing the diversity – hence *variegation* – of accumulation regimes within the world market. This variegation is not reproduced through mechanical repetition but through continuing re-organization based on the structural coupling and co-evolution of co-existing varieties of capitalism. This trend points to an emerging *single, but fractally[3] organized, variegated capitalism* rather than a more or less enduring set of *national varieties* of capitalism. Second, these alleged varieties are often studied in terms of their respective forms of internal coherence on the fallacious assumption that they can be investigated in relative isolation from each other. Yet the scope for rivalry, antagonism, complementarity, or co-evolution among ways of organizing capitalism also matters greatly for world market dynamics. It is important to identify and explain zones of relative stability in terms the complex 'ecology' of accumulation regimes, modes of regulation, and spatio-temporal fixes – noting how more stable regimes defer and/or displace contradictions and crisis-tendencies into the future and/or into zones of relative incoherence, instability and even catastrophe.

Third, locating conventional VoC in a globally variegated capitalism highlights the connection of relatively successful performance in certain economic spaces not only to their external and internal conditions of existence but also – and crucially – to the costs they impose on other spaces and future generations. Fourth, the VoC literature tends to assume that all VoC are equal and that, if one proves more productive and progressive (or less inefficient and exploitative) than others, then it could (and should) be adopted elsewhere and, indeed, everywhere, with the same results, as if the whole world economy could be organized along the same lines. This is inherently implausible given the complexities of the global division of labour and the diversity of material, institutional, and sociocultural conditions associated with different kinds of specialization. In sum, rather than studying individual varieties of capitalism, we should study their variegated articulation and co-evolution in a wider ecology that is both the presupposition and posit (result) of accumulation on a world scale.

This account improves on two alternative claims, namely: (1) there are only separate VoC that co-exist within a differentiated world economy; or (2) there is a single world system that, operating through the logic of capitalist competition, tends to drive all capitals and their associated 'space economies' to converge around a single model. But recognizing 'variegated capitalism' is only a first, albeit important, step to analyzing the world market. For the latter tends not only to connect particular branches of capitalist production and their different forms of social (dis)embedding but also to link them, positively or negatively, with pre- or non-capitalist forms of production. Relevant here are subsistence production, petty commodity production, household production, informal productive and reproductive labour. These are connected in the world market through the increasing dominance of accumulation on a world scale. Indeed, the more strongly integrated is the world economy, the stronger do the contradictions of capital accumulation operate on a world scale. This has both positive and negative effects through the dynamics of uneven and combined development as spur and fetter for differential accumulation.

This provides a new way of thinking about Marx's claim that the world market is the arena where all relevant forces interact. This did not imply a singular logic operating with singular directionality at the level of the world market (the mistake made in cruder versions of world system theory). Instead Marx regarded the world market as the most developed mode of existence of the integration of abstract labour with the value form – 'the place in which production is posited as a totality together with all its moments, but within which, at the same time, all contradictions come into play' (Marx 1973: 227). In short, the ultimate theoretical and practical horizon for engaging with capitalism should be 'variegated capitalism' at the level of the world market.

3 A Minsky moment?

Given these comments, how might we explain the North Atlantic crisis? For such a complex phenomenon, there is no easy but compelling answer, although many have tried to provide one. Several commentators predicted the North Atlantic crisis in terms drawn from heterodox post-Keynesian analysis à la Minsky and several business analysts and journalists referred to the tipping point into crisis as a Minsky moment. This seemed plausible because the crisis first surfaced on the economic scene in a manner that could be described in Minskyan terms as the collapse of the Ponzi stage of a financial cycle. Let us consider the case for this interpretation.

Minsky (1919–1996) was a financial Keynesian who is best-known for the idea that 'stability is unstable' or, better, that 'stability is de-stabilizing'.[4] But his work also covered many other topics. These included: the periodization of capitalism (commercial, then financial, then 1933–1937 New Deal welfare, and, most recently, money manager capitalism[5]), with each having its own crisis dynamics related to specific institutional features of the real and financial economies; poverty and full employment policy (with government proposed as the employer of last resort for the unemployed at the minimum wage); the role of big government in contemporary economies; the importance of narrow banking; and the contribution of community banks to local economic development and social solidarity.

According to Minsky's financial instability hypothesis, unusually long periods of relatively stable growth encourage false optimism. This leads economic actors to borrow excessively and to pay inflated prices for assets. Prudent investors who had hitherto engaged only in *hedging* finance (in other words, who expected to meet all their debt obligations, i.e. interest and principal, from reliable cash flows) become less risk averse and/or new investors are seduced to enter financial markets using borrowed money. This is the stage of *speculative* finance in which interest payments can be met from cash flow but capital repayments now depend on asset appreciation – with the result that, if economic movements do not turn out as anticipated, speculative borrowers may have to take fresh loans to repay the original loan. A third stage begins with *Ponzi* finance when even the repayment of interest depends on continuing asset price inflation that enables Ponzi borrowers to refinance a debt whose eventual repayment is always being postponed. Over the course of a cycle, huge portfolios of financial instruments are accumulated and levered and an increasing proportion of these portfolios are based on Ponzi finance. Minsky also noted that, over the course of a financial cycle (from hedging through speculative to Ponzi finance), financial institutions, which also become less risk averse, engage in financial innovation to get round regulations and prudential controls intended to prevent speculative frenzies because they expect the boom to last (Minsky 1992). This observation has been elaborated by Thomas Palley, based on Minsky's own insights, into a theoretical model of Minsky 'super-cycles', i.e. a series of hedging to Ponzi financial cycles, with each successive cycle resolved through bailing out the most indebted borrowers, so that, when the next cycle begins, moral hazard has been reinforced, the purgative effects of crisis have not been allowed to work themselves through, and financial innovation to avoid regulation has been consolidated (Palley 2011; also Minsky 1995, Moseley 2009).

A *Minsky moment* is the point in a business and or credit cycle when overindebted investors are forced to sell good assets to repay their loans, causing sharp declines in financial markets and hikes in the demand for cash. This leads in turn to a liquidity and even solvency crisis, which can force central bankers to extend credit (Minsky 1975, 1982, 1986, 1995). The result is a one-sided sellers' market and market collapse – sometimes called a 'Minsky meltdown' – unless bankers or other economic actors come to the rescue.

A 'Minsky moment' was not a term employed by Minsky himself (although it is implicit in his work) but is generally attributed to Paul McCullery of PIMCO, a global investment manager, who used it to describe the 1998 Russian financial crisis. It was adopted in 2007 by George Magnus, a senior economic adviser at

UBS and regular media economic pundit, to describe the outbreak of the North Atlantic crisis and warn that the crisis could well spread far beyond the mortgage market thanks to the preceding euphoria and the interconnectedness of markets (2007a, 2007b). Indeed, more and more market sectors were discovered to be directly involved in, or exposed to contagion effects from, Ponzi finance – which included not only those who took out sub-prime loans in 2005 and 2006 but also those who took second mortgages to finance consumption or investments, leveraged hedge and private equity funds and their investors, other highly leveraged investment banks, over-invested unit trusts with tiny cash reserves to meet redemptions, and speculators trading on margin in shares, bonds, and commodities. The result is many forced sellers in major asset markets: foreclosures, margin calls, redemptions (Financial Reality 2007). And this can introduce a downward spiral as more borrowers resort to distressed sales (even of good rather than toxic assets) to meet creditors' demands. This could lead to a debt-default-deflation crisis of the kind analysed in the Great Depression by Irving Fisher (1933) and, later, by Minsky (1995) and Rasmus (2010).

More recently, worries have been voiced about new Minsky moments. Magnus returned to the fray in May 2011 with worries about a *Chinese Minsky moment*. This threat is evident, he said, in the Chinese economy's dependence on investment for growth (47 per cent of GDP in 2011), of which around half went to property investment. Still more worrying, he argued, is that this investment is based on increased borrowing, leading to dependence on growing credit-intensity (the amount of credit expansion required to generate a given increase in output). Magnus cautioned that

> a Chinese Minsky moment would hit global growth and resource markets, and shock the consensus about steady appreciation of the *renminbi*. It would also undermine China's aim of rebalancing its economy towards consumers; and raise the risk of political unrest.
>
> (Magnus 2011)

In December of 2011, another PIMCO analyst raised the spectre of an impending *Minsky moment in the Eurozone and European Union* more generally (Parikh 2011). In the same month, the Governor of the Bank of Canada, Mark Carney, declared that a *global Minsky moment* had arrived. In an official speech, he emphasized the great challenge that confronts the world economy as crisis-managers seek growth while trying to reduce debt. As debt tolerance has turned decisively, '[t]he initially well-founded optimism that launched the decades-long credit boom has given way to a belated pessimism that seeks to reverse it'. He continued that '[c]urrent events mark a rupture. Advanced economies have steadily increased leverage for decades. That era is now decisively over' (Carney 2011: 4).

Minsky's financial instability thesis and its culmination in a crisis of Ponzi finance resonated strongly in this conjuncture and the term 'Minsky moment' became as contagious as panic in periods of financial fragility. It was adopted in many quarters, being employed by bloggers, leader writers, and journalists in the quality press (e.g. *Financial Times, Frankfurter Allgemeine Zeitung, Le Monde Diplomatique, La Repubblica, The Wall Street Journal*), and business channels such as Bloomberg, Business News Network, and CNBC (for examples, see Cassidy 2008, Chancellor 2007, Lahart 2007, and, in more academic terms, Whalen 2007). This led *The Economist* to describe the crisis as a whole as 'Minsky's moment' (Buttonwood 2009). Indeed, he was 'a cult hero among more bearish commentators after his model of a credit-driven asset-bubble, proposed back in the 1970s, was almost uncannily played out shortly after he died' (Wilson 2007).[6] Ivanova has also suggested that, for Wall Street insiders, 'Minsky's moment' is linked to the utility of his instability theorem in explaining the inevitability of financial crises and the consequent need to rescue banks deemed too big and/or interconnected to fail (2011: 21).

Interestingly, Minsky himself thought it unlikely that 'it' would recur, i.e. another financial cycle would implode, because, he believed, the authorities had learnt their lesson well from the 1930s. The state had learnt how to engage in expansionary fiscal policy, which boosts demand and profits, setting a floor to their decline; and, in addition, Central Bank intervention as lender of last resort would prevent a financial crisis from spreading, through a generalized liquidity squeeze. Consequently, 'the likelihood of a collapse in profits, such as what happened in the 1929–1933 period in the United States, decreases almost to the vanishing point' (Minsky 1995: 89).

What Minsky did not fully anticipate is how far neo-liberal forces would succeed in weakening the state's ability to engage in Keynesian demand management and otherwise undermine the counter-cyclical operations of big government. Nor did he foresee how far a combination of de-regulation and regulatory capture plus financial innovations such as securitization would lead to a finance-dominated regime in which investment in the 'real economy' at home was no longer the primary determinant of corporate profits. Instead cost-cutting, off-shoring, rent-seeking based on intellectual property rights and/or cost-plus government contracts, and financial engineering have become more important. Financial innovation has vastly increased the amount of leverage in the system and, contrary to Minsky's view that households relied on hedge finance to sustain their consumption and to purchase housing, it has enabled them to engage in speculative and Ponzi borrowing on a massive aggregate scale – encouraged to do so through lenders' new-found ability to securitize these loans and off-load their risks (on household consumption, see Ivanova 2011). This overwhelms the capacity of central banks to act as lender of last resort and/or has prompted the socialization of toxic assets at fictitious prices (compared to their mark-to-market valuation) and the transformation of private Ponzi debt into public and/or sovereign debt. This has changed the forms of appearance of the crisis and the allocation of its costs and consequences but it has not resolved it.

This raises the following questions. Can the North Atlantic Crisis and the potential global crisis – initiated this time from China rather than the USA (though both are pathologically interlinked in the economic space some call

'Chimerica') – be understood in terms of a financial and speculative crisis à la Minsky, which then spreads through contagion and policy errors to the real economy (debt-deflation-default) dynamics? Do these crises also have their origins in the real economy, leading to crises in the financial sector, which would indicate that there may also be an important Marxian moment – with moment being interpreted this time as aspect rather than event or trigger – to the crisis? Or, again, does the role of political action in creating the conditions for financial de-regulation and predatory finance indicate that there is also a Weberian moment (aspect) to the crisis in the role of political rather than rational capitalism, whether in the form of rational production or financial speculation? Or, perhaps, are these different aspects interrelated and, if so, how?

Minsky's financial Keynesian studies seem persuasive when compared with the neoclassical-Keynesian synthesis (Papadimitrou and Wray 2008). His analysis captures important financial features of market economies and he explores the institutional framework in which financial stability leads to financial fragility (Minsky 1995; Ferri and Minsky 1992). In the 1980s and 1990s he also explored the implications of securitization and money manager capitalism. Some Marxist commentators have suggested combining Minsky's analysis of *financial crisis tendencies* with Marx's analysis of *crisis-tendencies in the real economy* to produce a more comprehensive and more persuasive analysis (e.g. Crotty 1986;[7] criticized by Moseley 2009). Others have censured Minsky for assuming that the real economy cannot be the cause of crises. This is because he accepted Jerome Levy's and Michał Kalecki's financial analyses of national accounting identities and their implications for profits and unemployment,[8] conflated the real and the financial, and concluded that real economic crises are the reflection of financial crises rather than financial crises a reflection of crises in the real economy (Moseley 2009; Crotty 1986). Specifically, Minsky's analysis rests on the Levy-Kalecki equation of gross capital income with financed gross investment (Minsky 1995: 89). Minsky developed 'an investment theory of the business cycle and a financial theory of investment' (Minsky 1982: 95). Investment leads, profits follow, and these in turn shape investment (Minsky 1982: xvii, xix; cf. 1995: 89). Or, as he noted at greater length:

> The gross profits of business depend not upon the "productivity" of capital in any technical sense, but upon the amount of investment. The profitability of existing capital – and profit expectations from investment – can only decline if investment and expected investment decline. Thus we have to look elsewhere – to arguments other than those derived from assumed properties of production functions and hand waves with regard to over-investment – to explain why the marginal efficiency of investment falls. The natural place to look within the Schumpeter–Keynes–Kalecki vision is to the impact of financing relations – relations which involve both the financing of positions in the stock of assets and investments.
>
> (1983: 13)

This proposition is presented by Marxist critics as contrary to Marx's analyses of the circuits of capital. In particular, once commodity production based on wage labour and machinofacture has become the dominant form of economic organization, productive capital becomes its primary driving force. This criticism is easily overdrawn, however, because, for Marx, capitalist commodity production was always-already monetized and dependent on credit–debt relations (making it hard to differentiate the 'real' from the 'financial' sector) (e.g. McNally 2011).

A different and more compelling version of this criticism that bears directly on the limits of financial crisis-management has recently been advanced by Ivanova (2011). Commenting on the structural causes of the 'Great Recession' that has followed what I term the North Atlantic Financial Crisis, she claims that it originated not in the US financial sector but in the system of globalized production. Moreover:

> the belief originally fathered by Proudhon, reinvented by Keynes, and avowedly embraced by Minsky, that social problems have monetary/financial origins, and *ergo* could be resolved by tinkering with money and financial institutions, is fundamentally flawed. Yet the very recurrence of crises attests to the limits of fiscal and monetary policies as means to ensure "balanced" accumulation.
>
> (Ivanova 2011: 1)

This point is taken further by other Marxist critics, who claim that Minsky's financial instability thesis is neither empirically convincing nor theoretically compelling[9] and, in addition, fails to address the global rather than national character of the current crisis (Brenner 2006). In contrast, they argue, Marx not only analysed the crisis tendencies and antagonisms in the circuits of productive capital – which Minsky had ignored – but also recognized the abstract possibility and actual occurrence of *sui generis* financial crises and their potential impact on the real economy – in ways that prefigure Minsky's analysis.

In a complementary criticism, Carchedi contrasts the class perspectives of Minsky and Marx in their analyses of crisis. He writes:

> Minsky (following Keynes) sees the economy 'from the boardroom of a Wall Street investment bank',[10] Marx from the perspective of labour. Therefore, for Minsky, the economy's instability is basically *financial* instability. This is due to the 'subjective nature of expectations about the future course of investment'.[11] Investments here are basically financial investments because they are determined by borrowing and lending. For Marx, the economy's instability is an objective feature, the result of the crisis-prone tendency in the real economy, first in that sector and then in the financial and speculative ones.
>
> (Carchedi 2011)

Indeed, Carchedi further suggests that the economic and social standpoints of Minsky and Marx are reflected in contrasting views not only about the determinants of investment and employment but also about the possibilities of effective state intervention to manage the effects of financial crisis. Whereas Minsky makes investment and profit flows depend on portfolio decisions by different kinds of borrower, for Marx they depend on the rate of exploitation and expectations of future profits. Moreover, whereas Minsky believes that the big government and demand management can resolve crises by compensating for private sector deleveraging and declining demand and, in this way, raising profits and employment, Marx analyses the contradictory impact of state policy on profits and their realization respectively. In short, he argues, that because Minsky erases classes, class interests, and class struggle, his and Marx's accounts of financial crisis are not so much complementary as radically alternative. His final blow is that everything in Minsky relevant to financial crises and bubbles can also be explained [presumably better] by applying Marxian categories and analyses to the present (Carchedi 2011).

There are certainly strong similarities, as we shall see, between Minsky's analysis of financial portfolio movements, including the three types of borrowing relative to interest and principal repayments, and Marx's analysis of interest-bearing capital and the expansion of fictitious capital. It may also be possible to subsume Minsky's insights into a Marxian analysis without buying into his 'boardroom' perspective. But reconstruction is not the same as claiming that Marx fully anticipated Minsky's analyses even if he provides tools to recontextualize them. So, before dismissing Minsky out of hand, we should provide a more detailed review of Marx's analysis of money functions, money forms, and currency pyramids.

4 A Minsky moment or a Marx moment?

As noted above, adopting a logical-historical approach to the critique of political economy, Marx distinguished abstract potentials for crisis from their concrete causes in specific conjunctures. The real economy was, for Marx, always-already monetary. It involved generalized commodity production and the ever-present possibility that the exchange C-M-C (in terms of the conventional Marxian annotation: commodity-money-commodity) would be broken through the hoarding of money and/or for other reasons. Thus, even before he focused on capitalist production relations, Marx showed a theory of money and credit was an essential foundation for developing a theoretical account of crisis-tendencies. Money was essential to simple commodity circulation (C-M-C) and became more important still when money was transformed into capital (M-C-M'), i.e. allocated to the production of commodities in ways that enable surplus-value to be created and realized, leading to a larger sum of money at the end of the process than was initially invested. It is this transformation that, for Marx, underpins the modern system of financial markets and institutions (Marx 1981: 379–727). In brief, the real economy was the fundamental basis of crisis-tendencies and monetary-cum-financial crises were essentially supplementary factors. Nonetheless, in certain circumstances, financial crises could emerge on the basis of relatively autonomous financial movements with major repercussions on productive capital. Thus, while *profit* fluctuations are critical to monetary crises that are directly rooted in industrial and commercial crisis, some monetary crises have own causes and affect wider economy through contagion and feedback effects (Kenway 1980; for a recent review, Lehner 2010).

To interpret these initial comments on Marxian crisis theory, we need to consider his analysis of the functions of money, the forms of money, and, when we come to crisis-tendencies at the level of the world market, his views on world money and bullion (Jessop 2012). Two critical distinctions, often overlooked in exegeses that highlight the fundamental role of the 'tendency of the rate of profit to fall' in generating capitalist crises, are, first, that between money as money and money as capital; and, second, in this context, that between functioning capital and capital as property.[12] Marx and Minsky agree on the importance of money's function as a means of (deferred) payment and, hence, the role of credit–debt relations. Minsky cycles can be understood in terms of a shift in the role of money as capital from *functioning capital* towards *capital as property*. In Minsky's analysis, the role of hedging in the expansion of economic activities can be seen as one aspect of money as functioning capital. In contrast, in speculative and Ponzi finance, money operates in the guise of capital as property, i.e. as interest-bearing capital. Marx also suggested that the advance of credit is critical to the expanded reproduction of capital (serving to *pre*-validate investment and production – Minsky's hedging role – but vulnerable for this reason to ruptures in the C-M-C and M-C-M' circuits). He added that a period of growth facilitated in this way encourages further expansion of credit–debt relations. However, an increasing volume of credit-debt also makes the economy more vulnerable or, to cite Marx, 'oversensitive' to the eventual downturn (Marx 1981: 706). In this context, Marx observes a pro-cyclical flight to safety, 'a violent scramble for means of payment' (Marx 1981: 621), which others would later call 'a Minsky moment', threatening a downward spiral of debt-default-deflation:

> [When the rate of profit falls,] this disturbance and stagnation paralyzes the function of money as a means of payment [of debt], which is given along with the development of capital and depends on ... presupposed price relations. The chain of payment obligations at specific dates is broken in a hundred places, and this is still further intensified by the breakdown of the credit system.... All this, therefore leads to violent and acute crises, sudden forcible devaluations, and actual stagnation and disruption in the reproductive process and hence to an actual decline in reproduction.
> (Marx 1981: 363)

In times of pressure, when credit contracts or dries up, money suddenly confronts commodities absolutely as the only means of payment and the true existence of value. Hence the general devaluation of commodities and the difficulty or even impossibility of transforming them into money ... millions' worth of commodities must be sacrificed for a few millions in money.... As long as the social character of labour appears as the monetary existence of the commodity and hence as a thing outside actual production, monetary crises, independent of real crises or as an intensification of them, are unavoidable (Marx 1981: 649).

In short, differential accumulation and crisis dynamics rest on the interaction among (1) *abstract forms of crisis* (the abstract potential of crisis) in *commodity circulation* (especially of capitalist commodities), (2) the basic *crisis-tendencies* of capitalist *production* (which may be expressed in various ways), (3) the basic crisis-tendencies in the form and functions of money in circulation and the organization of production, and (4) the potential for the *autonomization of finance* when it circulates in the guise of capital as property rather than as functioning capital and, hence, the scope for short-term parasitism and predation by finance capital on the value created within the circuits of productive capital. These complexities make it misleading to explain crises in terms of initial or immediate causes. The specific crisis events and moments that trigger the crisis are contingent relative to the necessity of crisis.

These contingencies can be seen in the effects of financialization. This tends to transform the role of finance from its conventional, if crisis-prone, intermediary function in the circuit of capital to a more dominant role oriented to rent extraction through financial arbitrage and innovation. This weakens the primacy of production in the overall logic of capital accumulation, works against the long-term stability of accumulation and its regulation, and eventually runs up against the limits of a parasitic, rather than intermediary, role. This can be seen in the most recent wave of financial innovation associated with the rise of derivatives. These are new examples of capital as property, i.e. as fictitious capital that is valued (assumes a price form) on the basis of discounted future revenues or simple speculation on more or less volatile markets in financial instruments. Derivatives as forms of financial innovation integrate production on world scale and, via their role in all functions of money apart from means of immediate exchange, contribute to market completion on a world scale in real time. For example, they: (1) overcome the frictions of national boundaries; (2) open national economies to foreign competition; (3) help to overcome the clumsiness of production; and (4) enhance the role of finance in promoting competition. They generalize and intensify competition in relation to the means of production, money capital, specific capitals as units of competition, and social capital (Bryan and Rafferty 2006). In short, in so far as derivatives promote the completion of the world market, they also serve to activate 'all the contradictions' of capital accumulation (see Marx 1847; 1973; and Marx and Engels 1976).

Among other effects, these 'financial weapons of mass destruction' (Buffett 2003: 16) multiply the volume of opaque, highly leveraged, largely unregulated financial transactions. The expansion of these markets (especially when hidden in shadow banking activities or conducted off-shore) means that they now dwarf the role of financial intermediation and risk-management and therefore play a pro-cyclical, heavily de-stabilizing role via financial speculation and risk-taking by highly leveraged financial institutions (see Broadbent 2011; Haldane and Alessandri 2009). It is hardly surprising, therefore, that they played a crucial role in the North Atlantic Financial Crisis and its global repercussions, inflating the financial bubble to a degree unimaginable to the layperson and hard to calculate even for experts.[13]

The importance of the state emerges clearly in these conditions. Specifically, when it becomes apparent that the flight to safety is impossible without precipitating another Great Depression due to the excess of credit generated through leverage, capital as property that has become a toxic asset is purchased through central bank activities and/or is socialized at fictitious prices through the creation of state fiat money backed by the state's taxing powers. The massive expansion of public and sovereign debt in response to the North Atlantic Financial Crisis has rescued an over-leveraged, over-extended private financial sector largely through displacing the problem to the state and inter-state level. This is evident in the USA, Ireland, and the United Kingdom and, with a different dynamic, in the Eurozone. Without the expected purgative effects of a real depression, this postpones the forcible re-imposition of the unity of the circuits of capital through the elimination of excess production capacity relative to effective global demand (one effect of the neo-liberal offensive against labour) and of excess credit relative to the underlying expansion of the 'real economy' (one effect of the rampant financialization promoted through neo-liberalism). Whilst Marx could not anticipate the specific forms of the current crisis, his analysis of the abstract possibilities of crisis does describe their general form.

A function of money that Minsky largely ignores is that of world money, i.e. as a means of international settlement (conventionally through transfers of gold bullion and/or currency reserves deemed 'as good as gold'). This function becomes more important, the more the world market is integrated through trade, through direct investment that widens and deepens the international division of labour, and through financialization. In the absence of a bullion-based world money such as the gold standard or dollar exchange standard, the socialization of toxic financial assets by the US federal government threatens massive contagion effects on a world scale thanks to the continuing but diminishing role of the dollar as the de facto world money. Similar points hold for the euro and Renminbi as a key negotiated currency and emerging top currency respectively. This is where the hierarchy of monies (commodity money, bank money, central bank money, state money, and world money) provides important advantages to the capitals and states that effectively control the de facto world money or, in the case of the euro, the *de jure* regional money and potential challenger to the dollar. This brings us back, again, to the importance of foreign trade, the state, the world market, and crises in providing a comprehensive account of the contradictions and crisis-tendencies of capitalism.

5 Some oddly Weberian conclusions

The recent and continuing North Atlantic Financial Crisis and its uneven global repercussions have finance-dominated, neo-liberal accumulation at their core. This characterization refers to the articulation of the circuits of finance and production and is not intended to re-assert the misleading distinction between finance and the 'real economy'. The crisis was made in the USA and first broke out there, spreading via a mix of contagion and endogenous crisis-tendencies to other parts of the world market, even when these had not undergone neo-liberal regime shifts or had even taken defensive measures against the effects of neo-liberalism. Yet the ecological dominance of neo-liberalism in the world market, i.e. its role as problem-*maker* rather than problem-*taker*, has survived the global financial crisis. This reflects the global weight of the American economy, the continued dominance (despite declining hegemony) of the US federal state in the world political order, the lobbying power of financial interests in an increasingly corrupt US legal and political system, and the ecological dominance of the world market within world society. This is exemplified by the pathological co-dependency of the US and Chinese economies and its global ramifications. It is also exemplified on a regional scale (also with global repercussions) in the growing tensions in the Eurozone between the dominance of German neo-mercantilism associated with its export-oriented growth model and the operation of a crisis-prone Eurozone onto which neo-liberal austerity policies are being imposed and may even be entrenched in changes to the European constitution. These problems are reflected, as seen above, in concerns about Minsky moments in the USA (as the NAFC first broke out there), in neo-liberal economies more generally, in Europe, China, and, indeed, the world market, with recent fears being expressed about a 'global Minsky moment'.

> The world is becoming universally capitalist. Because of today's communications, record keeping, and computational capabilities, global financial integration is likely to characterize the next era of expansive capitalism. The problem of finance that will emerge is whether the financial and fiscal control and support institutions of national governments can contain both the consequences of global financial fragility and an international debt deflation.
> (Minsky 1995: 93)

At least in later work, then, Minsky noted the importance of what Marx analysed as the growing integration of the world market and he (i.e. Minsky) called 'the world becoming universally capitalist'. He also noted the scope for financialization based on financial innovation tied to changes in information and communication technologies and, one might add, the scope for time-space distantiation and time-space compression that they offer to superfast, hypermobile capital (see also Minsky 1987). This suggests that some Marxist critics have misrepresented his capacity to anticipate novel features of the current crisis. Indeed he anticipated the scope for what the Governor of the Canadian Central Bank would later call a 'global Minsky moment'. In this sense, I believe that we can describe certain aspects of the North Atlantic Financial Crisis in terms of Minsky's financial instability hypothesis and, indeed, describe the moment when the crisis finally became evident with the accelerating flight to safety as a 'Minsky moment'. This is in part because he correctly diagnosed some of the reasons why 'it' has happened again – but in the counterfactual sense of identifying the constraints introduced after the Great Depression in post-war America that prevented 'it' from happening again. What he missed was the shift in the balance of economic and political forces in the 1980s and 1990s that enabled the dismantling of these constraints, the defeat of organized labour, and the gradual but accelerating erosion of the welfare state. Interestingly, he did capture aspects of finance-dominated accumulation in his account of money-manager capitalism and his discussion of securitization.

This does not mean that Minsky's theory in any of its versions elaborated over 30+ years can fully explain the current financial crisis even in terms of its abstract possibilities, let alone its concrete causes and specific unfolding. But nor does a putative Marxian account. The more important question is whether Minsky provided powerful insights into the overall circuits of capital and the variable interaction between the circuits of productive and financial capital. Here, because of his one-sided focus on finance, the answer must be no. In this regard Marx has more to offer provided that his work is adapted and updated to the contemporary world market.

I conclude by returning to my opening remarks on the blinkers of mainstream economics and on the diversity and varieties of capitalism, invoking again Weber's typology of modes of orientation to profit. First, if mainstream economics seeks to treat capitalism as eternal and the causes of crisis as external, we might add that:

> [E]conomics ignores criminogenic environments. The weakness comes from three sources. Economic theory about fraud is underdeveloped, core neo-classical theories imply that major frauds are trivial, economists are not taught about fraud and fraud mechanisms, and neo-classical economists minimize the incidence and importance of fraud for reasons of self-interest, class and ideology.
>
> (Black 1995: 1)

Second, in this context, to explain the North Atlantic crisis, we should add a Weber moment. Both Minsky and Marx focused on aspects of what Weber classified as the two modes of rational capitalism. Their analysis of the abstract possibilities of crisis largely missed Weber's modes of political capitalism. Yet a growing theoretical and investigative literature shows that the financial crisis could become as serious as it has done because of unusual deals with political authority that enabled the dismantling of prudential controls, the rise of shadow banking and off-balance sheet transactions, and the weakening of state crisis-management capacities (Nersisyan and Wray 2010). There is also growing evidence of predatory profits based on fraudulent activities ranging from control fraud through corruption and insider trading to systematic infringement of laws about real estate titles, foreclosure processes, and so on (Black 2005, 2009; Smith 2010).

Profits from force and domination may have mattered less in generating this crisis but they have been important in other crises linked to military intervention and/or the imposition of market opening, structural adjustment, and financial conditionalities in the Global South and, recently, Southern Europe. In short, if one were to take a broader, world market perspective that considers not only varieties of 'rational capitalism' (and their inherent irrationalities) but also 'political capitalism', very different conclusions would follow about the world market and crises. This reinforces the relevance of Marx's six-book plan on condition that one takes the state and politics more fully into account.

Notes

1 This chapter derives from my ESRC-funded Professorial Fellowship on the Cultural Political Economy of Crises of Crisis-Management (RES-051–27–0303). It has gained from discussions with Maria Ivanova, Julian Jessop, Oliver Kessler, Brigitte Young, and Randall Wray. All errors of interpretation and explanation are mine.
2 Cf. Minsky on 'dirty rotten scoundrels' (1991: 5) or how money manager capitalism accentuates 'the predatory nature of current American capitalism' (1996: 363).
3 It is fractally organized in the sense that variegation operates on many scales – it is not just evident at the global scale.
4 Minsky (1995) attributes this formulation to Abba Lerner.
5 Wray (2009) gives a good Minskyan review of money manager capitalism.
6 As Minsky died in 1996, this must refer to the East Asian Crisis and/or the Russian crisis with its resulting collapse of Long Term Capital Management. He himself noted earlier examples in the USA and beyond that did not lead to another Great Depression.
7
> Minsky's work on financial markets ... is broadly consistent with Marx's unfinished effort to develop a sophisticated theory of finance that could be integrated with his analysis of production to form a general theory of growth and instability in the capitalist economy.
>
> (Crotty 1986)

8 For a brief survey of their views, see Levy (2000).
9 One wonders whether Brenner still believed this after the 2007 Minsky moment.
10 Minsky (1982: 61).
11 Minsky (1982: 65).
12 For a useful discussion of this distinction, see Meacci (1988).
13 Although there is no central register of derivatives, recent calculations suggest that the total global *notional* (non-cleared) stock of derivatives (exercised or not, regardless of term) has reached one quadrillion USD, which is 20 times global GDP.

References

Black, W.K. (2005) 'When fragile becomes friable: endemic control fraud as a cause of economic stagnation and collapse', Paper presented as IDEAS conference, New Delhi, 19–20 December www.pragoti.in/node/2976, accessed 24 April 2012.

Black, W.K. (2009) 'How the servant became the predator: finance's five fatal flaws', *Next New Deal: the Blog of the Roosevelt Institute*, www.nextnewdeal.net/how-servant-became-predator-finances-five-fatal-flaws, accessed 24 April 2012.

Broadbent, B. (2012) 'Deleveraging', Speech, 15 March, London: Bank of England, www.bankofengland.co.uk/publications/Documents/speeches/2012/speech553.pdf, accessed 24 April 2012.

Buffet, W.E. (2003) 'Chairman's letter', in *Berkshire Hathaway Inc. 2002 Annual Report*, Omaha, NE: Berkshire Hathaway Inc.

Buttonwood (2009) 'Minsky's moment', *The Economist*, 4 April.

Carchedi, G. (2011) 'Behind and beyond the crisis', *International Socialism Journal*, 132: 121–55.

Carney, M. (2011) 'Growth in the age of deleveraging', 12 December, www.bankofcanada.ca/wp-content/uploads/2011/12/speech-121211.pdf, accessed 20 April 2012.

Cassidy, J. (2008) 'The Minsky moment', *The New Yorker*, 4 February.

Chancellor, E. (2007) 'Ponzi Nation', *Institutional Investor*, 7 February.

Crotty, J. (1985) 'The centrality of money, credit and financial intermediation in Marx's crisis theory', in S. Resnick and R. Wolff (eds), *Marxian Political Economy*, New York: Autonomedia.

Crotty, J. (1986) 'Marx, Keynes, and Minsky on the instability of the capitalist growth process and the nature of government economic policy', in D.F. Bramhall and S.W. Helburn (eds), *Marx, Schumpeter and Keynes*, Armonk NY: M.E. Sharpe.

Dymski, G.A. (2009) 'Does heterodox economics need a unified crisis theory? From profit-squeeze to the global liquidity meltdown', in J.P. Goldstein and M.G. Hillard (eds), *Heterodox Macroeconomics: Keynes, Marx, and Globalisation*, London: Routledge.

Ferri, P. and Minsky, H.P. (1992) 'Market processes and thwarting systems', *Structural Change and Economic Dynamics*, 3: 79–91.

Financial Reality (2007) 'Minsky has his moment', 29 July, http://alamedalearning.com/reality/2007/07/29/minsky-has-his-moment/, accessed 20 April 2012.

Fisher, I. (1933) 'The debt deflation theory of great depressions', *Econometrica*, 1: 337–57.

Freeman, A. (2010) 'Marxism without Marx: A note towards a critique', *Capital & Class*, 34(1): 84–97.

Haldane, A.G. and Alessandri, P. (2009) 'Banking on the state', Basel: Bank of International Settlements, www.bis.org/review/r091111e.pdf, accessed 20 April 2012.

Ivanova, M.N. (2011) 'Marx, Minsky, and the Great Recession', Paper for the Second International Conference in Political Economy, Istanbul, 20–22 May, www.iippe.org/wiki/images/4/45/CONF_2011_Maria_Ivanova.pdf, accessed 20 April 2012.

Jessop, B. (2012) '"The economists ... know more about the future than about the present": Preliminary reflections on Marx, the world market, and the current crisis', Paper given at Political Studies Association conference, Belfast, 5 April.

Kenway, P. (1980) Marx, Keynes and the possibility of crisis', *Cambridge Journal of Economics*, 4: 23–46.

Lahart, J. (2007) 'In time of turmoil, obscure economist gains currency', *Wall Street Journal*, 18 August.

Lehner, M. (2010) 'Marx, money and modern finance capital', *Fifth International Journal*, 3(4): 53–128.

Levy, S.J. (2000) 'Profits: the views of Jerome Levy and Michal Kalecki', *Working Paper No. 309*, Annandale-on-Hudson, NY: Levy Economics Institute of Bard College.

Magnus, G. (2007a) 'The credit cycle and liquidity: Have we arrived at a Minsky moment?', *Economic Insights – By George*, 6 March. London: UBS Investment Research.

Magnus, G. (2007b) 'What this Minsky moment means', *Financial Times*, 22 August.

Magnus, G. (2010) *Uprising: Will Emerging Markets Shape Or Shake the World Economy*, Chichester: John Wiley & Sons.

Magnus, G. (2011) 'China risks credit-fuelled Minsky moment', *Financial Times*, 3 May.
McCulley, P. (2007) 'The plankton theory meets Minsky', *Global Central Bank Focus*, March, London: PIMCO Bonds.
McNally, David (2011) 'Marx, Marxists and the financial forms of the crisis', *International Journal of Management Concepts and Philosophy*, 5: 112–17.
Marx, K. (1847) 'Speech of Dr Marx on protection, free trade, and the working classes', in *Marx-Engels Collected Works, vol 6*, London: Lawrence & Wishart 1976.
Marx, K. (1973) *Grundrisse*, Harmondsworth: Penguin.
Marx, K. (1981) *Capital: Volume 3*, Harmondsworth: Penguin.
Marx, K. and Engels, F. (1976) *The German Ideology*, in idem, *Marx-Engels Collected Works, vol 5*, London: Lawrence & Wishart.
Meacci, F. (1998) 'Fictitious capital and crises', in R. Bellofiore (ed.), *Marxian Economics: a Reappraisal, Vol. 1*, Basingstoke: Macmillan.
Minsky, H.P. (1975) *John Maynard Keynes*, New York: Columbia University Press.
Minsky, H.P. (1982) 'Can "it" happen again?' *Essays on Instability and Finance*, New York, M.E. Sharpe.
Minsky, H.P. (1983) 'Money and Crisis in Schumpeter and Keynes', Hyman P. Minsky Archive, Paper 334, http://digitalcommons.bard.edu/hm_archive/334, accessed 24 April 2012.
Minsky, H.P. (1986) *Stabilizing an Unstable Economy*, New Haven, CT: Yale University Press.
Minsky, H.P. (1987) 'Securitization', Annandale-on-Hudson, NY: Levy Economics Institute Policy Note No. 2, 12 May.
Minsky, H.P. (1991) 'The Transition to a Market Economy', Working Paper No. 66, Annandale-on-Hudson, NY: Levy Economics Institute of Bard College.
Minsky, H.P. (1992) 'Schumpeter and finance', in S. Biasco, A. Roncaglia, and M. Salvati (eds) *Market and Institutions in Economic Development*, Basingstoke: Macmillan.
Minsky, H.P. (1995) 'Longer waves in financial relations: financial factors in the more severe depressions II', *Journal of Economic Issues*, 29(1): 83–96.
Minsky, H.P. (1996) 'Uncertainty and the institutional structure of capitalist economies', *Journal of Economic Issues*, 30(2): 357–68.
Moseley, F. (2009) 'Marx, Minsky and Crotty on crises in capitalism', in J.P. Goldstein and M.G. Hillard (eds), *Heterodox Macroeconomics: Keynes, Marx, and Globalisation*, London: Routledge.
Nersisyan, Y. and Wray, L.R. (2010) 'Transformation of the financial system: financialization, concentration, and the shift to shadow banking'. In D. Tavasci and J. Toporowski (eds) *Minsky, Crisis and Development*, Basingstoke: Palgrave Macmillan.
Palley, T.I. (20011) 'A theory of Minsky super-cycles and financial crises', *Contributions to Political Economy*, 30: 31–46.
Papadimitriou, D.B. and Wray. L.R. (2008) 'Introduction', in H.P. Minsky, *John Maynard Keynes*, New York: McGraw-Hill.
Parikh, S.H. (2011) 'PIMCO cyclical outlook: deleveraging, austerity and Europe's potential Minsky Moment', Newport Beach, CA: PIMCO, available at http://media.pimco.com/Documents/CyclicalOutlook–Parikh–December 2011–Global.pdf, accessed 5 April 2012.
Rasmus, J. (2010) *Epic Recession*, London: Pluto.
Shaikh, A. (1978) 'An introduction to the history of crisis theories', in U.R.P.E., eds, *U.S. Capitalism in Crisis*, New York: URPE, 219–41.

Smith, Y. (2010) *E-Conned*, Basingstoke: Palgrave Macmillan.
Swedberg, R. (1996) *Max Weber's Economic Sociology*, Princeton: Princeton University Press.
Weber, M. (1961) *General Economic History*, New York: Collier.
Whalen, C. (2007) 'The U.S. credit crunch of 2007: a Minsky moment'. Annandale-on-Hudson, NY: Levy Economics Institute Public Policy Brief, No. 92.
Wilson, S. (2007) 'Have we reached a Minsky moment?', *Moneyweek*, 5 April.
Wray, L.R. (2009) 'The rise and fall of money manager capitalism: a Minskian approach', *Cambridge Journal of Economics*, 33: 807–28.

3 Beyond the political economy of Hyman Minsky

What financial innovation means today

Anastasia Nesvetailova

> *It is a fact that financial crises have become rarer and less acute and indeed have almost disappeared since the early 1930 ... Financial crises are a childhood disease of capitalism, not an affliction of an old age.*
> (Goldsmith, 1982, 'A Comment on Minsky's Financial Instability Hypothesis')

1 The global crisis

Sparked by the collapse of the US subprime mortgage industry, the global financial crisis erupted in August 2007, mutated into an international banking collapse in autumn 2008 and at the time of writing (April 2012), is continuing in its third phase, the crisis of the Eurozone. According to some estimates by the Bank of England (2010), the global financial crisis has brought about $4 trillion in temporary loss of world output; it has eroded the banks' market value by $5 trillion; and has cost governments world-wide around $15 trillion in direct financial assistance to banks and markets. (At the time of writing in April 2012, this figure is already a conservative estimate, considering the amount of liquidity the European Central Bank has been providing to banks in the Eurozone during 2011–2012).

There is no doubt that a highly complex set of factors – historical, geopolitical, economic, social and even cultural – have shaped the preconditions for the meltdown. Schematically, conceptual accounts of the crisis fall into three overlapping categories. First, there is a group of structural explanations of the crisis. This current interprets the crisis as either as an outcome of deep-seated worldwide imbalances (of savings, markets and, broadly, economic power). Alternatively, in a more 'localized' version, as the crisis of a particular stage of capitalism that had been dubbed money-manager capitalism, debt capitalism or consumer capitalism of the Anglo-Saxon type (Wade 2008; Gamble 2009).

Second, institutionalist readings of the global credit crunch diagnose it mainly, as a failure of a particular industry, market practice or governance mechanism. In the context of the financial market, the credit crunch is a crisis of the practice of securitization and re-securitization. In terms of economic policy, the crisis has demonstrated a vivid failure of financial regulation, either corrupted by the market forces or simply made impotent by the massive efforts of the financial lobby to liberate finance from intrusive oversight or regulation. Alternatively, critics also interpret the credit crunch as an outcome of a colossal failure of the whole neoliberal paradigm of economic policy, particularly prominent in the Anglo-Saxon economies (Soros 2008).

The third group of theories can be summed up under the heading of 'behavioural' explanations. In formal economics, these types of analyses underline the skewed structure of incentives in the financial industry that has produced a suboptimal outcome. Outside the boundaries of economic orthodoxy, behavioural accounts emphasize the prominent presence of the human factor, and more precisely, human failure, in precipitating and escalating the global crisis. Stressing the role of sheer incompetence, greed and fraud, behavioural accounts reveal incompetent senior management at individual financial institutions; unaccountable traders and salesmen who knowingly sold risky products to their customers, often betting against the client; the financial space exploited by individual crooks of various calibre; the many warnings about the risk of the coming malaise being dismissed or silenced; and finally, the untrained, unskilled and not sufficiently savvy regulators, statesmen and even academics who did not see or were not sufficiently clued-in into the real-life developments in finance (cf. Nesvetailova 2010; Lawson 2009).

The three sets of theoretical explanations for the meltdown are certainly not mutually exclusive. All three groups of theories would concur that the crisis came as the end of a (super)-bubble of financial excesses; all three, to a larger or lesser degree, note how overpowering the sense of success and the magic of easy money had been for both the cast and the audience in the big financial spectacle of 2002–2007. Importantly, all three would also recognize that the crisis was caused by financial innovation. (Politically and ideologically however, interpretations of this problem do vary significantly.) At the same time however, the three schools of thought do differ fundamentally in the explanatory emphasis they place on the collective and systemic factors of the crisis, vis-à-vis its isolated and idiosyncratic characteristics.

Unsurprisingly, given the scale of the collapse and the costs it has imposed on the economies of the Anglo-Saxon world, observers chart parallels between the credit crisis of 2007–2012 and the Great Depression of the 1930s, evoking both theoretical accounts of the crisis and its policy lessons drawn over time (e.g. Almunia *et al.* 2010; Grossman and Meissner 2010). Along with the specter of the Great Depression, the credit crunch has resurrected a major theorist of financial crisis from the obscurity of heterodox political economy. Hyman Minsky (1919–1996), an original scholar of financial instability and a skeptic of financialized capitalism, foresaw the danger of another Great Depression in advanced economies as early as the 1980s (1982, 1986). Pondering the role of the post-war institutional transformations in US finance, or what he called 'money-manager capitalism,' Minsky concluded that it is the presence a 'Big Bank' and 'Big Government' that can help avoid another major depression. At the same time, he argued that in an economy where financial services are deregulated and where financial institutions are able to embark on a spiral of financial innovation, there is an inherent cumulative tendency towards financial fragility and crisis.

Minsky's theory of financial fragility is aptly tuned towards explaining the major dynamics of the global crisis. An historical significance of the global credit crisis lies in the fact that it became the first systemic rupture of risk-trading capitalism (Bernstein 1996; Shiller 2004). The ability to identify, locate, price and then shift risk from one's books lies at the very foundation of today's 'originate and distribute model' of banking (ODM) that since the late 1960s, has been crowding out the more traditional 'originate and hold' model of banking. The ability to trade risk has been the engine of securitization industry in finance, including the subprime mortgage market. The key to the financial institutions' ability to shift risky products to other parts of the financial system, in turn, lay in their newly-found ostensible control over risk and ability to create 'liquidity.' 'There was this sense that we had found this fantastic technology which we really believed in and we wanted to take to every part of the market we could' (Bill Winters, one of the senior officers behind the creation of a credit derivative at JP Morgan; cited in Tett 2009: 6).

During the last few decades, the very essence of financial innovation and securitization more narrowly, was to transform inherently illiquid assets into liquid securities. For a while, the alchemy seemed to have worked wonderfully: banks reaped more and more profits as they were able to remove credit risk from their books; customers and clients were happy as they felt better-off; credit ratings agencies, while occasionally suspicious, were glad to charge high fees to their stamps of approval; politicians, especially in the countries of Anglo-Saxon capitalism, were content as they gained on the political benefits of the economic boom. The continually expanding frontier of liquid assets, as well as rhetoric of a global liquidity glut or 'excess liquidity' during 2002–2007, only reinforced the idea that financial innovation creates liquidity, and therefore, wealth.

As far as financiers were concerned, their mission was to capitalize on this abundant liquidity by expanding their trades and products. Success bred arrogance, and many warnings about the riskiness of new financial practices and products were simply dismissed: 'the possibility that liquidity could suddenly dry up was always a topic high on our list but we could only see more liquidity coming into the market – not going out of it...' (anonymous risk manager, cited in *The Economist*, August 9, 2008).

On the one hand, the financial structure of capitalism of the 1970s and the 1980s analysed by Hyman Minsky in his original works pales in comparison with the degree of sophistication of the financial system of the early twenty-first century. In the time of Minsky, financial products, while complex, were less esoteric; the world economy was still divided into capitalist and Communist-ruled blocs; financial markets were much less integrated. In fact, it is interesting that recent revisions of Minsky's *financial instability hypothesis* (FIH) have argued that his framework is most adequately tuned to explaining the cumulative fragility of industrial business units, rather than modern financial firms as such (Bellofiore and Halevi 2010; Toporowski 2009).

Indeed, at first cut, the subsequent burst of the bubble in the summer of 2007 was simply, the unravelling of a grandiose liquidity illusion and wealth (Nesvetailova 2010). However on the other hand, the function and performance of 'liquidity' – long a confusing subject in political economy and financial theory – is itself a story of how a naïve dream became a monstrous creation, how youthful arrogance and short-sight first became systemic, and then unleashed a wave of destruction world-wide. In this regard, Minsky's insight into the political economy of the crisis, with its focus on the process of liquidity-stretching financial innovation that tend to destabilise the system, helps fill the void left by mainstream theorisations of finance that have come *to assume* the perfect liquidity of the contemporary financial markets.

2 'Liquidity' and the crisis of invented money

With the advance of financial globalization most analyses, from within the academe and beyond, have come to locate the concept of 'liquidity' in the realm of the financial market. Here, liquidity measures the degree of convertibility of an asset into a form of money, or likelihood that a trade can be executed reasonably swiftly without a loss in value. This conception makes liquidity a function of a right price: if you can price an asset, it means that there is a market for this asset. If there is market for the asset, in turn, it means that the asset is liquid. If the asset is liquid, you can expand the market and reap larger profits from the growing asset trade. As the practice of financial innovation seemed to affirm these theoretical assumptions, liquidity has come to be assumed to be synonymous with the general spirit, the vibrancy of market trade, or more simply, with confidence.

Out of the many conceptual problems with this reading of liquidity, one stands out in particular. Locating liquidity in the realm of the financial market avoids the question of whether liquidity is a quality inherent in an asset, or whether it is a quality that the asset possesses due to the operation of some external mechanism (Berle and Pederson 1934). Through pricing, marketing and shifting assets (i.e. risk) around the system, techniques of securitization made the question of the inherent liquidity of *assets*, irrelevant. The power of financial innovation was overwhelming. Or so it seemed.

In this instance, lessons about the nature of liquidity drawn in the wake of another financial disaster – the Great Depression – are instructive. Then, early theorizations of liquidity, having interrogated its contentious role in financial capitalism, conceived of it as organic fabric of political economy which weaves together not only individual trades in the financial markets, but the very process of production, consumption and accumulation of capitalism (Mueller 1953). This organisism makes liquidity a function of the future: while in many instances, liquidity actually denotes currentness, generally, it is the *prospective* liquidity that is meant when a degree of an asset's liquidity is being discussed (Brown 1940: 7, emphasis in the original). As such, liquidity in the economic sense provides a crucial link not only between various transactions that constitute financial exchange, but crucially, the connectivity between past, present and future. In other words, liquidity is 'merely the fruit of a desire to continue into the future the immediate ability to meet the desires of the moment' (Berle and Pederson 1934: 69).

In the heyday of the recent financial boom, the 'desire of the moment' was to generate higher fees and profits through finding new ways to trade risk. The success of the credit derivatives industry placated more conservative market players, prompting them to dismiss with more restrictive notions of liquidity and more cautious approaches to risk. 'Liquidity' was no longer about a cushion of capital that a bank needs to set aside for a rainy day; liquidity was not even about matching bid and ask prices in the market for your asset. Liquidity was, simply, 'appetite for risk' (McCulley 2008).

During the boom years, this appetite was infectious and liquidity was ostensibly infinite. The success of financial innovation led market players to think that now they could compete with gods (Bernstein 1996), while the ability to manipulate future led them to forget – if ever they remembered – the sombre lessons of history and bubbles. Maverick financial institutions, such as Goldman Sachs or Lehman Brothers, were seen as pioneers of the new era, while more old-fashioned banks that valued 'relationship banking' and conservative approaches to risk, like JP Morgan, were 'stodgy' and 'elitist' (Tett 2009). Young traders and the brains behind the derivatives deals, in turn, epitomized the new brave face of finance, while loan officers and risk analysts asking annoying questions about risks were 'the dinosaurs' of the old-age banking (Partnoy 1997).

In this respect, the global credit crunch verified the otherwise ill-timed metaphor of Goldsmith (1982). The meltdown became the disease of new-age capitalism, the brave and arrogant new world of financial command over risk and hence the future, reigned by the talents of over-specialized yet short-sighted geeks who believed (indeed many still do) that they have discovered the Holy Grail of financial alchemy: the way not only to predict, but manipulate, the future.

The problem is conceptual. 'Liquidity' is a very fluid, complex, multi-dimensional notion. It describes a quality – of an asset, portfolio, a market, an institution or an economic community. Liquidity also denotes a quantity – most often associated with the pool of money or credit available in a given system at any given time. 'Liquidity' is also a probability – a calculated chance of a transaction being completed in time without inflicting a major disruption to the prevailing trends in the market. 'Liquidity' is also the depth (of a market for a particular class of assets) *and* speed (with which a certain transaction can be completed).

To make things just a bit more complicated, 'liquidity' can also comprise also all these things together, and describe several layers of economic activity at the same time – for instance, the liquidity of an individual bank, a segment of the market, national economy and finally, the global financial system as a whole. Furthermore, 'liquidity' is also an inter-temporal category: 'liquidity' in good economic times is not the same as 'liquidity' in bad times. Or, as economists like to stress, liquidity to sell is not always the same as liquidity to buy. The liquidity that was widely assumed to be abundant during the pre-crisis period was not the same liquidity that disappeared during the crisis. Assets that are easy to sell when investors are confident about their profitability and risk profiles often turn out to be unwanted and expensive bundles of poor quality, illiquid debt when the sense of confidence and optimism evaporates. Liquidity can vanish literally overnight.

This is exactly what happened to trillions of dollars of securitized loans and a plethora of highly sophisticated and opaque financial instruments over 2007–2009. At the height of the 2002–2007 credit boom, financial institutions employed armies of young MBAs, awarding them fancy job titles and handsome pay. Bankers could confidently sell highly complex instruments in bulk to clients around the world. Not many buyers, it transpires, took the trouble to learn about the nature of these instruments fully. All they seemed to care about was that the market for these products appeared highly liquid and that they and, importantly, their competitors were making money. When the boom came to a halt, synthetic financial products became exposed for what they actually were – toxic parcels of debt – and their market liquidity evaporated. So did the markets for these products: whereas in 2007 $2,500 billion of loans were securitized the USA, in 2008 almost none were sold to private sector buyers (Tett and van Duyn 2009). The new generation of finance professionals turned out to be but a highly motivated sales force, bent on persuading even the most suspicious of clients to part with their hard cash for bundles of securitized loans.

These and many other puzzles of the credit crunch centre on the problem of liquidity and its metamorphoses in the modern financial system. Most chronicles of the crisis concur that the global meltdown has been centred on or, at least, started off as, liquidity drainage from the markets. There is no clear consensus, however, as to what the concept of liquidity actually implies today. As the field of credit crunch studies expands, the diversity of views becomes ever more apparent.

Not that long ago, things were somewhat simpler. In the brief age of Keynesian economic stability, 'liquidity' was generally assumed to describe a quality of *an asset*, and ultimately, was related to the notion of money. And even though to this day the concept of 'money' is probably the most controversial subject in the study of economics and finance, most students of finance at the time would concur that 'liquidity' is a property of an *asset*. As such, it is conditioned by the market context but crucially, it is intimately related to the notion of money: liquidity is 'an asset's capability over time of being realised in the form of funds available for immediate consumption or reinvestment – proximately in the form of money' (Hirchleifer 1986: 43).

But over time, the real life of the financial markets complicated things. In 1971, the post-war system of fixed exchange rates and financial controls was dismantled. As a result of the financial innovations that led to this collapse, the state lost its monopoly over the process of credit creation. The financial sector has been transformed from being part of the service economy, intermediating between lenders and investors, into an industry of trading and optimizing risk. In parallel, the concept of liquidity has undergone its own chain of mutations.

First, the transformation of 'liquidity' has paralleled the rise of private financial markets. During the centuries of metal-based money, and later in the era of the gold standard and even the fixed exchange rates of the Bretton Woods, 'liquidity' was tightly associated with, first of all, state-generated credit money and, secondly, the banking system's ability to extend credit. With the collapse of the Bretton Woods regime and the rise of private financial markets, the notion of liquidity, both functionally and conceptually, has been gravitating closer to the realm of financial markets themselves. A key factor in this trend has been the emergence in the late 1960s of the unregulated financial space, the Euromarket. Created by commercial banks to escape national regulations, the Eurocurrency market became the global engine of liquidity creation and debt-financing, and became prone to overextension of credit. Most dramatically, this trend manifested itself in the global debt crisis of the 1980s (Guttman 2003: 32).

The second mutation of 'liquidity' has been the so-called securitization revolution. Theoretically, securitization is a technique to create securities by reshuffling the cash flows produced by a diversified pool of assets with some common characteristics. By doing so, one can design several securities (tranches) with different risk-reward profiles which appeal to different investors (Cifuentes 2008). The idea behind this principle is that of economic flexibility: by securitizing previously non-traded products and putting them on the market, financial institutions attach a price to these assets, widen their ownership and, hence, by expanding the web of economic transactions, strengthen the robustness of the economy as a whole. In theory therefore, securitization is supposed to enhance liquidity and economic stability.

The business of securitization has been assumed to bring many benefits to the economy. Boosted by the resolution of the debt crisis of the 1980s, the securitization of credit became a process through which often poor quality, obscure loans have been transformed into securities and traded in the financial markets. Facilitated by technological and scientific advances, as well as the spread of derivatives markets, the securitization of credit has greatly increased the variety and volume of trades in the global financial markets, creating the sense of much greater liquidity of these markets and the depth of the credit pool (Guttman 2003: 40–1). With banks rapidly becoming major players in this global financial market, and with their heavier reliance on securitization techniques in managing their portfolios, the notion of 'liquidity' as tied to the pure credit intermediation mechanism or a state-administered monetary pool, began to fade away.

It is interesting in this respect that earlier political-economic conceptualizations of liquidity, while emphasizing its evasive and multi-dimensional character (Keynes 1936), have viewed liquidity necessarily as a two-fold concept, describing a property of assets and markets, and were based on the notion of an asset's proximity to a form of money. More recent examinations of liquidity as a category of finance have moved away from associating it with notions of money or cash, instead stressing the link between market liquidity and risk (Allen and Gale 2000). The reasons behind this change in the analytical approaches are to be found in the financial developments of the post-1971 era. Specifically, the privatization of financial and economic risks and the de-nationalization of money have shifted the process of liquidity creation away from the public sphere of political economy and into the realm of private financial markets (Holmstrong and Tirole 1998: 1).

The policies of financial deregulation and liberalization reinforced this tendency, thereby institutionalising 'liquidity' firmly as a category and instrument of the market and its pricing mechanism. As a result, over the past few decades, analyses of finance in the macroeconomy have assumed 'liquidity' as no longer primarily a property of assets but rather, as an indicator of the general condition and vitality of a financial market. As for instance, a web-based financial dictionary suggests, liquidity describes 'a high level of trading activity, allowing buying and selling with minimum price disturbance. Also, a market characterised by the ability to buy and sell with relative ease' (Farlex Free Dictionary).

The outcome of this chain of mutations – both analytical and market-based – is that in most contemporary readings, the connection between the notions of 'money' and 'liquidity' has waned away. After all, the global financial system is based on credit and a multitude of economic transactions. With 'money' itself becoming increasingly dematerialized, it may seem odd to link liquidity to categories of cash, high-powered or state-backed money. Instead therefore, 'liquidity' has been presumed to relate to the complex mechanism of financial transactions taking place in the markets and confronting a variety of risks. This in turn, has produced several inter-related assumptions that have shaped finance theory and policy in the run-up to the global credit crunch.

The first trend concerns the expansion of the global credit system and can be described as a process of *demonetized financialization*. It encapsulates two intertwined tendencies in contemporary capitalism: first, the deepening of the financial sector and the growing role of finance-based relations in shaping the nature of socio-political developments today, or what social scientists have understood as financialization. And second, the process of securitization, depicted above, centred upon financial initiations' ability to transform illiquid loans into tradable securities, reaping profits in the process. In terms of understanding what 'liquidity' is and how it behaves, an important assumption correlated with this trend. As financialization advanced, both in spatial and inter-temporal terms, 'liquidity' has progressively lost its public good component. Just as 'money' itself is, therefore, marked by the inherent contradiction between money as a public good and as a private commodity, liquidity has increasingly assumed the features of a private device of financial markets – in the sense that it is created by agents seeking to benefit individually from that privilege (Guttman 2003: 23). The expansion of the credit system and the accumulation of financial wealth or financialization therefore, have been progressively abstracted from the dynamics of productivity, trade, real economic growth and, crucially, from the developments in the sphere of state-backed or high-powered money.

Second, analytically, mainstream finance theory and practice supported and guided these trends, by embedding the new credit system in a paradigm of *scientific finance*. In this vision, the key function of the financial system as a whole is no longer the intermediation between savers and borrowers as such; that role has been assigned to only one sector of the financial system, commercial banking. Rather, the ultimate aim of the financial system today is to manage and optimise risk, in a three-step manner. First, by identifying and pricing risks (for instance, by pooling a bunch of subprime mortgages from several mortgage lenders); second, by parcelling them into specific financial vehicles (like tranches of mortgages, or structured financial products), and third, by re-distributing the risk to those who are deemed most able and willing to hold it (i.e. by selling it off to third and fourth parties, often institutions specializing in trading these particular products, or placing them off the balance sheet, as happened with many highly risky securitisation products) (e.g. Toporowski 2009).

This complex chain of financial innovation is known in mainstream finance theory as the process of *market completion*. In the context of the subprime market for instance, risk-optimizing and market-creating financial innovation has been seen as key to enhancing social welfare more generally:

> The subprime market provides a market-opening and -completing opportunity.... The subprime market allows funding to those who would otherwise not be homeowners. By pricing the risks of different types of credit quality, prime lenders can target some applicants who otherwise might not be qualified.... The prime mortgage market allows all borrowers meeting a particular threshold to be qualified.... Adding a subprime market provides a welfare gain, even to applicants able to qualify in a prime-only market. Those applicants obtain a welfare gain by having more choices and flexibility.
>
> (Chinloy and Macdonald 2005: 163–4)

Ultimately, as Alan Greenspan envisioned, 'financial innovation will slow as we approach the world in which financial markets are complete in the sense that all financial risks can be effectively transferred to those most willing to bear them' (cited in Wigan 2009). Financial innovation, therefore, by relying on scientific approaches to risk management and calculative practices, is believed to create new facilities for risk optimization and thus complete the system of markets. As the theory holds, securitization, for instance, transforms previously un-priced and typically illiquid assets – such as real estate, car or student loans or subprime mortgages – into tradable and liquid financial securities, thereby optimizing risks and enhancing the liquidity of the financial system as a whole (Cifuentes 2008). According to Alan Greenspan, this process – reaching far beyond the subprime market – symbolized 'a new paradigm of active credit management' (in Morris 2008: 61).

Third, the spiral of demonetized financialization has been underpinned by institutional and operational advances in financial innovation. In addition to the structural shift towards the 'originate and distribute' model of banking, there has been a remarkable rise of hedge funds; the growing sophistication and specialization of offshore financial centres and techniques (Palan 2003); the expansion of the so-called shadow banking industry; the spread of new methods of risk management and trade, such as value-at-risk (VAR) models, all leading to the extraordinary growth of variety and complexity of financial products themselves.

What is striking about the wave of financial innovation that defined the last two decades of the global financial system is that many newly created products of risk-management became so specialized and tailor-made that they were never traded in free markets. Indeed, as Gillian Tett writes, in 2006 and early 2007, no less than $450 billion worth of 'collateralised debt obligations of asset-backed securities' (CDOs of ABSs) was created. Yet instead of being traded, as the principle of active credit risk management would imply, most of them were sold to banks' off-balance-sheet entities such as structured investment vehicles (SIVs) – or simply left on the books. Generally, she argues, a set of innovations that were supposed to create freer markets and complete the system of risk optimization actually produced an opaque world in which risk was becoming highly concentrated; worryingly, in ways almost nobody understood. Officials at Standard & Poor's admit that by 2006, it could take a whole weekend for computers to carry out the calculations needed to assess the risks of complex CDOs (Tett 2009).

What does the combination of the three trends imply for our understating of the global credit crunch? It appears that most existing analytical and policy frameworks of the global financial system have been based on a strong and relatively straightforward assumption. Namely, they conceived 'liquidity' as, fundamentally, a property of the market or an institution, rather than a quality of assets as such. At the level of financial institutions themselves, the axiom that financial innovation and engineering have the capacity to *liquefy* any type of asset – or more accurately, debt – has resulted in the now mainstream notion of liquidity that is divorced from any attribute of assets per se. And although some recent analyses have drawn a distinction between market and systemic liquidity (Large 2005), or between search and funding liquidity (ECB 2006), in the Anglo-Saxon economies, it is the concept of *market* liquidity – describing the depth of markets for the sale or loan of assets or the hedging of risks that underlie those assets – that have come to inform most recent frameworks of financial governance (Crockett 2008: 13–17). Here, in turn, liquidity is most commonly understood as 'confidence' of the markets, able and willing to trade at a given point in time at a prevailing price level (Warsh 2007).

This conceptualization of liquidity, in turn, has produced a sequence of analytical fallacies which have contributed to the great illusion that is the real cause of the global credit crunch. The first fallacy is the assumption that it is the market-making capacity of financial intermediaries to identify, price and trade new financial products that create and distribute liquidity in the markets. Second is the view that the general market trade and turnover is synonymous with market liquidity. The third and corresponding fallacy is the notion that market liquidity itself – when multiplied across many markets – ultimately is synonymous with the liquidity (and financial robustness) of the economic system as a whole. Altogether, this chain of reasoning has been underpinned by the notion that financial innovation, in its various forms, ultimately enhances the liquidity of the financial system as a whole.

This misunderstanding, I believe, originates in a hollow notion of liquidity itself and, consequently, in the flawed vision – academic as well as political – of the dynamics of the relationship between private financial innovation and the liquidity and resilience of the financial system generally. Therefore, the hollow notion of liquidity lies at the heart of the great illusion of wealth and the belief in financial markets' capacity to invent money that are the real causes of the global meltdown.

3 Financial innovation and systemic fragility

'Stability is always destabilizing,' Hyman Minsky famously stated in his financial instability hypothesis. Amidst the ostensible rehabilitation of his name, it is this message from his scholarship that seems to attract most commentaries on the credit crunch. According to Minsky, 'good' times breed complacency, exuberance and optimism about one's position in the market, which leads to heavier reliance on leverage and underestimation of risks. Indeed, as stated famously by Citi's Chuck Prince in July 2007: 'When the music stops, in terms of liquidity, things will be complicated. But as long as the music is playing, you've got to get up and dance' (cited in Soros 2008: 84). Most observers concur that the major factor in the global credit crisis has been the progressive underestimation, or mis-understanding, of risks by financial agents based, in turn, on the general sense of stability, economic prosperity and optimistic forecasts that pervaded North Atlantic economies and financial markets.

Indeed, regardless of their intellectual and policy affiliations, most commentators on the credit crunch have recognized the tendency to under-estimate the risks in a bearish market or a bubble. Many US observers continue to believe that at the root cause of this problem was the liquidity glut coming from the emerging markets. Economists analysing the crisis do recognize the role of a liquidity crunch in the first stage of the crisis (August 2007–September 2008), notably, again, drawing the link between the supply of capital from abroad and the housing bubble in North America:

> The creation of new securities facilitated the large capital inflows from abroad.... The trend towards the 'originate and distribute model' ... ultimately led to a decline in lending standards. Financial innovation that had supposedly made the banking system more stable by transferring risk to those most able to bear it led to an unprecedented credit expansion that helped feed the boom in housing prices.
>
> (Brunnermeir 2009: 78)

The BIS went perhaps furthest in analysing the repercussions of this collective underestimation of risks for liquidity and admitted that, essentially, this phenomenon constitutes an illusion of liquidity, or a situation in which markets underprice liquidity and financial institutions underestimate liquidity risks (CGFS 2001: 2). In other words, the illusion of liquidity is being understood as a false sense of optimism a financial actor (be that a company, fund manager or a government) has over the safety and resilience of her portfolio, and/or market as a whole. As the credit crunch revealed, this illusion can have very real – and destructive – social, economic and political consequences. In this sense, many emergent theories of the global credit crunch appear to have strong Minskyan undertones, as now commonplace references to a 'Minsky moment' in finance or the crisis of Ponzi finance suggest.

And yet once we consider the contentious place of 'liquidity' in the crisis, it appears that only a fragmented, and highly selective, version of Minsky's theory of finance resonates in current readings of the global meltdown. While noting the risk effects of the general macroeconomic environment and investor expectations, most mainstream analysts of the crisis overlook the core of Minsky's framework. Very few of them, indeed, cast a critical eye on the very ability of private financial intermediaries to stretch the frontier of private liquidity, ultimately accentuating financial fragility in the system and thus accelerating the scope for a structural financial collapse and economic crisis.

According to Minsky, the web of debt-driven financial innovations has a twofold effect on the system's liquidity. On the one hand, as financial innovations gain ground, the velocity of money increases. Yet on the other, Minsky warned, 'every institutional innovation which results in both new ways to finance business and new substitutes for cash *decreases the liquidity of the economy*' (Minsky 1982: 173). The latest bout of securitization, propelled by the belief that clever techniques of parcelling debts, creating new products and opening up new markets creates additional and plentiful liquidity, in fact has driven the financial system into a structurally illiquid, and crisis-prone, state.

At the level of the financial system, securitization has produced an incredibly complex and obscure hierarchy of credit instruments, whose liquidity was assumed but in fact never guaranteed. What is astonishing about this is that some market players seemed to be aware of this danger. Just as the securitization bubble was beginning to inflate, one of the big investors warned about specific liquidity risks faced by his company. Although the firm's securitization strategy had been based on the assumption that collateralized mortgage obligations (CMOs) will be more liquid than their underlying collateral – the properties – he forewarned that this assumption was far too short-sighted and over-relied on the market's shared sentiments: 'as a guide to market discipline, we like the expression, "sure they're liquid, unless you actually have to sell them!"' (Kochen 2000: 112).

A notable outcome of the credit crunch is that it seems to have raised the importance of liquidity in the hierarchy of concerns of some policy-making bodies.[1] However most ensuing discussions of liquidity in the crisis, by focusing on the problem of valuations and risk mis-pricing, diagnose the evaporation of liquidity as a result of market failure rather than a systemic tendency. None of the studies, indeed, makes the connection between the excesses of private financial innovation and its liquidity-decreasing effects. Yet the evidence of these is abundant. For instance, in October 2008, the Bank of England documented a depletion of sterling liquid assets relative to total asset holdings of the UK banking sector, stating that:

> The ongoing turmoil has revealed that, during more benign periods, some banks sought to reduce the opportunity cost of holding liquid assets by substituting traditional liquid assets such as highly rated government bonds with highly rated structured credit products. This has been part of a longer-term decline in banks' holdings of liquid assets in the United Kingdom, which has been replicated in other countries.
>
> (2008: 39–40)

In this instance, one important question about the credit crunch continues to linger. If the participants of the credit boom themselves did admit that some of the foundations of their innovative techniques were shaky, and if a whole body of scholarship in heterodox political economy explains the dangers of financial euphoria and innovations, how come the illusion of liquidity and wealth had been sustained over a prolonged period of time, to lead people like Alan Greenspan to celebrate 'the new era in credit risk management'?

Part of the answer lies in the power of the paradigm of a self-regulating financial system, and the way it understand the concept and phenomenon of liquidity.

4 Financial innovation and the paradigm of self-regulating credit

In narrow terms, the global meltdown is a crisis centred on the US subprime mortgage industry; in its broader international dimension, it is a crisis of securitization. It is important to realize in this instance that securitization itself has become a functional form of the paradigm of self-regulating, efficient finance that has constituted mainstream thinking on finance and financial regulation for the past decades. The way 'liquidity' has been understood in this framework is representative of many other important assumptions of the paradigm of self-correcting financial markets.

Liquidity is the absolute essence of any market exchange and is paramount to the functioning of any financial system. Some scholars have even suggested that liquidity is synonymous with the greater meaning of 'capitalism' itself: ultimately, it is argued, 'liquidity' is about desire for, ownership of, and transferability of one's claims on wealth (Berle and Pederson 1934). In the era of highly financialised capitalism, dominated by sophisticated trading techniques and products, and defined by the notion that every eventuality can be priced, securitized and transferred to others in the market (Shiller 2008), liquidity of financial markets has often been assumed, yet not necessarily warranted.

The key reason for this lies in the ideology of perfect markets and the theory of market-completing financial innovation. Like in any other area of economic activity, innovation in finance has always been driven by the desire for faster and greater profits, but also, crucially, by the search for greater 'liquidity'. Yet precisely what this 'greater liquidity' implies remained a somewhat blurry notion. On the one hand, most financial innovations have for a long time been perceived to be liquidity-enhancing: by pooling a greater variety of assets into the market exchange, by pricing them and then transferring them on to their new willing and able owners, financial engineers and traders have expanded the reach of the financial markets, thereby increasing market turnover and, in popular terminology, liquidity.

On the other hand however, critics of the financial orthodoxy, from Minsky and beyond, have long argued that the relationship between new financial products and the liquidity of the economic system as a whole is far less straightforward. The process of inventing, valuing and introducing new credit instruments, markets and institutions has been driven by the search for greater liquidity across the global financial markets. At the same time, new financial instruments, while adding to *a sense* of greater liquidity in the markets, also rely on the liquidity of the underlying assets. Securitization for instance – the latest wave of financial engineering – both relies on and enhances liquidity. It 'enhances the liquidity of underlying receivables by transforming them into tradable securities. On the other hand, the funding of a large number of market participants involved in the securitisation process depends crucially on market liquidity being permanently sustained' (Banque de France 2008: 11).

Securitization has had its own controversial effects on the idea and functioning of liquidity in the markets. Theoretically, securitization has been understood to be 'a technique to create securities by reshuffling the cash flows produced by a diversified pool of assets with some common characteristics. By doing so, one can design several securities (tranches) with different risk-reward profiles which appeal to different investors.' (Cifuentes 2008). Advocates of the technique argue that the key economic functions of securitization have been to provide an alternative form of financing for companies with predictable cash flows, and to help lending institutions manage the credit exposure more efficiently, thus allowing them to make more loans. Generally, therefore, by creating securities out of illiquid assets, securitization has been believed to increase liquidity across the financial system and the economy as a whole.

This idea did not emerge out of the blue. Historically, much like other important financial segments (say, the Eurodollar market that has emerged almost through accident but later become widely established), securitization has been the banking sector's reaction to the introduction of the Basle II accord of financial regulation. Plainly, the Basle requirements made it unprofitable for banks to hold safe and liquid assets on their balance sheets (Wigan 2009). Unsurprisingly, banks reacted to the new regulations by accelerating debt origination on the basis of the capacity to move assets off-balance-sheet by selling them off. In practical terms, then, securitization meant that risky (but profitable) assets were removed from the balance sheets of banks into the unregulated realm of the financial system.

This trend in turn, has had its own – ultimately destructive – repercussions for the stability of the financial system as a whole. Chiefly, it was transmitted through its impact on liquidity. As Minsky foresaw, in a deregulated financialized economy, the ability to expand the debt chain leads to progressive illiquidity of the financial system as a whole:

> to the extent that either the most liquid assets leave the banking system for the portfolios of other financial institutions or the debts of the newly grown and developed financial institutions enter the portfolios of banks, the liquidity of the banking system declines.
>
> (Minsky 1984: 174)

In this regard, according to Victoria Chick, the experience of the first Basel accord illustrates the law of unintended consequences. Regulations intended to strengthen the balance sheets of banks by weighting assets on the basis of their riskiness (thus rewarding the holding of safe assets), actually drove risky assets off the balance sheet. As a result of the introduction of the Basel rules, securitization was undertaken not just as a small part of bank operations when banks needed liquidity, but on such a scale as to change the whole manner in which banks operate (Chick 2008).

This shift, in turn, has itself become a major institutional transformation of the global financial system. At the centre of this process lay a transformation of the US banking system (Kregel 2007, 2008). As noted above, securitization reflects the way risk has been modelled, valued and traded, by banks and financial houses since the liberalization reforms were introduced in the 1980s in the USA and in other countries.[2] These reforms led to the rise of a new type of banking, now known as the 'originate and distribute' (ORD) model. Under the new mode of operation, the bank is no longer an institution focused on taking deposits and giving out loans. Instead, it is a competitive financier seeking to maximize fee and commission income from originating assets, managing those assets in off-balance-sheet affiliate structures such as special investment vehicles (SIVs), underwriting the primary distribution of securities collateralized with those assets, and servicing them. Crucially in a discussion of financial fragility, the banker today has no motivation to conduct proper credit evaluation, simply because the interest and principal on the loans originated will be repaid not to the bank itself, but to the final buyers of the collateralised assets. In the words of Robert Wade, banks and hedge funds became careless because they were acting as intermediaries, not as principals (Wade 2008: 32–3), thus spreading moral hazard around the financial system.

The adoption of the ORD model of risk-trading has underpinned a phenomenal rise in commission fees and income from capital-market-related activities for banks. The incentive to be a prudent lender has been replaced by an overarching drive to reap commissions, bonuses and profits. In recent years, the gap between the capital of a bank and its managers has widened. Lenders have become progressively indifferent to risk and obsessed by reward (*Credit Magazine* 2008). According to one estimate, between 2004 and 2006, earnings from derivatives trading and capital-market-related activities at the top ten global investment banks have risen by almost two-thirds, from $55 billion in 2004 to $90 billion in 2006.[3] Reflecting these changes, the profits from the sales and trading operations had not only been growing, but also assuming a greater share of the investment banks' revenues (over 90 per cent for the Americas, over 80 per cent for Europe, the Middle East and Africa, and just over 40 per cent for Asia Pacific).

The concern with creating the new markets for their products prompted financial institutions – both in the official, visible banking sector and in the so-called shadow banking system – to embark on a spate of financial engineering unprecedented in its scope and sophistication. The resulting series of financial innovations that created a *sense*, though not a warranty, of abundant liquidity in the subprime-related financial markets and of the financial wealth being created and spread around. Politically, this trend has been commonly viewed as a sign of a more efficient financial system and a foundation for economic stability. In 2006, the Bank of England for instance noted that while the originate and distribute model 'does not alter the financial sector's aggregate credit exposure to the non-financial sector,' it promises to 'improve systemic stability if risk is held by those with the greatest capacity to absorb losses' (Bank of England 2006, cited in Langley 2010).

In the wake of the global meltdown, it seems too naïve and short-sighted to draw a straightforward and linear link between securitization and systemic stability. At the peak of the credit boom, however, things were much murkier. Here again, it is the idea of, or more accurately, the illusion of, liquidity, that disguised many fallacies – conceptual and political – at the time. As Paul Langley writes, the mainstream political discourse that paralleled the expanding credit boom invariably

> represented the markets as efficient ... and liquid. Such representations of finance meant that a 'liquid' market became an object that investors increasingly regarded as a given fact, external to them. Since the subprime industry seemed to exemplify what was possible in an era of liquid finance, there was little to suggest that markets for assets named 'liquid' would be any different from the norm.
>
> (Langley 2010)

With regard to how liquidity has been approached within the regulatory architecture, a particular emphasis within the Basle II Accord proved critical, and fatal, in the lead-up to the global credit crunch. Basle II has been built upon the presumption that a functioning financial market is *always* liquid. As a result, the accord established a whole system of regulatory principles that delegated to individual institutions themselves the management of their portfolios of risks. Specifically, the central parameters of international financial governance were founded upon regulatory developments in the private sphere: when eventually Basel I proved ineffective, the solution was sought in private risk-management tools (Wigan 2009). With the assumption of an infinitely liquid market there was no need to install systemic provision to guarantee its liquidity. The key concern for policy-makers at the time was market efficiency and the efficiency of individual banks (Davies 2009). Through the alchemy of financial engineering, the banks were assumed to optimise their own risk strategies; while the market as a whole – founded upon financial innovation and competition – was made liquid.

Mainstream finance theory, in turn, has guided this trend, arguing that this new approach to managing risks enhances market liquidity and the financial robustness of the economy. Politicians reaped the benefits of this process, partly capitalizing on the contribution of the financial sector to the economy, partly by advocating the social welfare gains of new, democratized finance. Like most illusions, however, the illusion of liquidity eventually came to a destructive end.

Notwithstanding the variety of explanation of the crisis mentioned above therefore, the global financial crisis, centred on the grandiose misunderstanding of financial innovation and a massive misrepresentation of risks, is an example of a colossal failure of modern economic theory and policy. Increasingly abstract, detached from reality and lacking a systemic vision of finance and the economy, orthodox economics has been unable and unwilling to ponder the possibility of a multifaceted structural rupture caused by the advance of innovative, yet murky, financial techniques and products, and the ideology that supported these inventions. What is perhaps most worrying in the wake of the credit crunch, is that the crisis has not prompted the economics profession to consider its role in precipitating the crisis. It is really disappointing, therefore, that a discipline that has its origins in the study of moral philosophy has become so self-engrossed as to have failed to provide any timely insight into the possibility of a crisis that would prove to the largest financial and economic collapse of the past 75 years.

Notes

1 Most notably, the BIS, the ECB, FSF and the IMF. Occasional studies of 'liquidity' have been published by other central banks in the wake of the crisis. The Bank of England for instance, noted in October 2008 that liquidity regulation 'can play an important role in requiring banks to build larger defences against crystallisation of roll-over risk' (2008: 39).
2 In this element, Kregel notes, the ongoing financial crisis does differ from the context Minsky identified originally. Jan Kregel, *Minsky's Cushions of Safety. Systemic Risk and the Crisis in the US Subprime Mortgage Market*, Policy Brief, Levy Economics Institute (2007).
3 Data from *The Economist*, May 17, 2007.

References

Allen, F. and D. Gale, 2000, 'Bubbles and Crises,' *The Economic Journal*, 110 (January).
Almunia, N., A. Bénétrix, B. Eichengreen, 2010, 'From Great Depression to great credit crisis: similarities, differences and lessons,' *Economic Policy*, 25:62, April.
Bank of England, 2006, *Financial Stability Report*, July, Issue No. 20, London: Bank of England.
Bank of England, 2008, *Financial Stability Report*, October.

Bellofiore, R. and J. Halevi, 2010, 'Magdoff-Sweezy, Minsky and the Real Subsumption of Labour to Finance,' in D. Tavasci and J. Toporowski, eds., *Minsky, Crisis and Development*, Basingstoke: Palgrave.

Berle, A. and V. Pederson, 1934, *Liquid Claims and National Wealth*, New York: Macmillan.

Bernstein, P., 1996, *Against the Gods, The Remarkable Story of Risk*, New York: John Wiley.

Brown, C., 1940, *Liquidity and Instability*, New York: Columbia University Press.

Brunnermeir, M. 2009, 'Deciphering the 2007–2008 Liquidity and Credit Crunch,' *Journal of Economic Perspectives*, 23:1.

CGFS, 2001, 'Structural Aspects of Market Liquidity From a Financial Stability Perspective,' CGFS Discussion Paper, BIS: Committee on the Global Financial System, June.

Chick, V., 2008, 'Could the Crisis at Northern Rock Have Been Predicted? An Evolutionary Approach,' *Contributions to Political Economy*, 28:1, May.

Chinloy, P. and MacDonald, N. 2005, 'Subprime Lenders and Mortgage Market Completion,' *The Journal of Real Estate Finance and Economics*, 30:2.

Cifuentes, A., 2008 'Insight: Securitisation Isn't the Villain,' *Financial Times*, 10 November.

Credit Magazine, 2008, 'Talking point – Are we facing a Global Economic Slowdown?' June.

Crockett, A., 2008, 'Market Liquidity and Financial Stability,' *Financial Stability Review (Special Issue on Liquidity)*, Paris: Bank of France, February.

Davies, P., 2009, 'On Cavendish Banana etc.' Keynote Address to the Workshop on Securitisation, Risk and Governance, City University London, 6–7 May, mimeo.

Gamble, A., 2009, *The Spectre at the Feast: Capitalist Crisis and the Politics of Recession*, Basingstoke: Palgrave Macmillan.

Grossman, R. And C. Meissner, 2010, 'International Aspects of the Great Depression and the Crisis of 2007: Similarities, Differences, and Lessons,' NBER Working Paper No. 16269, August.

Goldsmith, R., 1982, 'A Comment on Minsky's FIH,' in Kindleberger, C. and, Laffargue, J.-P., *Financial Crises. History, Theory and Policy*, Cambridge: Cambridge University Press.

Guttman, R., 2003, *Cybercash. The Coming Era of Electronic Money*, Palgrave Macmillan.

Hirschleifer, J., 1986, 'Liquidity, Uncertainty and the Accumulation of Assets,' CORE Discussion Paper 6810.

Holmstrong, B. and J. Tirole, 1998, 'Private and Public Supply of Liquidity,' *Journal of Political Economy*, 106:1.

Kochen, N., 2000, 'Securitization from the investor view: meeting investor needs with products and price,' in L. Randall and M. Fishman, eds., *A Primer on Securitization*, London and Cambridge, MA: MIT Press.

Kregel, J., 2007, 'The Natural Instability of Financial Markets,' Levy Institute Working Paper no. 523 (December), Levy Institute of Bard College.

Kregel, J., 2008, 'Minsky's Cushions of Safety. Systemic Risk and the Crisis in the U.S.Subprime Mortgage Market,' Public Policy Brief No. 93, Levy Institute of Bard College. Available at www.levy.org.

Langley, P., 2010, 'The performance of liquidity in the sub-prime mortgage crisis,' *New Political Economy*, 15:1.

Large, A., 2005, 'A Framework for Financial Stability,' Speech at the International Conference on Financial Stability and Implications of Basle II, Istanbul, 18 March.

Lawson, T., 2009, 'The current economic crisis: its nature and the course of academic economics,' *Cambridge Journal of Economics*, 33, pp. 759–77.

McCulley, P., 2008, 'The Liquidity Conundrum,' *CFA Institute Conference Proceedings Quarterly*, March.
Minsky, H., 1982 (1984pb), *Can 'It' Happen Again?*, New York: M.E. Sharpe.
Minsky, H., 1986, *Stabilizing an Unstable Economy*, New Haven, Conn.: Yale University Press.
Morris, C., 2008, *The Trillion Dollar Meltdown*, New York: Public Affairs.
Mueller, F., 1953, 'Corporate Working Capital and Liquidity,' *The Journal of Business of the University of Chicago*, Vol. 26, No. 3, July, pp. 157–72.
Nesvetailova, A., 2010, *Financial Alchemy in Crisis: the Great Liquidity Illusion*, London: Pluto.
Palan, R., 2003, *The Offshore World*, Ithaca and London: Cornell University Press.
Partnoy, F., 1997, *F.I.A.S.C.O. Guns, Booze and Bloodlust: The Truth About High Finance*, London: Profile Books.
Shiller, R., 2004, *The New Financial Order: Risk in the 21st Century*, Princeton: PUP.
Soros, G., 2008, *The New Paradigm for Financial Markets*, New York: Public Affairs.
Tett, G., 2009, *Fool's Gold*, New York: Free Press.
Tett G. and A. van Duyn, 2009, 'Under restraint,' *Financial Times*, 7 July.
Toporowski, J., 2009, *'It's Not About Regulation...'*, DIIS Working Paper 2009:08, Copenhagen: Danish Institute for International Studies.
Wade, R., 2008, 'The First World Debt Crisis of 2007–2010 in Global Perspective,' *Challenge*, July–August.
Warsh, K., 2007, 'Market Liquidity – Definitions and Implications,' Remarks at the Institute of International Bankers Annual Washington Conference, Washington DC, 5 March.
Wigan, D., 2009, 'Financialisation and Derivatives: Constructing an Artifice of Indifference,' *Competition and Change*, 3:2.

4 The problematic nature of the Economic and Monetary Union

Malcolm Sawyer

1 Introduction

It is widely acknowledged that there is a crisis of the Eurozone with its continued existence called into doubt, and questions raised on whether it can function effectively. In this chapter we outline a view of the nature of the Eurozone crisis which can be summarised as arising from 'design faults' of the Economic and Monetary Union and a balance of payments crisis with large current account imbalances between countries. In section 3 we argue that the policy remedies (in the form of the 'fiscal compact') which are being put into place will not work in their own terms and will make the economic performance of the Eurozone countries worse. In section 4, we sketch some Keynesian remedies for the crisis in terms of alternative policy proposals for the operation of the Economic and Monetary Union. Section 5 concludes the chapter.

2 The nature of the Eurozone crisis

There can be little doubt that there is a Eurozone crisis. At one level, there are economic and financial crises, high levels of unemployment and recession in many of the countries of the Economic and Monetary Union (EMU). At another level, there is a crisis of the Economic and Monetary Union with many now doubting whether it can continue in its present form and if it does whether it would inevitably involve continuing severe unemployment. The focus of this chapter is on Eurozone crisis in the second sense (without doubting the severity of the first and indeed the degree to which the first is arising from the second). In other papers (for example, Arestis and Sawyer, 2010a, 2010b) we have talked of the 'design faults' of the EMU and also of its 'dysfunctional nature'. We have argued that the Eurozone crisis should be viewed through the lens of the design and nature of EMU, and not through that of 'bad behaviour' by some member governments. These 'design faults' can be seen as related to many writers who warned (in the 1990s) that the EMU would be subject to many strains and stresses through the way it was constructed and the constructed policy framework (notably the Stability and Growth Pact with attempted constraints on national government budget deficits and the independence of the European

Central Bank). Some pointed to the 'optimal currency area' (OCA) literature, and the lack of correspondence between the criteria of that literature and the conditions in the Eurozone. The OCA literature had highlighted that the formation of a single currency removes a country's ability to change its exchange rate (in case of fixed exchange rate) or a market adjustment process (in the case of floating exchange rate) in the face of 'shocks' to the economy. For example, a downturn in the demand for a country's products can be adjusted for through a depreciation of the exchange rate. The OCA literature pointed to alternative adjustment processes such as price flexibility and factor mobility, and doubt was cast on the scale of labour mobility in the Eurozone (apart from any issue over the desirability of large scale migration). The lack of an EMU level fiscal policy and transfers was also noted by many, which could have acted to cushion the impact of downswings in individual countries and also served to redistribute income between countries.

The role of the central bank (European Central Bank, ECB) was a matter of concern in at least two ways (leaving aside issues over 'independence' of central bank – see Arestis and Sawyer, 2010a). First, the operation of monetary policy in the form of the setting of a policy interest rate raised concerns over the 'one size fits all' problem. This is an inevitable issue relating to monetary policy in that monetary policy involves the setting of an interest rate which applies across the whole of the currency area, and in diverse economy the interest rate appropriate for the conditions in one part of the area may not be appropriate for other parts. The extent of the problem depends on matters such as the degree of convergence of the business cycle and of inflationary conditions, and the similarities between the regions of the currency area in the workings of their economies and the transmission of monetary policy.

Second, the ECB was an EMU-level body, whereas fiscal policy was operated by national governments (subject in principle to the constraints of the Stability and Growth Pact SGP on the size of budget deficits, which were in the outturn frequently broken). Within a national state, there is usually a close relationship between the fiscal authority (central government) and the monetary authority (central bank). The monetary authority will always accept central government (and other levels of government) debt as collateral in exchange for currency, and central government debt is underpinned by its acceptance by the central bank. Further, directly or indirectly, the central bank will always monetise a budget deficit if required, and the central government will always be able to finance its deficit and its debt position through the central bank's willingness to supply currency to the central government. In this position, the central government can always meet its debt obligations and need never default, provided that the debt is denominated in the national currency. In the EMU, the ECB is not obligated to accept the debt of member national governments as collateral, and is explicitly prohibited from monetising national government deficits.

Others pointed to the current account imbalances between member countries, and the lack of mechanisms through which those imbalances could be resolved without resort to deflation in the deficit countries. A country can run a trade deficit provided that other countries are prepared to lend to it. The current account deficit covering the trade deficit, interest and related payments on borrowing would then tend to rise (relative to GDP). Apart from any fickleness of capital inflows, there is the problem of financing rising current account deficits. A fixed exchange rate regime (which a single currency is par excellence) does not permit the use of the exchange rate changes to respond to a current account deficit. At some stage, a country with a large trade deficit is likely to encounter difficulties in financing the current account deficit, and yet in the absence of the ability to change the nominal exchange rate will be pushed towards deflation to lower income and imports and to lower domestic prices (to change the real exchange rate).

The pattern of current account deficits and surpluses also involved, of course, a pattern of capital account surpluses and deficits. Given the pattern of current account deficits and surpluses, this implied as a broad generalisation lending by Northern European countries and borrowing by Southern European countries. The imbalances of current account positions and their development prior to the financial crisis is illustrated in Figure 4.1 where the current account position relative to GDP (in per cent) for the original 12 Eurozone members are given. The creation of the Eurozone facilitated that pattern of lending and borrowing in that within a single currency area neither the lenders nor the borrowers faced exchange rate risks. Further, for the lending countries interest rates (particularly

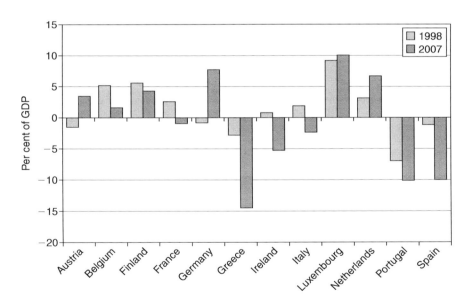

Figure 4.1 Current account position as per cent of GDP for Eurozone countries (original 12 members) (source: figures derived from OECD, *Economic Outlook*, December 2011).

in nominal terms) were significantly lower than previously experienced. There appeared to be little difficulty in the deficit countries borrowing to cover their current account deficits.

The Maastricht convergence criteria referred to similar inflation rates, interest rates, stability of exchange rate, and budget deficit and government debt levels. There was much concern expressed as to how far these convergence criteria were the relevant ones, and how far there were important convergences and divergences which were left unmentioned with little apparent attention paid to them by the policy makers. There was little consideration of the convergence of cycles in economic activity which is particularly relevant for the operation of a 'one size fits all' macroeconomic policies. Whilst there was a requirement for convergence of inflation rate at a particular time, there was no requirement for the convergence of expectations on and attitudes to inflation nor to the wage and price setting mechanisms and their implications for the inflationary processes. These omissions were to come to haunt the EMU in that there were significant divergences of inflation between member countries with consequences for the evolution of relative competitiveness. There were the more general omission of the compatibility of differences of general policy outlooks (e.g. role of industrial intervention policies, perspectives on macroeconomic policies including fiscal policy), of industrial structures (e.g. with regard to export performance and competitiveness), and institutional arrangements (e.g. with regard to operation of labour markets).

The Economic and Monetary Union was formed without sufficient consideration being given to whether there was sufficient convergence amongst the member countries to warrant the operation of a single currency. There were many dimensions of convergence/divergence which were over-looked: we have pointed here to lack of attention to convergence of business cycle and economic conditions, to inflationary mechanisms and to political, social and institutional perspectives. There was also a lack of concern over current account imbalances and their correction, and a major problem which the EMU now faces is how to correct those imbalances without resort to long periods of austerity.

We now turn to the policy remedies which are currently under discussion, which we argue will be ineffectual and indeed likely to be damaging. This is followed by an outline of some alternative policy proposals.

3 The quack remedies

The remedy to the Eurozone crisis which is currently being brought into force is embodied in the Treaty on Stability, Coordination and Governance in the Economic and Monetary Union (European Union, 2012) (hereafter referred to as the Treaty) of which the 'fiscal compact' is the central part, and the associated so-called 'six pack' of policy measures.[1] The argument here is that the fiscal compact is no more than a quack remedy which cannot work in its own terms and will bring considerable economic damage, and could be more accurately labelled a 'fiscal suicide pact'.

The essential features of the 'fiscal compact' for the discussion here are:

i   The imposition of a 'structural budget deficit' rule such that that notion of budget deficit does not exceed 0.5 per cent of GDP. Under Article 1 'the budgetary position of the general government of a Contracting Party shall be balanced or in surplus' and this is interpreted as 'the annual structural balance of the general government is at its country-specific medium-term objective, as defined in the revised Stability and Growth Pact, with a lower limit of a structural deficit of 0.5% of the gross domestic product at market prices. The Contracting Parties shall ensure rapid convergence towards their respective medium-term objective. The time-frame for such convergence will be proposed by the European Commission taking into consideration country-specific sustainability risks'.

ii A stricter policy imposed on countries with debt ratio exceeding 60 per cent of GDP. The Treaty (following the Six Pact) makes it 'possible to open an EDP [excessive deficit procedure] on the basis of the debt criterion. Member States with government debt ratios in excess of 60% of GDP should reduce this ratio in line with a numerical benchmark, which implies a decline of the amount by which their debt exceeds the threshold at a rate in the order of 1/20th per year over three years. If they do not, they could be placed in EDP depending on the assessment of all relevant factors and taking in particular into account the influence of the cycle on the pace of debt reduction.' (Article 4). The precise impact of this would depend on the rate of nominal growth, and the imposition of the EDP is possible rather than mandatory. However, in a slow growth economy with a debt ratio of say 120 per cent of GDP, this approach would involve a budget surplus of the order of 3 per cent of GDP (and a primary surplus which was substantial greater when interest payments on debt considered).

iii The deficit requirement is to be written into a country's national constitution or equivalent. 'The rules set out ... shall take effect in the national law of the Contracting Parties at the latest one year after the entry into force of this Treaty through provisions of binding force and permanent character, preferably constitutional, or otherwise guaranteed to be fully respected and adhered to throughout the national budgetary processes. The Contracting Parties shall put in place at national level the correction mechanism ... on the basis of common principles to be proposed by the European Commission, concerning in particular the nature, size and time-frame of the corrective action to be undertaken, also in the case of exceptional circumstances, and the role and independence of the institutions responsible at national level for monitoring compliance with the rules set out. ... Such correction mechanism shall fully respect the prerogatives of national Parliaments.' (Article 3.2)

The 'fiscal compact' could be viewed as a development of the Stability and Growth Pact in which the intention to balance the budget deficit over the cycle is superseded with a balanced structural deficit rule, with the addition of the stricter policy rule as under (ii). Further, the sanctions for breaking the 'fiscal compact' are re-inforced after the failures under the Stability and Growth Pact for the rules on budget deficits to be followed. The fascination with a 60 per cent debt-to-GDP ratio remains, though there is no significance to be attached to the figure of 60 rather than any other, and the inconsistency between a 60 per cent debt-to-GDP ratio and a budget on average near balance remains. There are some exemptions from adherence to these rules in 'exceptional circumstances' which: 'refers to the case of an unusual event outside the control of the Contracting Party concerned which has a major impact on the financial position of the general government or to periods of severe economic downturn as set out in the revised Stability and Growth Pact, provided that the temporary deviation of the Contracting Party concerned does not endanger fiscal sustainability in the medium-term.' (Article 3.3). But 'exceptional circumstances', whether an event such as financial crisis which drastically depresses demand or a major natural disaster which requires large public expenditure to deal with the disaster, does not change the 'structural' levels of public expenditure nor the 'structural' tax revenues (based on the level of potential output, as indicated below), and hence would not change the structural budget position.

The writing of requirements on the achievement of a structural balanced budget into the national constitution or equivalent has two points of significance. First, it embeds economic policy into the constitution whereas ideas on appropriate economic policy are not unchanging over time. It seems a folly to incorporate ideas that some, but no means all, think are appropriate policies into a document which is difficult to change, especially when those ideas are mistaken. It can also be seen as an attempt to tie the hands of the electorate and future governments on economic policies – what is the point of a party presenting a manifesto committed to raising public expenditure when the constitutional court would rule the implementation of such a commitment illegal?

Second, the implementation of a balanced structural budget requirement will be made difficult by disputes over the measurement of the structural budget position. The implementation of a requirement that there be a balanced annual budget (as is the case with the European Union itself) does not face such difficulty as the annual budget outcome can be readily measured, though it is the ex post annual budget which can be measured but not the ex ante budget. The structural budget is 'structural' public expenditure (that is some 'normal' level of expenditure excluding any one-off forms of expenditure) less the tax revenues which would be generated from the 'normal' set of tax rates when the economy operates at some 'average' level (which will be described as 'potential output' in line with the literature). Each of the elements of the structural budget is a matter of estimates and dispute, and notably what constitutes 'potential output'.

The preamble to the Treaty notes the 'European Commission's intention to present further legislative proposals for the euro area concerning, in particular, *ex ante* reporting of debt issuance plans, economic partnership programmes detailing structural reforms for Member States under an excessive deficit procedure as well as the coordination of major economic policy reform plans of Member States' (p. 3). Under Article 5,

> A Contracting Party that is subject to an excessive deficit procedure under the Treaties on which the European Union is founded shall put in place a budgetary and economic partnership programme including a detailed description of the structural reforms which must be put in place and implemented to ensure an effective and durable correction of its excessive deficit.

Within the Treaty, 'structural reforms' are not defined. But there can be little doubt as to what is in mind. In an interview with the Wall Street Journal, Mario Draghi, President of the ECB stated that the most important structural reforms were

> first is the product and services markets reform. And the second is the labour market reform which takes different shapes in different countries. In some of them one has to make labour markets more flexible and also fairer than they are today. In these countries there is a dual labour market: highly flexible for the young part of the population where labour contracts are three-month, six-month contracts that may be renewed for years. The same labour market is highly inflexible for the protected part of the population where salaries follow seniority rather than productivity.[2]

This echoes the sentiments which have been repeatedly expressed by the European Central Bank in their Monthly Bulletin. For example, writing in December 2009, ECB (2009) argued that

> With regard to structural reforms, most estimates indicate that the financial crisis has reduced the productive capacity of the euro area economies, and will continue to do so for some time to come. In order to support sustainable growth and employment, labour market flexibility and more effective incentives to work will be needed. Furthermore, policies that enhance competition and innovation are also urgently needed to speed up restructuring and investment and to create new business opportunities.
>
> (p. 7)

The nature of the intended 'structural reforms' can be also seen by reference to those imposed on Greece in terms of privatisation and labour market 'reforms' (notably drastic reduction of minimum wage).[3]

Anti-democratic

All tiers of government operate subject to a budget constraint in the sense that expenditure (current and capital) minus revenue has to be covered by borrowing, and for many tiers of government limits are placed on the scale of borrowing (e.g. limited to cover capital expenditure, subject to approval by higher tier of government). The limits on borrowing may be imposed by 'higher authority' (e.g. national government over local government) or may be self-imposed. Placing such limits on borrowing is not inherently undemocratic, and depends where the effective decision-making lies. The features of the 'fiscal compact' which are troublesome in this regard are, first, the ways in which policy decisions on being imposed on national governments, and most clearly this has been the case for Greece already, but further the Treaty seeks to impose a specific range of policy decisions ('structural reforms') as a condition of membership of EMU. Second, the writing of the 'fiscal compact' conditions into national constitutions unnecessarily binds future governments and future perspective governments with regard to issues of taxation and public expenditure.

It must be questioned whether economic policies should be embedded into constitutions or quasi-constitutional legislation which limit the necessary flexibility to change economic policies as conditions and ideas on policies change. The ideas of 'independent central banks' and of 'balanced structural budgets' are not universal panaceas and indeed many of us would argue that the idea of 'independent central banks' is highly problematic. It is also an idea which could be viewed as a current fashion whose attraction is fading. If an economic policy is to be given the force of law, it should be capable of precise definition such that whether the policy has been implemented can be accurately judged. Further, it should be a policy which is capable of being achieved. In the following two sections it is first argued that the idea of 'structural budget' is ambiguous and correspondingly a 'structural budget position' cannot be exactly measured. Second, it is argued that a balanced structural balanced budget is often not achievable – that is a budget which is balanced when the economy is operating at potential output.

The ambiguity of the structural budget

A structural budget deficit (which appears to be left without a precise definition in the 'fiscal compact', and lacking any clear indication of the methodology to be used in its estimation) can be viewed as the deficit which would result from the application of current tax rates (where here transfer payments are treated as negative taxes) and prevailing public expenditure levels if the economy were operating at some 'normal' level of output, which has come to be linked with the level of 'potential output'. We put inverted commas around 'potential output' to signify that this term is used in a specific way in this literature as explained below, and does not correspond to the everyday usage of the term potential which would signify capability and capacity. We use the term structural budget deficit (SBD) below though cyclically adjusted budget deficit is also used in the 'fiscal compact' and elsewhere, and the two are treated as synonymous. Thus the structural budget deficit (SBD) is given by:

$$SBD = G^* - t(Y^*) \qquad (1)$$

where G^* is underlying ('structural') level of government consumption and investment, t as tax function relating to prevailing tax rates with income transfers regarded as negative taxation and Y^* 'potential output'. There would generally be some issues over exact measures of G^* as to elements which could be regarded as temporary or discretionary and hence not included. In a similar vein, there would be issues over the tax function to be used to reflect prevailing tax rates – for example, with an income tax system involving tax free allowances and tax rates which vary with the level of income, what is assumed about the adjustments of the tax free allowances and levels of taxable income at which tax rates change in the face of inflation and changing aggregate income levels. Here we leave those issues on one side to focus on the more major issues.

There are two key major measurement issues here, and the interaction of them (combined with measurement issues over 'potential output') generate considerable ambiguity over the measurement of structural budget deficit such that it is not a suitable concept to embed in law.

The first is that a structural budget deficit is a hypothetical calculation and the question as to whether a consistent estimate of the SBD can be made (for some measure of potential output). The difficulty here can be readily seen by reference to the national accounts relationship which is here written as:

$$G - T = S - I + M - X \qquad (2)$$

Where G is government expenditure, T tax revenue, S private savings, I private investment, M imports and X exports (including net income). In terms of out-turns, a balanced budget with the left hand side equal to zero would require the right hand side to be similarly equal to zero.

Suppose the SBD in conditions appertaining at time t was calculated as equal to α. For reasons of consistency and sustainability this would mean that:

$$S_1^* - I_1^* + M_1^* - X_1^* = \alpha \qquad (3)$$

Where a * after variable signifies the level of the variable which would correspond to 'potential output', e.g. S^* is intended level of savings which would be forthcoming at potential output.

Now consider the case where the policy intention is to change the SBD through changes in tax rates and levels of public expenditure, and the target is β. Then it not only would SBD=β, but the following equation would also need to hold:

$$S_2^* - I_2^* + M_2^* - X_2^* = \beta \qquad (4)$$

This would be possible if there were relevant changes in 'structural' savings, investment, imports and exports, e.g. if for example intentions to save diminished between (3) and (4) (in the case of $\alpha > \beta$). This could arise with a strong form of Ricardian equivalence – the intention to reduce a structural budget deficit would be exactly matched by corresponding changes in private expenditure.

The second issue relates to the concept of 'potential output' itself. It must first be said that the term 'potential output' is used in a number of different ways which need to be distinguished, and that it is a theoretical notion for which there may not be a counterpart in the real world. Further, any estimation of 'potential output' (for a given definition) is inevitably backward looking in the sense of using past data, but the measure of 'potential output' which is relevant for policy is the current and future levels.

The term 'potential output' is generally linked with the supply-side of the economy. In common usage the term potential would suggest some form of maximum output. When we speak of someone's potential we are thinking of the most they could achieve or be capable of. In economic terms 'potential output' can be linked with productive capacity. As such 'potential output' could be interpreted as the (sustainable) physical capacity output, though more usually some notion of costs would be involved such as the level of production at which costs would start to rise 'sharply'. This approach to 'potential output' is closely related to some upper limit to the level of output. However, the notion of 'potential output' which is common in the current dominant paradigm in macroeconomics, that is the 'new consensus in macroeconomics' is more akin to some average level of output around which the economy fluctuates, and more recently has tended to be aligned with the level of output at which inflation would be constant.

It is also apparent that the estimation of 'potential output' requires data – that is the estimation can only be conducted after the events. It is only if past estimates of potential output can be used to project forward future potential output can estimates of potential output be derived. As output tends to grow over time, this would clearly involve not only scaling potential output against actual output, but also deriving estimates of the growth of potential output.

The more general theoretical framework within which 'potential output' is cast is one of the independence of demand and supply factors. The actual level of output is viewed as determined in the short run by the level of aggregate demand, whereas potential output is set on the supply side of the economy, and in general that the growth of 'potential output' is unaffected by what happens on the demand side, and that the level of demand fluctuates around potential output (and hence output gap tends to average out as zero).

It is often implicitly assumed that the economy operates on average at the potential output level, and also that the economy *should* operate at that level. This is formalised in the quadratic loss function which appears in the 'new consensus in macroeconomics' where the loss function to be minimised is quadratic in inflation (minus inflation target) and output gap. Thus inflation below target is treated in same way in terms of welfare losses as inflation above target, and positive output gap in same way as negative output gap. Actual output above potential generates losses comparable to those from actual output below potential.

The zero output gap (actual equals potential output) does not in general correspond to full employment of labour. There are two distinct reasons here. First, potential output is often taken as akin to the average level of output (trend adjusted), and hence sometimes actual output is above and sometimes below potential output. Full employment of labour is more akin to a ceiling for employment and thereby economic activity: we do not see full employment as the average level of employment (unfortunately). Second, potential output can be taken to be the level of output which would correspond to the employment rate which can be deduced from the NAIRU or NAWRU. The NAIRU is simply the rate of unemployment which is deemed to be consistent with constant rate of inflation, and should not carry with it any connotation of full employment. The estimates of the NAWRU produced by the OECD (and also labelled 'structural unemployment' in OECD *Economic* Outlook): for example, the figures for 2007 (used to avoid influence of financial crisis) were: France 8.4 per cent, Germany 8.4 per cent, Italy 6.3 per cent, United Kingdom 5.3 per cent and the euroarea average 7.6 per cent.[4]

The impossibility of balanced structural budget

The question here can be simply posed in terms of the conditions for a structural balanced budget (the argument would apply with minimal adjustment to conditions for a structural budget deficit of say 0.5 per cent of GDP). Drawing on the national accounts equations above, the condition for a structural balanced budget would be:

$$G - t(Y^*) = S^* - I^* + M^* - X^* = 0 \tag{5}$$

In other words, the savings, investment, net exports which would be forthcoming at 'normal' savings, investment rates and when output is at the potential level are consistent with this equation. The 'fiscal compact' asserts in effect that condition is always fulfilled – at each point in time and for every country (at least those within the Economic and Monetary Union). The actual budget deficit could diverge from this balanced position as private aggregate demand fluctuates – for example, through a change in the propensity to invest, leading to change in level of output, and thereby in tax receipts. But it is asserted that if investment demand were at some 'normal' level (along with savings and net export behaviour correspondingly) then equation (7) would be satisfied.

The key argument here is that there is little reason to think that equation (7) would indeed be satisfied. In Sawyer (2012) the argument is developed at length. One part of the argument is that of historic experience. The occurrence of budget deficits has been the norm in many countries without clear evidence of 'overheating' and the average budget has been in deficit – indeed government debt levels of the order of 40 to 80 per cent of GDP would not have been the norm within EMU countries without a history of budget deficits. Another part of the argument is the absence of forces which would equate savings and investment at a high level of economic activity. The pace of investment is closely linked with the pace of growth of the economy: in the simple case the net investment ratio to GDP will be around the capital-output ratio times the growth rate. Savings depends on the desire of households to save, often linked with pension provision, and the saving by corporations. The forces at work on investment and those on savings are rather different, and there is little reason to think that there will be factors bringing savings and investment into line.

Structural reforms and labour market 'flexibility'

A full evaluation of the imperatives for structural reforms which are advocated in the Treaty would be well beyond the length of this chapter, but in any case would require rather more precisely definition than is currently available. Here we make three general points.

First, there is the view expressed that structural reforms will somehow lead to lower budget deficits and to the removal of 'excessive' deficits. The mechanisms by which this could arise are not spelt out, and there would seem little reason to think that an increase in labour market 'flexibility' would, for example lead to a lower deficit. By reference to equation (2) above, it can be seen that the budget deficit would tend to fall if there is an increase in the desire to invest, a decrease in the propensity to save, or an increase in net exports. Many of the measures associated with labour flexibility (such as a more stringent approach to unemployment benefits, reduction of minimum wages) would tend to reduce the wage share in national income, tend to depress demand and to increase the budget deficit. The budget deficit could then only be expected to decline (following a more 'flexible' labour market) if an investment boom were stimulated. A similar argument is deployed by Tridico in relating labour market flexibility with the financial crisis.

> The flexibility agenda of the labour market and the end of wage increases ... diminished workers' purchasing power. This was partly compensated with increased borrowing opportunities and the boom of credit consumption, all of which helped workers to maintain unstable consumption capacity. However, in the long term, unstable consumption patterns derived from precarious job creation, job instability and poor wages have weakened aggregate demand. Hence, labour market issues such as flexibility, uneven income distribution, poor wages and the financial crisis are two sides of the same coin.
> (Tridico, 2012, p. 17)

Second, there is an underlying neo-liberal assumption that 'structural reforms', which are directed towards labour market de-regulation, reduction of employment and wage protection measures, privatisation and product market de-regulation, will have beneficial effects on the economy concerned (and on the size of budget deficits which is the centre of policy attention). However, that case is far from being established. For example, Glyn, Howell and Schmitt

(2005) found the evidence linking 'various indicators of the implementation of labor market reforms and unemployment' to be unconvincing. This was following up on Baker *et al.* 2004, 2005 who have challenged the robustness of the findings that 'rigidity effects of labor market institutions explain the pattern of unemployment across developed countries' (pp. 20–1). They conclude that

> proponent of labor market deregulation have not produced robust evidence of systematic positive effects of their proposed reforms on cross-country employment performance, though this result has evidently not dimmed the confidence with which such reforms are promoted.... Deregulationists often argue that demonstrating any negative effect of labor market institutions on the unemployment rate is sufficient to pare back or eliminate those institutions. In fact, since these institutions typically provide substantial economic and social benefits, the burden of proof should be set much higher

A recent OECD study (OECD, 2012) is, not surprisingly, more sympathetic to a structural reform agenda, but concludes that 'the benefits from reforms often take time to materialise' though 'concerns about possible negative short-term effects of structural reforms seem exaggerated'. However,

> cyclical conditions matter for the short-term effects of reforms. There is some evidence that in "bad times", certain labour market reforms (of unemployment benefit systems and job protection in particular) can make the economic situation temporarily worse. In still depressed economies, such reforms would therefore be more quickly beneficial if carried out only once the labour market shows clear signs of recovery.

'In view of wide remaining spare capacity, constrained macroeconomic policies and impaired fiscal positions in most OECD countries, policy priority should be given to reforms that offer comparatively strong short-term gains, especially in terms of strengthening the jobs recovery' (OECD, 2012, p. 166) with the promotion of active labour market policies.

Third, there is a strong sense of seeking to impose a 'one size fits all' set of policies on member countries under the banner of 'structural reform'. The Treaty also speaks of 'benchmarking best practices and working towards a more closely coordinated economic policy' (Article 11). The 'varieties of capitalism' literature provides a strong argument that there are major differences in institutional arrangements and policy approaches between market capitalist economies. Amable (2003), for example, provides a five-way classification, of which the first four are relevant for EMU: market based, Continental European capitalism, Social Democratic economics, Southern European capitalism and Asian capitalism. The Treaty threatens to pose 'structural reforms' whether or not they are appropriate to the institutional, social and political arrangements of the country concerned. It has yet to be established that a neo-liberal agenda is the appropriate one for all countries (and whether it would be acceptable to the peoples of the countries).

92 *M. Sawyer*

4 The Keynesian medicine

In this section we outline what we will term as Keynesian medicine for the ills of the Eurozone – the term Keynesian is used in order to have some label and to signify that the medicine pays much attention to the conditions of aggregate demand, to the use of budget deficits (or surpluses) as a policy instrument to secure high employment and to avoid using deflation as a means of resolving current account imbalances. In doing so we have to recognise that the ideological 'climate' within the policy makers of the Economic and Monetary Union is virulently anti-Keynesian (which helps explain the current predicament of the Eurozone) and that the policies sketched below would face enormous ideological resistance from those policy-makers, substantial political resistance because of the implied transfer of resources and funding of national budget deficits and legal constraints arising from the application of the Treaty of Lisbon and the German constitutional court and interpretation of the German constitution (specifically the debt brake).

Current account imbalances

The scale of the current account imbalances has been illustrated in Figure 4.1. The EMU as a whole has run a current account position close to balance. The accounting relationship which comes from that is that broadly the surplus countries within EMU are directly or indirectly lending to the deficit countries. This though implies that without major changes in the current account position of EMU as a whole, reductions of the current account deficit in deficit countries will have to be accompanied by reductions of an equivalent amount in current account surplus of surplus countries.

A country with a current account deficit faces intense pressures over the deficit simply because to maintain a deficit requires borrowing from overseas or depletion of foreign currency reserves, whereas current account surplus countries do not face the same pressures. Keynes sought to devise a plan which would enable the adjustments to balance of payments imbalances (in the context of a fixed exchange rate system) to take place without imposing deflation. In the context of the Economic and Monetary Union, a change in the nominal exchange rate of a member country (vis-à-vis other member countries) is not possible, though changes in the real exchange rate are through changes in domestic prices and costs relative to prices and costs in other member countries. The possible responses to a current account deficit imbalance can be easily summarised in terms of finding ways to carry on borrowing, change real exchange rate through price adjustments, change real exchange rate through improving (non-price) competitiveness, change imports through domestic deflation.

These responses are not mutually exclusive. What is required is an agreed EMU set of policies which enable countries to continue to finance their trade deficit over say a five-year time horizon, with the promotion of industrial and regional policies to improve their competitiveness and abilities to export. There would need to be a recognition for the need for a change in relative prices between deficit countries and surplus countries, and that while prices may need to be lower in the deficit countries, the counterpart is for prices to be higher in surplus countries.

The challenge presently facing the EMU countries is how to resolve the present set of current account imbalances without resorting to deflation, and then to avoid the re-occurrence of the imbalances. It should be stressed that imbalances are a relative matter in the sense that reducing one country's current account deficit involves reducing another country's surplus, and within the context of the EMU it is likely (though not certain) that the reduction of the surplus involved will be that of fellow EMU members. It is then likely that one EMU country's attempt to reduce their deficit would be frustrated if other EMU countries respond in ways which prevents their surplus being reduced. For example, if a country with deficit lowers domestic prices and hence their real exchange rate, but other countries respond by similarly lowering their prices the change in the real exchange rate will be frustrated.

Fiscal policy and sectoral imbalances

There should be two basic principles underlying the approach to fiscal policy within EMU. First, the fiscal stance should be set to enhance the levels of output and employment, and not set in order to achieve some arbitrary balanced budget target (which we suggested above may be unachievable anyway). This applies to national and supra national fiscal policies though it is only the former which in operation at present. This will likely imply that not only should fiscal policy through augmented automatic stabilisers seek to dampen down economic fluctuations, but also that budget deficits will often be required on a long-term basis. For those countries where there is a tendency for savings to exceed investment, there will be, as argued above, a need for budget deficits to secure high levels of employment.

Second, there should not be any attempt to impose a 'one size fits all' fiscal policy on national government in the sense of imposing the same numerical limits on the scale of budget deficits (where a zero limit or any other). The fiscal policy and resulting budget position should be tailored to the requirements of the country concerned: some countries will require budget deficits whereas others may be able to operate successfully with budget surpluses. It is also evident from above that the current account positions vary substantially across countries, and the accounting identity in equation (2) above indicates the likelihood that differences in current account positions will to some degree be reflected in differences in the budget position.

There has long been the need for the development of an EMU-level fiscal policy with the scale of the EMU budget very much larger than the current EU budget (of just over 1 per cent of EU GDP, and with a requirement to be balanced). A significant question here is whether the EU itself would operate the larger scale budget. The EMU would be able to run budget deficits (or surpluses) to support the level of economic activity within the EMU. Others who have argued for a EMU-level fiscal policy which would serve to help stabilise economic activity across EMU have put the necessary scale of such a policy at 7.5 per cent of GDP (Commission of the European Communities, 1977), 5 per cent (Huffschmid, 2005, Chapter 16), 2 to 3 per cent of GDP (Currie, 1997; Goodhart and Smith, 1993).

An EMU-level fiscal policy should be used for stabilisation purposes for the euroarea as a whole. A progressive tax system applied across the euroarea would serve to operate as an automatic stabiliser. Further, an EMU-level fiscal policy would also cushion a region (or country) against economic shocks which hit the region (or country). An income tax system which is proportional or progressive (or even mildly regressive) will involve more tax revenue (per capita) being raised in higher income regions than would be raised in lower income regions. The degree to which fiscal transfers between countries are involved would depend on the progressivity of the tax system and the structure of public expenditure undertaken from the EMU-level budget. These fiscal transfers would serve to re-distribute spending power, and could go somewhere to easing current account imbalances. An EMU-level fiscal policy must involve the ability of EMU to levy taxes in its own right to help underpin borrowing by EMU. The relationship between EMU as a fiscal authority and the ECB as the central bank would be comparable to that between a national government and its central bank in terms of the support which the central bank can provide to fiscal policy and the ability of government to borrow.

Central Bank

We have argued elsewhere (Arestis and Sawyer, 2006) that the policy arrangements for the ECB currently have a range of drawbacks and problems. There is an urgent need to reformulate the position and role of the ECB in a manner which promotes employment and economic activity. Here we advocate three major elements of such a reformulation.

The first is to end the independence of the ECB and to integrate the ECB into a set of democratic policy making procedures. The ECB would retain charge of operational matters such as the implementation of interest rate decisions but would co-ordinate its decisions with other monetary and fiscal authorities. Whilst the ECB has been independent in the sense of a political independence, it has not been independent from a neo-liberal policy agenda, and it has frequently advocated (in terms of fiscal constraints and the promotion of more 'flexible' labour markets and pension 'reforms') a neo-liberal policy agenda. The integration of ECB into the policy-making arrangements would enable policy co-ordination which should lead to more effective policy making. The 'independence' of the ECB would appear to preclude co-operation and co-ordination between the different bodies responsible for aspects of macroeconomic policies. Yet, in a world of multiple objectives (including high levels of economic activity and employment, financial stability, inflation etc.) there is a need for multiple instruments, which are operated by different authorities, and where there should be some coordination.

The second arises from the dominance of inflation targeting as the prime policy objective. We have pointed elsewhere (Arestis and Sawyer, 2008, 2010c) to the general failures of inflation targeting, and also that the ECB has not in generally achieved the price stability target (interpreted as inflation between 0 and 2 per cent) albeit that the inflation rate has tended to be just over 2 per cent. A more significant issue has been the differential inflation rates between countries and the inability of monetary policy to address those differences in inflation rate. Further, monetary policy has had a perverse effect in that with a single policy nominal interest rate leads to lower real interest rates in higher inflation countries – exactly the reverse of the way in which inflation targeting is intended to work whereby real interest rate is high when inflation is high with the intention of damping down demand.

The pursuit of financial stability should become the prime objective of the ECB (and other central banks). This argument is based, in part, on the relative frequency of financial instability and the significant costs associated with financial crisis, which are several orders of magnitude greater than any costs of inflation. The instruments of policy have to be further developed. The key argument here though is that the pursuit of financial stability should become the prime focus of the ECB.

Third, the relationships between the ECB and national governments (and other fiscal authorities which may be developed) have to become akin to that between national central banks and the central government in most countries. The ECB should on all occasions stand ready to operate as 'lender of last resort' (which at present is allowable for the ECB but not compulsory). It should always accept the bonds and bills issued by national governments (within EMU) as part of open market operations in the way in which a national central bank would always accept the bonds of its government. It should also stand ready to directly lend to national governments (in exchange for bonds in euros of that government) if required. The general proposition is that the ECB should support the fiscal policies determined by EMU national governments, whether or not those policies involve deficits of which the ECB disapproves.

Inflation and competitiveness policies

Finding a way of effectively constraining inflation without resorting to deflationary measures has been a recurring issue throughout the post-war period. It has been indicated above and more extensively argued elsewhere (Arestis and Sawyer, 2008, 2012) that inflation targeting is ineffectual and alternatives have to be developed. However, as noted above, within the EMU there had been relatively low inflation but the inflation target of 0 to 2 per cent was frequently missed albeit by a small margin, and more significantly for EMU there were persistent differences of inflation between member countries. Within EMU it is argued here that mechanisms have to be developed which will in effect coordinate wage developments and prices across EMU countries. A key aspect here is that the evolution of competitiveness between EMU member countries. It is clear that monetary policy cannot address differential inflation problems.

There is then the need to develop wage and price coordination mechanisms at the EMU level through which not only the general pace of inflation can be addressed but more significantly the similarity of the pace of inflation across countries be ensured.

5 Concluding remarks

In this chapter, it has been argued that the roots of the ongoing euro crisis come from the ways in which the Economic and Monetary Union was constructed, and the failure of that construction to address the current account imbalances between the member countries. It has considered the proposed Treaty on Stability, Coordination and Governance and 'fiscal compact', and argued that the fiscal conditions which the Treaty seeks to impose are inadequately defined and the target of a balanced structural budget is unachievable and attempts to reach the conditions will impose continent wide austerity. The final section has outlined the elements of a Keynesian alternative which can restore prosperity to the EMU.

Notes

1 The 'six pack' entered into force on 13 December 2011, and involved five Regulations and one Directive (hence 'six pack') which constitutes EU secondary law. It applies to all 27 member states, with some specific rules for EMU members. The six pack covers not only fiscal surveillance, but also macroeconomic surveillance under the new Macroeconomic Imbalance Procedure. The crucial aspects of the six pack appear in the Treaty and are discussed under that head. For further information see http://ec.europa.eu/economy_finance/articles/governance/2012-03-14_six_pack_en.htm.
2 www.ecb.europa.eu/press/key/date/2012/html/sp120224.en.html, accessed 20 March 2012.
3 See European Commission (2012) for discussion of the measures imposed on Greece.
4 Figures taken from OECD, *Economic Outlook*, Statistical Annexe, December 2010.

References

Amable, B. (2003), *The Diversity of Modern Capitalism*, Oxford: Oxford University Press.
Arestis, P. and Sawyer, M. (2006), 'Macroeconomic policy and the European constitution' in P. Arestis and M. Sawyer (eds), *Alternative Perspectives on Economic Policies in the European Union*, Basingstoke: Palgrave Macmillan, pp. 1–36.
Arestis, P. and Sawyer, M. (2008), 'New consensus macroeconomics and inflation targeting: Keynesian critique', *Economia e Sociedade*, Campinas, 17, Número especial, pp. 629–54.
Arestis, P. and Sawyer, M. (2010a), 'The Design Faults of the Economic and Monetary Union', *Journal of Contemporary European Studies*, vol. 19(1), pp. 19–30.

Arestis, P. and Sawyer, M. (2010b), 'The problems of the Economic and Monetary Union: is there any escape?', *The Journal of Economic Analysis*, vol. 1 no. 1 pp. 1–14.

Arestis, P. and Sawyer, M. (2010c), 'What Monetary Policy After the Crisis?', *Review of Political Economy*, (2010) vol. 22: 4, 499–515.

Arestis, P. and Sawyer, M. (2012), 'Moving from Inflation Targeting to Prices and Incomes Policy', revised version of paper presented at Cambridge Journal of Economics conference on The Future of Capitalism 25–26 June 2011.

Baker, D., Glyn, A., Howell, D. and Schmitt, J. (2004), 'Unemployment and labor market institutions: the failure of the empirical case for deregulation', Report to the International Labour Organization.

Baker, D., Glyn, A., Howell, D and Schmitt, J. (2005), 'Labor market institutions and unemployment: a critical assessment of the cross-country evidence' in David Howell (ed.), *Fighting Unemployment: the Limits of Free Market Orthodoxy*, New York: Oxford University Press.

Commission of the European Communities (1977), *Report of the Study Group on the Role of Public Finances in European Integration*, chaired by Sir Donald MacDougall, Economic and Financial Series No. A13, Brussels: Belgium.

Currie, D. (1997), *The Pros and Cons of EMU*, London: HM Treasury (Published originally by the Economist Intelligence Unit, January 1997).

European Central Bank (ECB) (2009), *Monthly Bulletin*, December 2009, Frankfurt: European Central Bank.

European Commission (2012), 'The Second Economic Adjustment Programme for Greece', *European Economy*, Occasional Papers 94, March 2012.

European Union (2012), *Treaty on Stability, Coordination and Governance in the Economic and Monetary Union*, Brussels: European Union.

Glyn, A., Howell, D. and Schmitt (2006), 'Labor Market Reforms: the evidence does not tell the orthodox tale', *Challenge*, vol. 49, no. 2, pp. 5–22.

Goodhart, C.A.E. and Smith, S. (1993), 'Stabilization', *The Economics of Community Public Finance*, European Economy: Reports and Studies No. 5/1993, Brussels: Belgium.

Huffschmid, J. (ed.) (2005), *Economic Policy for a Social Europe A Critique of Neo-Liberalism and Proposals for Alternatives*, Basingstoke: Palgrave Macmillan.

OECD (2012), *Economic Policy Reforms 2012: Going for Growth*, OECD Publishing. http://dx.doi.org/10.1787/growth-2012-en.

Sawyer, M. (2012), 'The contradictions of balanced structural government budgets' in H. Herr, T. Niechoj, C. Thomasberger, A. Truger, and T.L. van Treeck (eds), *From crisis to growth? The challenge of imbalances and debt*, Metropolis Verlag, Marburg, forthcoming.

Tridico, P. (2012), 'Financial crisis and global imbalances: its labour market origins and the aftermath', *Cambridge Journal of Economics* vol. 36(1), pp. 17–42.

5 Financialization, income distribution and the crisis

Engelbert Stockhammer

1 Introduction

The advanced capitalist economies are experiencing the worst economic crisis since the Great Depression. The depth of the crisis as well as the ongoing hegemony of neoliberalism requires explanation. This chapter argues that a process of financialization has given rise to a finance-dominated regime of accumulation and that the crisis should be understood as the outcome of the process of financialization and the polarization of income distribution. The first part may be less controversial: financial deregulation is widely recognized as a cause of the crisis. We go further in arguing that financialization represents a profound transformation of the capitalist accumulation regime. The second part may be more innovative. We argue that the polarization of income distribution is a root cause of the crisis in the sense that it contributed to the imbalances that erupted in the crisis.

Epstein has described "financialization [as] the increasing role of financial motives, financial markets, financial actors and financial institutions in the operation of the domestic and international economies" (Epstein 2005, 3). This definition may lack precision, but it gives a good impression of the ubiquity and pervasiveness of financialization and is thus a good starting point. We will maintain that financialization has micro economic as well as macro aspects. In other words: financialization has transformed how economic actors (households, workers, firms and financial institutions) perceive themselves, what goals they pursue and what constraints they face. The macroeconomic transformations are no less profound: economies are increasingly driven by movements in the prices of real estate and financial assets and by the burden of servicing financial obligations, i.e. debt. And a change in the credit rating of a country's debt can horrify politicians and wreck public finances.

In discussing the finance-dominated accumulation regime, we highlight a further aspect: financialization, much like other incarnations of capitalism, creates its own dynamics of differentiation. Rather than analysing the US (or UK) experience as the purest, most advanced form of financialization, we emphasize that their development is part of a differential process. Other countries' experiences are of empirical as well as of theoretical interest (Becker 2002).

In a nutshell, our story is the following. Financialization has increased the size and the fragility of the financial sector (much like Keynes and Minsky would have predicted). How this impacted on the global accumulation regime turns out to be quite complex. Neoliberalism has led to a shift in power relations between capital and labour. As a consequence income distribution has shifted sharply in favour of capital. Socially this has left working class households struggling to keep up with consumption norms. Economically it had a potentially dampening effect on domestic demand (as demand is wage led in the world as a whole). Different countries have developed different strategies of coping with this shortfall of demand. Everywhere households (including working class households) have experienced rising debt levels. In Anglo-Saxon countries debt-driven consumption turned into the main demand engine, usually in conjunction with real estate bubbles. Financial deregulation has an international as well as a domestic dimension. The liberalization of capital flows has allowed countries to temporarily sustain large current account deficits – as long as financial markets were willing to provide the corresponding capital inflows. Indeed, for many countries (in particular developing economies), boom-bust cycles driven by capital inflows and currency crises have been the most important feature of the finance-dominated accumulation regime. As countries have been able to run substantial current account surpluses (while others run deficits) international financial liberalization has created a new scope for different trajectories across countries. A second group of counties has relied on *export-driven growth* (and subdued domestic consumption) and run substantial current account surpluses. Two key sources of the crisis, debt-driven consumption and international imbalances, are thus linked to the interactions of financial liberalization and the polarization of income distribution.[1]

The remainder of this chapter is structured as follows. Section 2 gives an overview of the present crisis and its metamorphoses. Section 3 visits debates around financialization and the nebulous borders between neoliberalism and financialization. Section 4 summarizes changes brought by financialization for the financial sector, businesses and households. Section 5 discusses changes in income distribution, financial globalization and the characteristics of the finance-dominated accumulation regime. In particular it highlights the emergence of two different growth models. Section 6 discusses the channels by which income inequality has contributed to the crisis and section 7 concludes.

2 The crisis 2007–2011

In mid 2006 house prices in the USA started to decline. With hindsight, that marks the beginning of the crisis, even if it attracted little attention at the time. Rapidly rising house prices, and the mortgage lending that came with it, had been the basis of a boom driven by credit-financed consumption and construction investment in the USA. But this section will give a brief overview of the unfolding of the crisis itself.

The crisis broke out in a seemingly obscure niche of the US financial system: the subprime market, which is the market on which derivatives on low-quality mortgage credit; thus the initial name of the crisis as *subprime crisis*. This is a rather small segment of the overall mortgage market, though it accounted for a substantial part of the credit growth in the years before the crisis. As subprime credit is, by definition, of low quality, it was the natural field for the kind of financial engineering, securitization, which was supposed to reduce risk. What was going on here was the extreme form of what happened on a much broader scale in the entire mortgage industry. In August 2007 the crisis spilt over into the interbank market, where banks lend to each other, usually very short term. The interbank market is at the very centre of the modern financial system. Interest rose to more than one percentage point above that on government bonds. This increase in the risk premium of lending meant that banks did not trust each other. And rightly so, as it turned out. Central banks reacted quickly and pumped billions (of dollars and euros) into the market to maintain liquidity.

However, while the interbank market stabilized the crisis evolved. In spring 2008 Bear Stearns, one of the leading investment banks, was bankrupt and could only be sold with the FED guaranteeing some US$20 billion worth of assets. A first (small) fiscal stimulus packet was implemented in the USA, but the impact on the real economy outside the USA was limited. In August/September 2008 the crisis turned into a full scale *financial crisis* – and it did so with a bang: Lehman Brothers, one of Wall Street's leading investment banks, went bankrupt. The end of the world (or at least of big finance) as we knew it, seemed to have arrived. Interest rates soared (interest spread rose to several percentage points) and liquidity froze.

Again economic policy reacted. The principles of neoliberal free-market economics were suspended for a few weeks. Central banks provided more liquidity, but that proved insufficient to stabilize markets. Governments had to intervene directly: AIG, an insurance firm that had insured huge volumes of credit derivates, was taken over by the state as were Fannie Mae and Freddie Mac, the two state-sponsored mortgage refinancing giants. Within a few weeks the recapitalization of financial institutions and massive guarantees for interbank credits became mainstream economic policy. Recapitalization meant that governments effectively nationalized (fully or partly) financial institutions – but governments abstained from interfering with the management banks despite obvious management failures. In late October 2008 an EU summit issued a statement that no systemically important financial institutions would be allowed to fail – a capitalism without bankruptcies (of big banks) was declared!

By fall 2008 the financial crisis had turned into a full blown *economic crisis*. Income in most developed countries shrank at a speed not seen since the 1930s (in most countries by around 5 per cent). And it not only hit those countries that had experienced property bubbles, but also countries like Germany and Japan (where property prices had been practically flat) and it spread to the emerging countries. Eastern European countries were particularly badly hit, with the Baltic countries suffering GDP declines by around 20 per cent. The IMF had to be called in to save Hungary, Pakistan and the Baltic states. But the most conspicuous symbol of the downturn was certainly the fall of GM: once the world's largest firm and employer, it now had to rescued by the state.

While complete meltdown seemed imminent in fall 2008, in the course of spring 2009 it became clear that the – historically unprecedented – scale of government intervention had prevented outright collapse. A cascade of bank breakdowns could be prevented by rescue packages that amounted to 80 per cent of GDP in the USA and the UK (UNCTAD 2009, Table 1.8) and by the FED expanding its balance sheet by one trillion US$, mostly by acquiring assets that it would not have touched in normal times. Risk premia remained elevated, banks were making phenomenal losses, unemployment started rising, but normality of a sort returned. And, apparently, the pressure to reform the system had receded. Earlier declarations of a fundamental restructuring of the financial system had been forgotten and the debate on reform turned into a specialists' debate on technicalities, with all but private bankers and central bankers being excluded from the decision-making circles. The arrogance of the financial elite, however, is best captured by the fact that, despite of the obvious disaster in finance, bankers' bonuses are back to pre-crisis levels.

But the normality that was about to restore itself was not quite the normality of before the crisis. After all, the crisis was by no means over. Indeed, for large parts of the population, it only had begun, when for the bankers it was almost over. Production fell and unemployment rose. In the USA foreclosures were rising. People lost their jobs and their homes. And there was another devastating effect of the crisis: budget deficits were increasing, surpassing 10 per cent of GDP in many cases. So in the course of 2009 the crisis thus took its next turn: a *fiscal crisis*. This has been lingering for several months, but its most prominent victim in winter 2009/2010 was Greece and with it the euro system.

In January/February 2010 Greece faced punitive interest rates on its (public) debt issues. Greece had fudged public debt statistics (with the help of leading Wall Street banks) and now had difficulties refinancing its debt. Indeed, what had been exposed was fundamental flaw in the construction of the euro system. With exchange rates frozen, the southern countries had, despite much lower inflation since adopting the euro, slowly, but steadily by lost competitiveness to Germany and its economic satellites. Germany's net exports (mostly to other euro countries) amounted to more than 5 per cent of GDP. This was achieved by wage suppression and, consequently, low inflation rates (Lapavitsas *et al.* 2010). The euro area had no instruments to deal with internal imbalances, other than trusting labour market flexibility to adjust the price levels. Greece received a €110 billion loan from the newly instituted European Financial Stability Facility (EFSF).

While it was relatively simple to blame the Greek crisis on irresponsible fiscal policy the structural problems of the euro area were illustrated by the Irish crisis shortly thereafter. Ireland had government surpluses before the crisis, but still needed a huge rescue package (€85 billion, more than half of Irish GDP). Like in Greece, the rescue package is really a rescue package for the European financial sector rather than for states. Ireland had experienced an enormous real estate bubble that burst und effectively bankrupted its banks. Because of the bank bailouts, Irish debt soared by 40 percentage points of GDP from 2007 to 2010.

Literally all of the obligations of the bust Irish banking system were guaranteed, which lead to an angry article by Eichengreen (2010).

The euro crisis is far from over (indeed at the time of writing it seems that Italy is engulfed next) and in the USA economics news indicates stagnation. What is somewhat euphemistically called 'deleveraging' has begun. Meantime fiscal policy has switched into reverse in all countries. What is more, in several cases (most notably the UK and Greece) it is becoming clear that the battle cry of sound fiscal policy is used to cover a re-structuring of the role of the state: a second wave of neoliberalism!

3 Financialization: concept, debate, delineation

Financialization has profoundly transformed advanced economies. The term used to summarize a broad set of changes in the relation between the 'financial' and 'real' sector which give greater weight than heretofore to financial actors or motives. The debate on financialization draws a range of different theoretical and methodological approaches and is thus difficult to summarize.[2] Cultural economists have highlighted the incompleteness and contradictions of the discursive strategies of financialization (Froud *et al.* 2006), while macroeconomists have tried to identify the conditions for viable growth regimes; economic sociologists have argued that (financial) markets have to be constructed by specific actors with specific interest (MacKenzie and Millo 2003), while post-Keynesian economists have highlighted the fragile nature of finance-led growth (see Ertürk *et al.* 2008 for a useful collection of seminal contributions and Stockhammer 2010 for a short survey).[3]

Before we turn to specific changes for different economic actors, let us highlight a common theme of the transformation brought about by financialization: Actors increasingly perceive themselves as financial institutions manipulating their balance sheets, as if they were managing a portfolio of assets. They compare relative rates of return and want to be able to trade in liquid assets. This represents an increasing commodification of social relations. These transformations have different implications for different sectors in the economy: financial institutions have shifted towards liquid assets; within firms this represents a shift in power relations from labour to capital, but the rule of capital has taken a new guise, that of shareholder value; for households, in particular working class households the transformation dissolved previous notions of working class consciousness and opened new ways for exploitation.

Let us illustrate these last points by quoting from Foucault's summary of labour in neoliberal analysis:

> An income is quite simply the product or return on a capital. Conversely, we call "capital" everything that in one way or another can be source of future income. Consequently, if we accept on this basis that the wage is an income, then the wage is therefore the income of a capital.
>
> (Foucault 2008, 224)

The worker becomes "an entrepreneur of himself" (Foucault 2008, 226). Bowles (1975) had offered as similar analysis of the indeological content of human capital theory earlier.

This represents an important shift in the ideological justification of capitalism. While, according to Marx's analysis of commodity fetishism, the wage contract appears as "fair" as it is agreed-up exchange of labour for money (Marx 1976, Chapters 1.4 and 6), it implicitly acknowledges the existence of a working class. In Foucault's analysis of neoliberalism, the worker himself becomes an entrepreneur. Modern capitalism isn't just fair; we're all capitalists now!

There are multiple overlaps between the concept of financialization and that of neoliberalism. Various (Marxist) authors have highlighted that financialization is one of the core parts of neoliberalism (Harvey 2005, Glyn 2006, Duménil und Lévy 2004) and that profits increasingly accrue in the form of financial incomes or in the forms of capital gains. In this analysis neoliberalism is essentially the latest offensive of capital to restore profitability.

This may understimate the novelty of neoliberalism. Already in the late 1970s Michel Foucault (2007) had suggested an interpretation of neoliberalism as form of *governance by competitive subjectification.* Based on a careful reading of the German ordo-liberal school and the US-American Chicago School he argues that neoliberalism differs radically from classical liberalism in that it does not aim at liberating markets, but at *creating* markets and subordinating government activity under this goal. Markets do not spontaneously spring into being, but have to be constructed and maintained – *by governments.* Contrary to classical liberalism neoliberalism thus requires permanent and profound state intervention.

Stockhammer and Ramskogler (2009) reached a similar conclusion based on an analysis of recent economic policy and of "New Keynesian" and Neo-Institutionalist developments in mainstream economics and call these developments *enlightened neoliberalism.* Many recent mainstream economics approaches differ from the old neoclassical general equilibrium theory not in their trust in the efficiency of markets, but argue that they have to be created and maintained rather than posited. The title of the World bank's (2002) World Development Report encapsulates this approach: *Creating Institutions for Markets.*

Our approach in the following will make use of the regulationist framework.[4] Before proceeding, three clarifications are in place. First, I am purposefully using the term regulationist "framework" rather than regulationist "theory" as the Regulation School, in my view, does not qualify as theory in the strong sense of the word, i.e. as positing specific causal explanations of a range of social or economic phenomena. Rather I regard it as an "intermediate theory" that offers a platform to analyse historically specific eras by encompassing socio-institutional as well as economic aspects and allows potentially for the (historically specific) integration of (among others) Keynesian and Marxian arguments. In this view the theoretical scope of Regulation Theory is limited; its practical usefulness, however, has been undervalued since its boom in the 1980s.

Second, we will use the term accumulation regime to describe the macroeconomic pattern of phases of capitalism, based on specific institutions settings or trajectories. The meaning of accumulation requires some discussion. Regulation theory was originally (Aglietta 1979) based on Marxian analysis. In Marxian analysis there is a certain ambiguity in the term accumulation as it can refer the growth of profits or to the growth of capital stock (i.e. reinvested profits). As we shall see, financialization drives a wedge between the two. One of the features of the finance-dominated accumulation regime is that there has been an increase in profits while, at the same time, there is sluggish growth of investment.

Third, our discussion will be structured by economic sectors instead of following the standard Regulationist script of the analysis of the mode of regulation and its institutional structures. This may reflect my macroeconomic interests, but it is mainly a device to highlight the effects of financialization. As any light also casts a shadow, this comes at a cost. Compared to a proper regulationist analysis the transformation of the capital-labour relation, the impact of globalization and the changes in the state get insufficient attention.[5]

4 Transformations brought about by financialization

Financialization was made possible by a series of measures to deregulate the financial sector and to liberalize international capital flows. Many of these measures were themselves reactions to increasing activities on the part of private agents to circumvent financial regulation. This section aims to give an overview of how financialization has affected different sectors of the economy. In doing so, we highlight changes in the constraints as well as in the aims of economic actors and we try to document differences across countries.

4.1 The financial sector

Changes in the financial sector have been quite dramatic. The first set of changes is about the actors and institutions which make up the financial sector. Non-bank financial institutions ranging from insurance firms to investment funds, money market funds, hedge funds, private equity funds and special purpose vehicles have gained weight. Typically these institutions are much less regulated than banks, though, thanks to financial innovation, they perform similar functions as banks and are thus often referred to as shadow banking system (Pozsar *et al.* 2010). The shadow banking system has also been an engine for financialization and in the form of offshore finance parts of it blatantly serve for tax evasion and money laundering (Shaxson 2010). One important aspect of the emergence of the shadow banking sector is financial innovation, i.e. the development of new financial instruments that often helped to circumvent traditional banking regulation. Pozsar *et al.* (2010) estimate that in the USA the shadow banking system is now larger than the regular banking sector (measured in terms of assets).

Within the banking sector there has been a shift towards fee-generating business rather than traditional banking that generates income as a result of the interest differential between rates on deposits and on loans. Part of this has been the emergence of what has been called the originate-and-distribute model of banking (in particular in the USA), where mortgages were quickly sold in the form of asset backed securities. In terms of lending, there has been a shift to lending to households rather than to firms. In particular mortgages are now by far the largest loan positions (Ertürk and Solari 2006, Lapavitsas 2009).

Supporters of financial deregulation have argued that financialization will provide a superior way of dealing with risk; e.g. securitization was supposed slice risk into different parts (by means of different securities) and allocate it to those who were best equipped to hold it. The financial system would thus be more stable (e.g. IMF 2006, 51) and society better off, a claim that sounds plainly embarrassing after the events of recent years. In contrast Keynesians have long argued that financial markets are intrinsically unstable and tend to generate endogenous boom-bust cycles (Minsky 1986). More recently, they have highlighted conflicts of interest and the dangers of the belief that risk could easily be sliced by means of looking at past correlations (Aglietta and Rebérioux 2005).

There are long-standing differences between financial systems across countries, which are often grouped into market-based and bank-based systems (e.g. Allen and Gale 2000, Schaberg 1999). While financialization has increased the size of financial sectors (as measure by assets as well as by the profits) in all countries, strong differences across countries persist e.g. in the size of stock markets, banks and institutional investors (Davis 2003), though in some areas the international activities of financial institutions may render these differences less important. The spread of the subprime crisis to the balance sheet of financial institutions across the globe is case in point, though (national) banking regulation and governance did make a difference for how banks were affected (Beltratti and Stulz 2009).

4.2 Non-financial businesses

One of the most important changes in the non-financial business sector is due to the increased role of shareholders. Lazonick and O'Sullivan (2000) argue that a shift in management behaviour from "retain and reinvest" to "downsize and distribute" has occurred. While there is broad agreement (in heterodox economics) that financial motives and actors have become more important within firms, there is a subtle difference in interpretation. Firms could be the victims of institutional investors, or shareholder value orientation could be a strategy of increasing exploitation. Either way, it is clear that interest and dividend payments have increased (Duménil and Lévy 2001, Crotty 2003). However only for few countries, namely for the USA, is data readily available.

More formally, Stockhammer (2004) shows that an increase in shareholder power will modify the desired profit-growth frontier for the firm and presents econometric evidence that financialization may explain a substantial part of the slowdown in accumulation. However, results vary widely across countries (strong effects in the USA and France, weak effects in Germany). Orhangazi (2008) finds evidence for this channel based on firm-level data for the USA.

Onaran *et al.* (2011) present econometric evidence for the negative effect of dividend and interest payments on investment.

A second change for investment behaviour has been in the economic environment that firms face. Volatility on financial markets has increased substantially in the course of financial deregulation. As a consequence firms face a higher degree of uncertainty which may make physical investment projects less attractive. In particular volatility of exchange rates seems to have had some effects on manufacturing investment. However, uncertainty is hard to measure and estimation results from the existing literature are not conclusive enough to suggest a clear order of magnitude of the effect (Carruth *et al.* 2000, Stockhammer and Grafl 2010).

The weak performance of investment compared to profits can be seen in Figure 5.1. The decline in the investment-to-profits ratio can be observed in all major economies, even if the peak values differ across countries (the mean peaks in 1980). The measure of operating surplus used in Figure 5.1 is based on the National Accounts and thus a broad one that includes all non-wage income. Part of the reason for the declining trend in the investment operating surplus ratio is due to a change in the composition of the operating surplus. Perhaps surprisingly stock market prices have very little effect on investment. Already in the early 1990s (Chirinko 1993), most empirical economists would have agreed that share prices have little, if any, effect on investment. In our view financialization has had a dampening effect on business investment due to negative effects of shareholder value orientation and increased uncertainty.

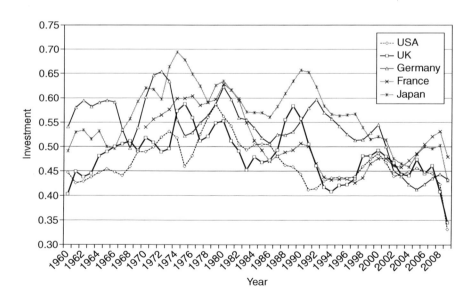

Figure 5.1 Investment-to-profit ratio for advanced economies (source: AMECO).

4.3 Households

Financialization has increased the access of households to credit, the most important form of which has been mortgage credit, which typically makes up 80 per cent of household credit. In combination with real estate booms this has often led to credit-financed consumption booms.[6] In the USA consumption expenditures have become the main driving force in GDP growth in the 1990s. Mainstream economists try to explain this increase in consumption assuming rational behaviour (in Anglo-Saxon countries). The falling saving rates were first explained by a wealth effect due to the rise in the value of financial assets because of the stock market boom. In the late 1990s a 5 per cent marginal propensity to consume out of financial wealth was often quoted (with some more qualification for European countries; e.g. Boone *et al.* 1998). The stock market crash in 2000, however, did not result in a slowdown in consumption growth. The unabated consumption boom in the USA was then explained by booming house prices. Residential property was now identified as the key source of the wealth effect as is more frequently accepted as collateral. Case *et al.* (2001), Catte *et al.* (2004) and Girouard *et al.* (2006) find substantially higher marginal propensity to consume out of property wealth than out of financial assets.[7]

There are two areas of disagreement between the mainstream economics and heterodox approaches regarding the analysis of household debt. First, the mainstream literature usually assumes that households rationally increased their debt ratios as their wealth increased. From a heterodox point of view a substantial part of the accumulated debt is due to households maintaining consumption levels that are unsustainable (and could therefore be considered irrational). As wages have stagnated in many countries consumption norms as represented in mass media have arguably increased, many households could have been driven into debt (Cynamon and Fazzari 2009). The second major disagreement is about the role of income distribution. Several heterodox authors have argued that the increase in household debt should be regarded as a substitute to increases in wages (Barba and Pivetti 2008). While consumption norms have increased, wages have not to the same extent. Consequently working class households were driven into debt.

Household debt is difficult to measure and international comparisons chronically suffer from deficiencies in comparability of data due to different financial institutions and practices in different countries. Table 5.1 reports a wide range of debt-to-GDP ratios across countries. However most European countries have experienced rising debt ratios since 1995, though at quite different levels. While the UK, the Netherlands and Denmark have debt ratios similar to those of the USA, most continental European countries have much lower levels. It is also clear, with hindsight, that strong increases in household debt ratios were driven by property bubbles (namely in the USA, the UK, Ireland and Spain).

Within the (old) European Union, debt levels have been rising most dramatically in the Mediterranean countries and in Ireland – exactly the group of countries that is now experiencing the crisis (see Table 5.1).

Table 5.1 Household debt in % of GDP

	2000	2008	2009	Change 2000–2008
USA	70.21	96.35	96.34	26.13
United Kingdom	75.16	107.43	110.00	32.27
Ireland		114.26	124.93	114.26
Greece	19.83	55.29	57.24	35.46
Spain	54.22	88.06	89.88	33.84
Portugal	74.96	102.34	107.48	27.38
Italy	35.29	53.61	56.54	18.32
Germany	73.41	61.70	63.91	−11.71
Austria	47.13	55.04	56.92	7.91
Switzerland	74.76	77.70	82.08	2.94
France	47.46	64.56	69.46	17.10
Belgium	40.85	50.25	54.08	9.40
Netherlands	86.98	119.81	130.45	32.83
Bulgaria	4.32	35.07	50.06	30.75
Estonia	12.14	61.35	69.27	49.21
Latvia	7.08	48.65	53.88	41.57
Lithuania	2.11	35.46	42.09	33.35
Hungary	9.04	39.51	40.65	30.47
Poland	8.29	32.77	33.03	24.48
Romania	3.28	29.24	31.23	25.96
Slovakia	12.70	38.29	47.77	25.59

Source: Eurostat, expect USA (Flows of Funds).

Note
Ireland 2001–2008.

5 The finance-dominated accumulation regime

5.1 Changes in income distribution

One of the hallmarks of neoliberalism has been the polarization of the distribution of income. The shift in power from labour to capital is clearly reflected in wage developments. Wage shares have been falling across Europe and in Japan and, to a lesser extent, in the USA and the UK. The Anglo-Saxon countries have, however, witnessed a strong increase of inequality in personal income distribution (Atkinson *et al.* 2010). Arguably, the exorbitant management salaries in the Anglo-Saxon countries should be considered a form of profits rather than wages. Indeed, subtracting the top 1 per cent of wage earners from the US wage share, a strong decline can be observed. Based (CPI-adjusted) data available from OECD (2008), median weekly wages in the USA have grown by a mere 2.8 per cent from 1980 to 2005, the bottom quartile of wages fell by 3.1 per cent and the top 10 per cent increased by 21 per cent.

While mainstream economics tends to identify the role of technological change has been the main cause of the decline in the wage share and that globalization has been a secondary cause (IMF 2007a, EC 2007), political economy approaches tend to highlight the financial globalization, trade globalization and the decline in union density. Rodrik (1998), Harrison (2002), and Jayadev (2007) econometric evidence for the effects of capital controls and capital mobility on income distribution. Stockhammer (2009) finds for OECD countries that financial globalization, trade globalization and the decline in union density have been the main forces behind the falling wage share. ILO (2008) argues that financial globalization has contributed to the decline in the wage share, but does not provide econometric evidence. Onaran (2009) shows that financial crisis have long-lasting distributional effects for several developing countries.

What are the likely macroeconomic effects of this redistribution on aggregate demand? From a Kaleckian point of view, one would expect a dampening effect on aggregate demand. As wage incomes are typically associated with higher consumption propensities than profit incomes, this ought to lead to a decrease in the consumption share. Stockhammer *et al.* (2009) find a saving differential of around 0.4 for the euro area.[8] Given that wage shares have declined by some 10 percentage points since 1980, consumption shares ought to have declined by some 4 percentage points (of GDP) over this period due to changes in income distribution. The background for macroeconomic developments in the neoliberal era is one of potentially stagnant demand.

5.2 International capital flows

For many countries, in particular in the developing world, the main experience of financialization has been that of exchange rate crises: Latin America in the 1980s and again in 1994, South-East Asia in 1997/1998. Typically these crises were preceded by periods of strong capital inflows and were triggered by a sudden reversal of capital flows (Reinhart and Reinhart 2008). All of them have led to severe recessions (at times with double digit declines in real GDP). The EMS crisis 1992/93 also shook developed economies and it lead European countries to speed up monetary unification and introduce a common currency, the euro. At first, the euro appears to have been a success. Not only was the new currency accepted by the public, it also substantially decreased inflation and (real) interest rates in the former soft-currency countries. However, since inflation differentials persist across European countries, there have been creeping changes in real exchange rates that have accumulated over the years. *Real* exchange rates have diverged since the introduction of the Euro. Germany has devalued by more than 20 per cent in real terms vis à vis Portugal, Spain, Ireland or Greece since 1999 and, unsurprisingly these countries have had large current account deficits (whereas Germany had large surpluses). Rather than preventing internal imbalances, the euro system has changed the nature of the ensuing crisis: Rather than an exchange rate crisis, the imbalances now lead to a sovereign debt crisis in a situation, where the affected country has neither the possibility to devalue its currency nor does it have a central bank of its own that could rescue its banks or finance its government.

When politicians like Jacques Delors pushed for the introduction of the euro, what they had in mind was the creation of a European state. While they have not succeeded in this, they have come rather close to destroying some of the old nation states. Monetary unification has thus in an ironic way politicized the crisis while at the same time there is no European polity to debate the crisis.

The flaw of the euro system is basically the following: There is a common monetary policy and fiscal policy is severely restricted. Exchange rate realignments are by definition not available to adjust to divergences across the euro zone. So how can countries adjust? Basically through wage moderation. But this fails to work in practice. First, labour markets simply are not as flexible as economic textbooks and EU treaties would like them to be. Second, the adjustment via labour markets has a clear deflationary bias – the country with the current account deficit will have to adjust and it has to adjust by wage restraint and disinflation. However, as overall inflation is limited to 2 per cent, any country that seriously wants to improve competitiveness would have to go through an extended period of deflation, which would require mass unemployment and falling wages. The present model requires that the deficit countries restrain inflation and growth whereas the surplus countries are allowed to proceed running surpluses (Stockhammer 2011b). But beyond its failure to deliver stability, this arrangement also has severe distributional consequences. Simply put, under the present arrangement Greek wages have fallen, but German wages do not have to rise. The system worked badly enough during the good times (in particular for the working classes), it's proving lethal in bad times.

International imbalances in trade balances (and the corresponding capital flows) are widely recognized as having played an important role in the building up of the bubble in the USA. Capital flows have provided vast amounts of capital in search of yield in US$ assets. These they found in various derivatives based on mortgage and commercial credit, thereby fuelling the credit-financed consumption boom. However, we want to highlight a more structural feature of financial globalization: it has increased the potential for different developments across countries – if only as long as international financial markets remain calm. Financial liberalization and globalization have allowed countries to run larger current account deficits, provided that they can attract the corresponding capital inflows. Figure 5.2 plots the standard deviation of the current account as a ratio to GDP (for OECD countries) as a measure of international imbalances. This shows that international imbalances have increased substantially since the mid 1980s.[9] Two things are remarkable about Figure 5.2. First, imbalances in the early 2000s were above the levels of the mid 1970s when the oil price shock gave rise to strong changes in current accounts across many countries; second the rise in international imbalance has been gradually building up since 1980.

5.3 The regime of fragile and slow accumulation

The debate on financialization is fuelled by the perception that finance is increasingly dominating real activity, with the exact meaning of this statement often being hard to pin down. However, there is ample evidence that financial activity has grown faster than real activity (as measured for example by GDP). For

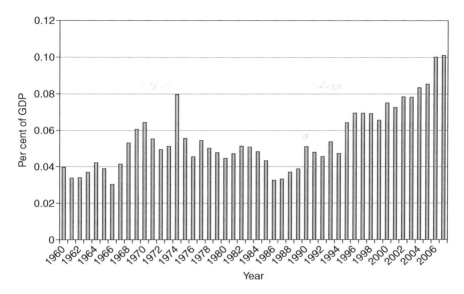

Figure 5.2 Standard deviation of the current account as % of GDP across OECD countries (source: AMECO).

example, in the USA stock market capitalization has increased from 58 per cent of GDP in 1988 to 163 per cent in 1999. The rise in stock market turnover is even more spectacular, rising from 33 per cent (of GDP) in 1988 to 383 per cent in 2008 (according to the World Bank Financial Structure Data Set). The ratio of financial and international profits to total corporate profits has risen from just above 12 per cent in 1948 to a peak at 53 per cent in 2001 (Bureau of Economic Analysis, National Income and Product Accounts, Table 6.16B-D). Finally, financialization has come with a dramatic increase in debt levels across different sectors. Figure 5.3 shows the debt of households, businesses and the financial sector (as a ratio to GDP). While the business sector has increased its debt from 52 per cent of GDP (in 1976) to 77 per cent (2009), household debt has increased from 45 per cent (1976) to 96 per cent (2009), with a clear acceleration in the early 2000s. Most spectacularly, the debt of the financial sector has increased from 16 per cent to 111 per cent (2009).[10] The popular perception of the increasing role of finance is clearly substantiated by economic data: activity on financial markets has increased faster than real activity; financial profits make up an increasing share of total profits; and households as well as the financial sector are taking on a lot more debt.

While there is evidence for a consumption boom in the USA (and previously for limited periods in some developing countries), for continental European countries one does not find the strong evidence of a consumption boom (related with a property price bubble) – despite the fact that household debt levels

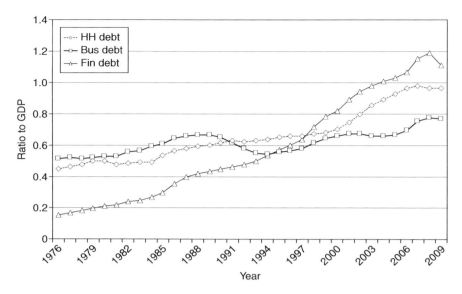

Figure 5.3 Debt of households, businesses and financial sectors (as ratio to GDP), USA (source: FED Flow of Funds, Table D.3 Credit Market Debt Outstanding by Sector; Household, business and financial debt are the total debt outstanding by households, businesses and domestic financial sectors respectively, all divided by GDP).

increased substantially.[11] Investment performance has been weak. In particular rising profits have not translated into rising investment. Presumably (but hardly conclusively) this is related to shareholder value orientation and increased uncertainty due to volatile financial markets. The liberalization of capital flows has relaxed current account constraints on countries and led to volatile exchange rates and frequent financial crises.

Overall the effects of financialization thus give rise to a finance-dominated accumulation regime that is one of *slow* and *fragile* accumulation. There are two related reasons to expect the finance-dominated accumulation regime to come with more volatility in output growth (and other macroeconomic variables). First, macroeconomic shocks from the financial sector have become more severe and more frequent. There is ample evidence that financial markets generate highly volatile prices. Overshooting is well established for exchange rates and the boom bust cycles of share prices has become evident (again) in the past years. Second, because of high debt levels, the fragility of the economy has increased. Financialization has encouraged households to take on more debt. This debt presumably either has fuelled consumption expenditures or was necessary to buy property in the face of soaring house prices. Either way, debt has to be serviced out of current income (or by ever increasing debt). Even temporary reductions in income may thus escalate if households have to default on their loans. While this need not happen necessarily, the *fragility* of the system has increased as the resilience of households against temporary shocks has decreased.

One would expect that this combination of more frequent crises on financial markets and high fragility of households to translate into macroeconomic volatility. IMF (2007b) presents evidence that business cycle have become more *moderate* since the 1970s. The devil, however, lies in the detail. While "output volatility (…) has been significantly lower than during the 1960s" (IMF 2007b, 85), recessions have become harsher in the Post-Bretton Woods era than in the Bretton Woods era (IMF 2002, Table 3.1). As output growth (and expansions) was much higher in the Fordist era than in the post-Fordist era, the IMF is correct in concluding that volatility has decreased. But this does not mean that recession have become less severe! Moreover, financial crises have become more frequent and more severe (Eichengreen and Bordo 2003).[12] The present crisis is not a rare exception, but only one of many in the age of deregulated finance.

It is important to note that state shares in GDP are still substantially higher than at the time of Great Depression. Automatic stabilizers are thus in place and government consumption forms a sizable part of value added. Moreover, central banks in developed countries (in particular the Fed) have been pro-active in reacting to dangers of financial crisis. The resilience of a sizable government sector and (by historical standards) a functional welfare state combined with active monetary policy may be the reason, why financial crises have so far not had a devastating effect on (advanced) economies and why the Great Recession has not yet turned into a Great Depression.

6 Income distribution and the underlying causes of the present crisis

Financialization and the rise in inequality have interacted in complex ways to provide the preconditions of the present crisis. The starting point for our discussion is the assertion that, other things equal, an increase in inequality leads to a lack of consumption demand. In the period of financialization, the increase in inequality and profits did not translate into an increase in investment expenditures. We highlight three channels through which inequality has contributed. First, in the USA, the median working class household has experienced stagnant wages. Consumption norms have increased faster than median wages and household debt has increased sharply. The property boom allowed households to take out loans that they could not afford given their income, but that seemed reasonable to banks which assumed that property prices would continue to increase. The USA (and other Anglo-Saxon countries) have developed a *credit-driven consumption boom* growth model – and debt-to-income ratios have increased faster for lower income groups than for higher ones. Typically these countries had current account deficits.

Other countries have also, albeit in somewhat different forms, experienced an increase in inequality. But some of them have developed a different strategy of coping with the shortfall in domestic demand that came with the polarization of income distribution. Here net exports played the key component of demand growth. Thus these countries developed an *export-led growth model*. The resulting capital outflows fuelled the property bubble and bubbles in other financial markets. Thus the second channel is the development of two growth models that were made possible by financial globalization. It's important to realise that the export-oriented model is also, in part, a response to macroeconomic problems caused by a rise in inequality.

A third channel is that a rise in inequality, more precisely a rise in wealth inequality, leads to an increase of the social propensity of speculation in the sense that the rich households will hold a riskier portfolio. Lysandrou (2010) provides more specific evidence for this channel. He argues that the rise of high net wealth individuals has fuelled the hedge funds that cater the very rich and hedge funds contributed to financial instability, first by their high degree of leverage and second by being the prime demand for subprime securities.

7 Conclusion

The chapter has argued that the crisis should be understood as the outcome of a process of financialization that has shaped the accumulation regimes in advanced economies and that has interacted with the effects of the polarization of income distribution. This analysis lends itself to two central demands for economic policy: a de-financialization of the economy and a pro-labour shift in the distribution of income. While there will be little disagreement that something needs to change in the realm of finance, the scope of the necessary changes is subject to disagreement. We go beyond the familiar call for more and better regulation and advocate de-financialization. This would imply a shrinking of financial sector, a stronger voice of stakeholders, such as labour unions, at the expense of shareholders in corporate governance; it would also aim at replacing the logic of profit (or shareholder value) maximization in many social areas by a democratically determined policy priorities and principles of solidarity.

The second part of our policy conclusions is even less conventional (by today's standards): wage moderation has been one of the structural causes underlying the present crisis, therefore higher wage growth is one condition for re-establishing a viable growth regime. Wages have to increase at least with productivity growth. This would stabilize domestic demand in the surplus countries and allow us to avoid a collapse of consumption demand in the deficit countries. A more egalitarian income distribution is not a luxury that can be dealt with once the economy has been stabilized; it is an integral part of a sound macroeconomic structure.

Notes

1 Horn *et al.* (2009) and Hein (2011a) develop a very similar argument.
2 One of the first prominent works to use the term financialization was Arrighi (1994) who identified long waves of economic development in global capitalism that involve hegemonic and geographic shifts. While the upswings of these long waves are characterized

by increased manufacturing and trade activity, in the downturns a process of financialization occurs: the leading power had initially established a competitive advantage in terms of production, but it shifts towards financial activities as its growth model gets exhausted and other players catch up. In contrast to Arrighi most of the recent debate uses the term more narrowly to refer to the period since the 1970s.
3 For contributions on the macroeconomics of financialization see Boyer 2000, Stockhammer 2005/06, Dutt 2006, van Treeck 2009, Hein 2011b.
4 Classical works of the (French) Regulation Theory include Aglietta (1979), Lipietz (1985) and Boyer (1990). There are similarities between the Regulation Theory and the (American) Social Structures of Accumulation approach (Gordon *et al.* 1982, Bowles, *et al.* 1983).
5 Vidal (2010) offers an interpretation of post-Fordism as Waltonism.
6 There is an additional channel through which financialization may have affected consumption expenditures. In many countries the pay-as-you-go pension systems are being reformed or have been questioned. Typically some version of a capital-based system is envisioned in which households have to invest their savings (usually via funds) in the stock market. This should lead to an increase in savings as households have to put more aside for retirement. I am not aware that this channel has been investigated empirically.
7 While there is substantial evidence for the USA (albeit based on a short period of observations!) to back up this story, the evidence on European economies was always much thinner. Typically the wealth effects estimated for European economies were not statistically significant and/or much smaller.
8 This value is in line with comparable studies for other groups of countries (Naastepad and Storm 2006/2007, Hein and Vogel 2008).
9 As our measure only includes OECD countries China as well as some other South-East Asian countries that run substantial current account surpluses are not included. Our measure thus underestimates the full extent of international imbalances.
10 These figures refer to *gross* debt. Typically debt will be used to acquire assets. The difference between the value of the assets and gross debt is net debt. It is useful to look at gross debt as the valuation of assets that may at times change dramatically as happened in 2008/2009, whereas the nominal value of debt is fixed.
11 However, given that income distribution has changed at the expense of labour, which should have decreased consumption ratios, it is plausible that debt-driven consumption has also fuelled demand in Europe to some extent.
12 In particular Eichengreen and Bordo report that there had been *no* banking crises in the 1945–1973 period.

References

Aglietta, M. (1979) *A Theory of Capitalist Regulation. The US Experience*. London: Verso.
Aglietta, M. and Rebérioux, A. (2005) *Corporate Governance Adrift. A Critique of Shareholder Value*. Cheltenham: Edward Elgar.
Allen, F. and Gale, D. (2000) *Comparing Financial Systems*. Cambridge, MA: MIT Press.
Arrighi, G. (1994) *The Long Twentieth Century*. London: Verso.
Atkinson, A., Piketty, T. and Saez, E., (2010) Top Incomes in the Long Run of History. *Journal of Economic Literature* 49(1): 3–71.
Barba, A. and Pivetti, M. (2009) Rising household debt: Its causes and macroeconomic implications – a long-period analysis. *Cambridge Journal of Economics* 33, 113–137.
Becker, J. (2002) *Akkumulation, Regulation Territorium. Zur kritischen Rekonstruktion der französischen Regulationstheorie*. Marburg: Metropolis Verlag.

Beltratti, A. and Stulz, R. (2009) Why Did Some Banks Perform Better During the Credit Crisis? A Cross-Country Study of the Impact of Governance and Regulation. NBER Working Paper No. 15180.

Boone, L., Giorno, C. and Richardson, P. (1998) Stock market fluctuations and consumption behaviour: some recent evidence. OECD Economics department working papers No. 208.

Bowles, S. (1975) The problem with human capital theory: a Marxian critique. *American Economic Review* 65(2): 74–82.

Bowles, S., Gordon, D. and Weisskopf, T. (1983) *Beyond the Waste Land. A Democratic Alternative to Economic Decline*, Garden City, NY: Anchor Press.

Boyer, R. (1990) *The Regulation School: A Critical Introduction.* New York: Columbia University Press.

Boyer, R. (2000) Is a finance-led growth regime a viable alternative to Fordism? A preliminary analysis. *Economy and Society* 29, 1: 111–145.

Carruth, A., Dickerson, A. and Henley, A. (2000) What do we know about investment under uncertainty? *Journal of Economic Surveys* 24 (2), 119–153.

Case, K., Shiller, R., Quigley, J. (2001) Comparing Wealth Effects: The Stock Market Versus the Housing Market. NBER Working Paper No.w8606 November 2001.

Catte, P., Girouard, N., Price, R. and André, C. (2004) Housing markets, wealth and the business cycle. OECD Economics Working Paper 394.

Chirinko, R. (1993) Business Fixed Investment Spending: Modeling Strategies, Empirical Results and Policy Implications. *Journal of Economic Literature*, 31 (4), 1875–1911.

Crotty, J. (2003) The Neoliberal Paradox: the impact of destructive product market competition and impatient financial markets on nonfinancial corporations in the Neoliberal Era. *Review of Radical Political Economics*, 35 (3), 271–279.

Cynamon, B. and Fazzari, S. (2009) Household debt in the consumer age: source of growth – risk of collapse. *Capitalism and Society*, 3 (2), Art 3 www.bepress.com/cas/vol. 3/iss2/art3/.

Davis, E. P. (2003) Institutional investors, financial market efficiency, and financial stability. EIB Paper 8, 1: 77–107.

Duménil, G. and Lévy, D. (2001) Costs and benefits of Neoliberalism: a class analysis. *Review of International Political Economy*, 8 (4), 578–607.

Duménil, G. and Lévy, D. (2004) *Capital Resurgent. Roots of the Neoliberal Revolution.* Cambridge, MA: Harvard University Press.

Dutt, A. (2006) Maturity, stagnation and consumer debt: a Steindlian approach, *Metroeconomica*, 57(3), 339–364.

Eichengreen, B. (2010) Ireland's reparations burden. [original appeared as Jämmerliches Versagen, Handelsblatt, 1 Dec 2010] www.irisheconomy.ie/index.php/2010/12/01/barry-eichengreen-on-the-irish-bailout/ (accessed 21 Jan 2011).

Eichengreen, B. and Bordo, M. (2003) Crises now and then: what lessons for the last era of financial globalization? In: P. Mizen (ed.): *Monetary history, exchange rates and financial markets. Essays in honour of Charles Goodhart, Volume two*. Cheltenham: Edward Elgar.

Epstein, G. (ed.) (2005) *Financialization and the World Economy*. Cheltenham: Edward Elgar.

Ertürk, I. and Solari, S. (2007) Banks as Continuous Reinvention, *New Political Economy*, 12(3). 369–388.

Ertürk, I., Froud, J., Johal, S., Leaver, A. and Williams, K. (eds.) (2008) *Financialization At Work. Key Texts and Commentary*. London: Routledge.

European Commission (2007) The labour income share in the European Union. Chapter 5 of: *Employment in Europe*.
Foucault, M. (2008) *The Birth of Biopolitics: Lectures at the College de France, 1978–1979*. Houndsmills: Palgrave Macmillan.
Froud, J., Johal, S., Leaver, A. and Williams, K. (2006) *Financialization and Strategy: Narrative and Numbers*. London: Routledge.
Girouard, N., Kennedy M. and André, C. (2006) Has the rise in debt made households more vulnerable? OECD Economics Working Paper 535 (ECO/WKP(2006)63).
Glyn, A. (2006) *Capitalism unleashed: Finance, Globalization and Welfare*. Oxford: Oxford University Press.
Gordon, D., Edwards, R. and Reich, M. (1982) *Segmented Work, Divided Workers. The Historical Transformation of Labour in the United States*, Cambridge: Cambridge University Press.
Harrison, A. (2002) Has globalization eroded labor's share? Some cross-country evidence, Mimeo, UC Berkeley.
Harvey, D. (2005) *A Short History of Neoliberalism*. Oxford: Oxford University Press.
Hein, E. and Vogel, L. (2008) Distribution and growth reconsidered – empirical results for Austria, France, Germany, the Netherlands, the UK and the USA. *Cambridge Journal of Economics*, 32 (3), 479–511.
Hein, E. (2011a) Distribution, 'Financialisation' and the Financial and Economic Crisis – Implications for Post-crisis Economic Policies, MPRA Paper 31180.
Hein, E. (2011b) 'Financialisation', Distribution and Growth. In: E. Hein and E. Stockhammer (eds): *A New Guide to Keynesian Economics and Economic Policies*. Cheltenham: Edward Elgar.
Horn, G., Dröge, K., Sturn, S., van Treeck, T. and Zwiener, R. (2009) From the financial crisis to the world economic crisis. The role of inequality. English version of IMK Report No. 41 IMK Policy Brief www.boeckler.de/show_product_imk.html?productfile=HBS-004528.xml.
ILO (2008) World of Work Report 2008. Income inequalities in the age of financial globalization. Geneva: ILO.
IMF (2002) Recessions and recoveries. Chapter 3 of World Economic Outlook 2002/1.
IMF (2006) Global Financial Stability Report April 2006. Washington: IMF 2006.
IMF (2007a) The globalization of labor. Chapter 5 of World Economic Outlook April 2007. Washington: IMF.
IMF (2007b) The changing dynamics of the global business cycle. Chapter 5 of: World Economic Outlook 2007/2.
Jayadev, A. (2007) Capital account openness and the labour share of income. *Cambridge Journal of Economics* 31, 423–443.
Lapavitsas, Costas (2009) Financialised Capitalism: Crisis and Financial Expropriation. *Historical Materialism* 17, 114–148.
Lapavitsas, C., Kaltenbrunner, A., Lindo, D., Michell, J., Painceira, J.P., Pires, E., Powell, J., Stenfors, A. and Teles, N. (2010) Eurozone crisis: Beggar Thyself and Thy Neighbour. RMF occasional report March 2010 http://researchonmoneyandfinance.org/media/reports/eurocrisis/fullreport.pdf.
Lazonick, W. and O'Sullivan, M. (2000): Maximising shareholder value: a new ideology for corporate governance. *Economy and Society*, 29 (1), 13–35.
Lipietz, A. (1985) *The Enchanted Word*. London: Verso.
Lysandrou, P. (2011) Global inequality, wealth concentration and the subprime crisis: a Marxian commodity theory analysis. *Development and Change* 42, 1, 183–208.

MacKenzie, D. and Millo, Y. (2003) Constructing a market, performing theory: the historical sociology of a financial derivates exchange. *American Journal of Sociology* 109: 107–145.

Marx, K. (1976) *Capital. A Critique of Political Economy* Volume One. London: Penguin Books.

Minsky, H. (1986) *Stabilizing An Unstable Economy*. New Haven: Yale University Press.

Naastepad, C. and Storm, S. (2006/07): OECD demand regimes (1960–2000), *Journal of Post-Keynesian Economics*, 29 (2), 213–248.

OECD (2008) *Growing unequal? Income distribution and poverty in OECD countries.* Paris: OECD.

Onaran, Ö. (2009) Wage share, globalization, and crisis: The case of manufacturing industry in Korea, Mexico, and Turkey. *International Review of Applied Economics*, 23(2), 113–134.

Onaran, Ö., Stockhammer, E. and Grafl, L. (2011) The finance-dominated growth regime, distribution, and aggregate demand in the US. *Cambridge Journal of Economics* 35(4): 637–661.

Orhangazi, Ö. (2008) Financialisation and capital accumulation in the non-financial corporate sector: A theoretical and empirical investigation on the US economy: 1973–2003. *Cambridge Journal of Economics* 32, 863–886.

Pozsar, Z., Adrian, T., Ashcraft, A. and Boesky, H. (2010) Shadow banking. Federal Reserve Bank of New York Staff Report No. 458.

Reinhart, C. and Reinhart, V. (2008) Capital Flow Bonanzas: An Encompassing View of the Past and Present. NBER Working Paper No. W14321.

Rodrik, D. (1998) Capital mobility and labor. Manuscript. http://ksghome.harvard.edu/~drodrik/capitalm.pdf.

Schaberg, M. (1999) *Globalization and the Erosion of National Financial Systems. Is Declining Autonomy Inevitable?* Cheltenham: Edward Elgar.

Shaxson, N. (2010) *Treasure Islands: Tax Havens and the Men who Stole the World.* London: Bodley Head.

Stockhammer, E. (2004) Financialization and the slowdown of accumulation. *Cambridge Journal of Economics*, 28 (5), 719–741.

Stockhammer, E. (2005/06) Shareholder value-orientation and the investment-profit puzzle. *Journal of Post Keynesian Economics* 28, 2: 193–216.

Stockhammer, E. (2008) Stylized facts on the finance-dominated accumulation regime. *Competition and Change* 12 (2), 189–207.

Stockhammer, E. (2009) Determinants of functional income distribution in OECD countries. IMK Studies, Nr. 5/2009. Düsseldorf 2009.

Stockhammer, E. (2010) Financialization and the global economy. Political Economy Research Institute Working Paper 242.

Stockhammer, E. (2011a) Neoliberalism, income distribution and the causes of the crisis. In: P. Arestis, R. Sobreira, J. Oreiro (eds): *The 2008 Financial Crisis, Financial Regulation and Global Impact. Volume 1 The Financial Crisis: Origins and Implications.* London: Palgrave Macmillan.

Stockhammer, E. (2011b) Peripheral Europe's debt and German wages. *International Journal of Public Policy* 7, 1–3: 83–96.

Stockhammer, E., Grafl, L. (2011) Financial uncertainty and business investment. *Review of Political Economy* 22, 4: 551–568.

Stockhammer, E., Onaran, Ö. and Ederer, S. (2009) Functional income distribution and aggregate demand in the Euro area. *Cambridge Journal of Economics*, 33 (1), 139–159.

Stockhammer, E. and Ramskogler, P. (2009) Post Keynesian economics – how to move forward. *Intervention* 5 (2): 227–246.

UNCTAD (2009) *Trade and Development Report 2009*. New York: United Nations.

Van Treeck, T. (2009) The political economy debate on 'financialisation' – a macroeconomic perspective, *Review of International Political Economy*, 16(5), 907–944.

Vidal, M. (2012) On the persistence of labour market insecurity and slow growth in the US: Reckoning with the Waltonist growth regime. *New Political Economy* forthcoming.

Worldbank (2002) *Building Institutions for Markets. World Development Report 2002*. Washington, DC: Worldbank.

Part II
Impact and consequences of the crisis

6 Labour market institutions and the crisis

Where we come from and where we are going

Sebastiano Fadda

1 When talking about labour market institutions it is necessary to remove a fundamental misunderstanding. That is to think that there are countries, or better economic systems, which rely on markets as opposite to countries which rely on institutions. In fact, markets themselves are sets of institutions, and labour markets in particular (let's mention Solow's essay "The labour market as a social institution") always operate with agents' decisions and interactions shaped by rules. Even the jungle has its "rules" and competitive markets often need special rules in order to protect their own existence. We may distinguish between formal and informal rules[1] and their relative weight, and we may make judgements about "good" or "bad" institutions, but we cannot imagine (nor define) an "institution-less" system. Nor we can assume that institutions are *per se* detrimental to the working of market forces: think of antitrust regulations or of the definition of property rights; they are institutions on which the working of efficient markets is based.

This consideration is important because it allows us to establish that it is not the presence of labour market institutions which reduces "economic freedom", but rather their quality that may be against or in favour of economic freedom. Otherwise we could easily place Zambia or Uganda (due to their lack of "formal" institutions) at the top of the rank of economic freedom and, say, Germany or Sweden at the bottom,[2] and jump to a conclusion that a negative relation exists between labour market freedom and the level of GDP per capita.

Having said that, the scheme of this chapter will be as following:

- To see "where we come from" I'll try to trace the evolution of the attitude towards labour market institutions starting from the OECD Jobs Study of 1994.
- Then I'll consider the burst of the recent financial crisis, trying to see if its origins reveal a link with the institutional set up of the labour market.
- At this point, a look at the effects of the crisis on the labour market would allow us to establish whether these may have been affected by differences in labour market institutions and whether a process of institutional change has been stimulated by the crisis.
- Finally, the study will consider whether the impact and the success of the measures to overcome the crisis may be influenced by the labour market

institutional set up and in which directions this should evolve in order to enhance the chances of success of the stimuli in overcoming the crisis.

2 The bulk of "structural reforms" that the OECD suggested in its well known "jobs study" of 1994 (OECD, 1994) in order to improve the performance of labour markets and employment all over the world can be actually boiled down to a set of measures directed at obtaining changes in the labour market institutions along the following lines: increase labour "flexibility"; reduce unemployment benefits; reduce employment protection and security provisions, increase the responsiveness of wages to market pressure, and improve labour market active policies. The soundness of these suggestions should be considered in the first place through their links with the theoretical framework and in the second place against the empirical evidence:

- Of all the dimensions of the so called flexibility (functional flexibility, freedom to change tasks and working time within the firm, and freedom to fire and hire) the last is the most significant and the one to which the best consequences in terms of labour market performance are generally attributed. It has been suggested though (Schivardi, 1999) that under certain conditions, removing restrictions to firing and hiring is neutral with regard to levels of employment, while it may affect the efficiency of the system through a better resource allocation. It's more interesting for the purposes of this chapter to consider the increase in flexibility under the perspective of the reduction of the adjustment costs that it implies, and particular to consider the effect of this reduction on the labour share in GDP. As P. Vermeulen (2007) states, "firing costs cause firms to fire less in recessions and hire less in booms, causing wage costs to fluctuate less cyclically than output, thus inducing variability and counter-cyclicality in the labour share". Redundancy or severance payments, legal restrictions to workers' dismissal and also the cost of mobility would therefore be contrary to the Kaldorian-stylized growth fact that the labour share is constant in the long run. Obviously, one consideration is the long run and the other is the cyclical movement; nevertheless, without specifying how long is the long run, we can observe deviations from this constancy for significant lengths of time. Of course it is of paramount importance, as we shall see, to establish whether movements in labour share can be explained through changes in institutional factors such as firing and hiring costs.
- Reducing unemployment provisions was a second pillar of the advocated structural reforms. The bulk of the argument against unemployment benefits does not lay in public budget considerations, but rather in their effect on the supply of labour (Burtless, 1990). As non-wage income, they would have a wealth effect reducing labour supply for any given wage level and would raise the reservation wage; the decrease in the cost of search would cause an increase in the duration of voluntary search-unemployment. One should take notice however that as for the labour supply, the traditional microeconomics

refers to hours worked and the effect is not directly transferable in the decision as to whether to participate at all in the labour force (intensive and extensive elasticities are different); and that, as for the job search intensity, the longer time devoted to job search could result in an improvement of the quality of job matches. Besides, differences in unemployment benefits duration, conditionality, eligibility, coverage and replacement rate may, after all, significantly affect the behaviour of labour supply (Schmieder, 2010).

- The reduction of employment protection legislation and security provisions is supposed to work in the same way as the increase in flexibility. In fact, the employment protection legislation can take several forms. It is possible to impose compulsory negotiations with worker representatives prior to dismissals, or administrative authorizations as necessary condition to proceed with dismissals, or to inhibit "unfair dismissals", or to impose severance payments, and so on; but all of these cases can be converted in terms of adjustment costs and therefore they have an impact on the labour market in the same way as the degrees of flexibility. An important point to make in this regard is related to the presence of "legislation", which might not be reflected in the actual behaviour of agents (and these patterns of behaviour, rather than the rules, should actually be considered as "institutions") (Fadda 2006), owing to the gap between formal rules and actual practice. Obviously, this aspect, although relevant under a theoretical profile, is most decisive in the field of empirical investigation. Under a theoretical point of view it is worth considering the employment protection legislation as a case of property rights definition. According to the Coase theorem, with freedom of bargaining and no transaction costs the distribution of property rights should be irrelevant with respect to efficient allocation. When this is applied to labour market, if the worker is attributed the right not to be fired, the firm will pay for the decisions according to the established restrictions; if the firm is attributed the right to fire, the firm itself will detain the profit from the decision. In this line it has been suggested (Freeman 2007), therefore, that any property rights distribution set by the employment protection legislation would possibly affect the income distribution, but not the efficiency of production.[3]

- A third suggestion mentioned by the Jobs Study is in favour of making wages more responsive to market pressures. Actually, the rationale and the meaning of this statement are far from clear. Are "market pressures" supposed to lead to an aggregate full employment equilibrium wage level? Do these pressures guarantee a perfectly competitive market so that the same market and the same occupation corresponds to same wage? Should marginal productivity of labour be the parameter for wage setting? Aren't "efficiency wages" in themselves a result of free market pressures? Are variables such as "power" part of the "market pressures" which influence wage bargaining? What this recommendation actually aims at seems to be a substantial reduction of the role of trade unions and collective agreements in wage setting, on the assumption that this would push wages above the "market" level. But on this point many questions can be raised. First, the role and weight of trade unions in wage setting is a vector of several variables which includes trade unions density, coverage of collective agreements, various degrees of centralization or decentralization, coordination devices, different parameters for wage setting. Second, the impact of such vector on labour market and economic performance is difficult to establish on theoretical terms, not to say on empirical grounds, due to the different influences and different weights of each component. It could be argued that "work councils", good industrial relations at firm level, with more knowledge diffusion and workers' participation, would favour wage moderation, but also the opposite: that centralized bargaining and social dialogue would make workers more aware of the constraints coming from balance of payments and prices stability.

Finally, the Jobs Study includes among the advocated structural reforms the improvement of active labour market policies. Obviously, this does not affect the aggregate demand for labour, but mainly through job search assistance, counselling and training, it may reduce frictional and structural unemployment. If measures for direct job creation or subsidies for self employment are adopted an impact on the overall labour demand may also be considered.

When from the level of theory we move to the level of empirical evidence unfortunately we do not receive much assistance in detecting the impact of the institutional variables mentioned above on the performance of the labour market and the economy in general. The results of empirical investigations are not univocal and even when significant relations are found, they are generally accompanied by warnings, caveats and particular assumptions. As it is easily understandable, the main reason lies in the difficulty to find countries which are similar in all the relevant economic variables except for that particular institution to which the difference in economic performance is to be attributed. Even within the set of institutions it is not possible to test the influence of one particular feature without taking into account the overall institutional set up. A study made in 2002 for the Center for European Studies (Baker, Glyn, Howell and Schmitt, 2005) deals in great detail with the main empirical cross country investigations and also multivariate analyses trying to establish a relationship between labour market institutions and economic and employment performance. The study puts under examination "the evidence for the widespread belief that labour market rigidities are largely responsible for high unemployment and that labour market deregulation is therefore the best route to raising employment rates". The study concludes that none of the links between the above mentioned elements of the so called "structural reform" suggested by the OECD and the labour market outcomes is empirically proved. In particular, the results of the examination

> suggest a yawning gap between the confidence with which the case for labor market deregulation has been asserted and the evidence that the regulating institutions are the culprits. It is even less evident that further weakening of

social and collective protections for workers will have significant positive impacts on employment prospects. The effects of various kinds of deregulation on unemployment are very hard to determine and may be quite negligible. Moreover such effects as there are may influence labor force participation rather than employment (e.g. lower wages and greater employment insecurity may lead workers to opt out of the labor force altogether, which could contribute to lowering the unemployment rate).

Nevertheless, in spite of this lack of empirical evidence, the traditional consensus has maintained its strength. Advices and recommendations have kept pouring in this direction, and several countries, particularly those more dependent on World Bank and IMF conditionalities, have taken measures to weaken "institutional rigidities".

3 The recent financial crisis: are some of the roots deepened in the labour market? While governments of different countries were busy implementing to a various degree the "structural reform" among these lines, the great financial crisis occurred. As is well known, it started creeping in the US financial sector, then exploded into a violent bust and spread its effects in the real sector nearly all over the world.

Although there was a common agreement in regards to the specific "mechanics" of the sequences that led to the explosion of the crisis, more open questions remain as to the root causes of it. Surely two facts have converged to determine the crisis: one is the financial disorder which has accompanied the financialization of the economy allowing for an unlimited buying of financial assets on credit (excessive leverage and spread of the risk in a variety of derivatives); the second is the expansionary monetary policy of the Federal Reserve, with low interest rates and easy credit which led to financial "euphoria". If this were the complete explanation of the crisis, the countermeasures should be sought at the financial level and they would be enough to stop a similar crisis from happening again. But a deeper insight shows that the root causes of the crisis lay in the structural aspect of the real sector, and to be precise, in the decline of household purchasing power, which would have implied a deficiency of aggregate demand had households not been able to keep up a high level of consumption demand through an increase in their indebtedness. It is this enormous increase, extended more and more to people who are unable to repay the debt mainly in the housing sector, accompanied by a wild deregulation of the financial markets which triggered the spiral of the financial boom and then led to the bust once the deleveraging process started to work. The aggregate demand required to sustain the growth of the economy was therefore financed out of private debt[4] rather than out of income (Cynamon and Fazzari 2008, Kumhof and Ranciere 2010), but this process could not last forever, and in fact it didn't. It is worth considering that once the aggregate purchasing power had fallen, either it had to be compensated by an increase in borrowing or it would have led straight to a recession in the real economy through a decline in the level of economic activity.

The question to be asked now is in regards to what has caused the decrease in the purchasing power. There is wide agreement in the literature that the cause is to be attributed to the increase in income inequality which has produced first a fall in the savings rate of households and second an increase in their indebtedness. No general awareness existed prior to the crisis regarding the risk that an increasing income inequality and a decreasing of the labour share in GDP could have led to such disastrous results, although the phenomenon was well known (Glyn 2006, 2007), and this is quite striking. Among the rare warnings that were made before the crisis, one should mention the paper by Barba and Pivetti (2006), which pointed out the long-term macroeconomic implications of the rise of households debt, underlining the great difference between private and public debt. Now the role played by the growth of income inequality seems to be widely recognized (Fitoussi and Saraceno, 2010), although the measures taken all over the world to overcome the crisis do not show alignment with this view.

But to see where we come from we must now ask if any role has been played by labour market institutions in determining the trend in income inequality. Three facts are empirically evident: first, the trend in income inequality is growing nearly everywhere in industrialized countries in recent decades; second, the United States show the greatest increase and the highest absolute level of inequality; third, the increase in income inequality is parallel to the decrease in the labour income share in GDP.

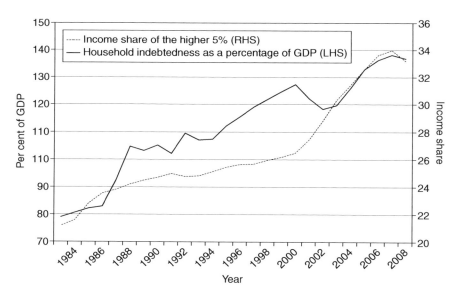

Figure 6.1 Income inequality and household indebtedness in the US (source, IMF 2010).

Notes
Income share of the higher 5% (right side).
Household indebtedness as a percentage of GDP (left side).

Labour market institutions and the crisis 129

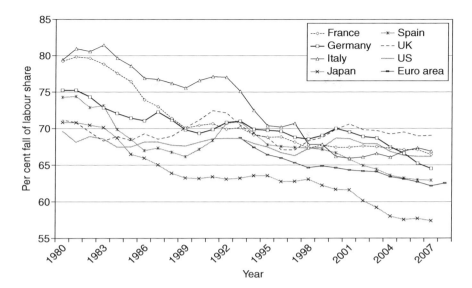

Figure 6.2 The fall in labour share (source: OECD (from Fitoussi 2010)).

In consideration of these facts we can observe the evolution of a few features of the labour market institutional set up.

The first feature is the level of employment protection legislation. With all the caveats regarding the OECD index we can see that while inequality was growing and labour share falling in the United States, EPL was kept constant and significantly lower than levels of other countries. In other countries the fall of labour share was accompanied by a fall in EPL, though remaining much higher than in the US. It's difficult to imagine a causal relationship going from the former to the latter.

A second relevant feature is the decrease of trade union power as expressed by Union Density data. The OECD data shows not only a decreasing trend of workers trade union participation but also a significant difference between the

Table 6.1 EPL index, selected years

	1985	1995	2008	2009		1985	1995	2008	2009
Austria	2.21	2.21	1.93	–	Italy	3.57	3.57	1.89	–
Belgium	3.15	3.15	2.18	–	Netherlands	2.73	2.73	1.95	–
Denmark	2.40	1.50	1.50	–	Portugal	4.19	3.85	3.15	2.88
Finland	2.33	2.16	1.96	–	Spain	3.82	3.01	2.98	–
France	2.79	2.98	3.05	3.04	Sweden	3.49	2.47	1.87	–
Germany	3.17	3.09	2.12	–	United Kingdom	0.60	0.60	0.75	–
Greece	3.56	3.50	2.73	–	United States	0.21	0.21	0.21	–
Ireland	0.93	0.93	1.11	–					

Source: OECD.

Table 6.2 Trade union density – selected countries

	Trade union density in %						
	1970	1980	1990	2000	2008	2009	2010
Australia	44	48	40	24	18	19	18
Austria	63	57	47	37	29	29	28
Belgium	42	54	54	49	52	52	–
Canada	31	34	34	28	27	27	28
Denmark	60	79	75	74	68	69	–
Finland	51	69	73	75	68	69	70
France	22	18	10	8	8	–	–
Germany	32	35	31	25	19	19	19
Greece	–	–	34	27	24	–	–
Iceland	–	66	93	89	79	–	–
Ireland	51	54	49	38	32	34	–
Italy	37	50	39	35	33	35	35
Japan	35	31	25	22	18	18	18
Luxembourg	47	51	46	43	37	–	–
Netherlands	37	35	24	23	19	19	–
New Zealand	57	69	49	22	21	21	21
Norway	57	58	59	54	53	54	–
Portugal	–	55	28	22	20	20	19
Spain	–	–	13	17	15	16	–
Sweden	68	78	80	79	68	68	68
Switzerland	29	28	23	21	18	18	–
United Kingdom	43	50	38	30	27	27	27
United States	27	22	15	13	12	12	11

Source: OECD employment outlook, various years.

United States (11.9 per cent in 2008) and main European countries in the same year (Sweden: 68 per cent; Belgium: 51.9 per cent; Italy: 33.4 per cent; Germany: 19.1 per cent).

A third feature is the degree of collective agreements coverage.

Table 6.3 Collective bargaining coverage in % – selected countries

	1980	1990	2000
Austria	95	95	95
Belgium	90	90	90
Denmark	70	70	90
Finland	90	90	80
France	80	90	90
Germany	80	80	90
Italy	80	80	80
Sweden	80	80	90
United Kingdom	70	40	30
United States	26	18	14

Source: OECD Employment outlook, various years.

Taking the Union Density data and collective bargaining coverage it is possible to see the relative position of the United States.

A fourth element is the degree of collective bargaining centralization, which is largely supposed to negatively affect wages inequality.[5] Even on this ground the United States show a lower degree of centralization compared with European countries.

The trend in wages and the wage share on GDP may also be seen against the growing of the so called non-standard work contracts.

It is clear at this point where we come from. We come from a labour market institutional set up which has depressed the share of labour in the economy and has created a "great moderation" of which even Bernanke declared, in a famous speech, to be proud. Undoubtedly this institutional evolution has taken place under the pressure of globalization, which on one side has granted the employers an increase in bargaining power in front of the employees due to the possibility and the threat of transferring abroad part of the production and on the other side has pushed the government to favour this process with the aim of resisting the strong competition from emerging countries. But the story has brought to light that such attempts to respond to low labour standards and in some cases social dumping in competitor countries through lowering of labour standards, in turn has far from succeeded in reaching the target. Thus the structural basis has been created for the slow building of the crisis which later exploded into a full blown financial crisis.

4 The effects of the crisis on the labour market have been widely analysed in the literature. According to ILO's global employment trends, the global unemployment rate rose between 2007 and 2009 from 5.6 to 6.3. But it's important to

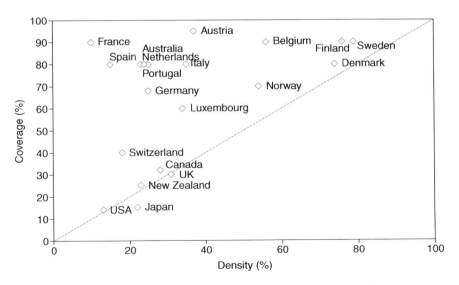

Figure 6.3 Trade union density vs. trade union coverage (source: OECD data).

Table 6.4 Centralization of bargaining index

	1970–1974	1975–1979	1980–1984	1985–1989	1990–1994	1995–2000
Australia	4	4	4	4	2	2
Austria	3	3	3	3	3	3
Belgium	4	3.5	3	3	3	3
Canada	1	1	1	1	1	1
Denmark	5	5	5	3	3	2
Finland	5	5	4	5	5	5
France	2	2	2	2	2	2
Germany	3	3	3	3	3	3
Greece						
Iceland						
Ireland	4	4	1	2.5	4	4
Italy	2	2	3.5	2	2	2
Japan	1	1	1	1	1	1
Luxembourg						
Netherlands	3	3	3	3	3	3
New Zealand	3	3	3	3	1	1
Norway	4.5	4.5	3.5	4.5	4.5	4.5
Portugal	5	4	3	3	4	4
Spain	5	4	4	3.5	3	3
Sweden	5	5	4.5	3	3	3
Switzerland	3	3	3	3	2	2
United Kingdom	2	2	1	1	1	1
United States	1	1	1	1	1	1

Source: OECD

compare the performance of the labour market between the US and the European countries. As shown by Eurostat (Statistics in focus, 20/2010), in the European Union, despite the stronger downturn of economic growth, the unemployment rate has risen sharply as a result of the economic crisis, but the increase has been much smaller than in the United States.

The following graph (Figure 6.4) shows the trend of unemployment in the EU and in the US (lower line) since 2000. In spite of being much lower at the start of the crisis, the US rate has overtaken the EU rate at its peak. The two subsequent graphs are a description of the relationship between the growth of GDP and the rate of unemployment respectively in the US and in the EU. What can be seen is that compared with the United States the crisis has had in Europe a greater impact on GDP but a smaller impact on unemployment.

The question which requires an answer is whether these different elasticities of unemployment with respect to cyclical fluctuations of GDP are connected to different labour market institutions. Subsequently it could be asked whether the crisis has influenced the evolution of labour market institutions themselves.

As for the first point, it seems possible to explain the different impacts on unemployment in Europe on the basis of its more rigid labour market institutions. It goes without saying that it is necessary to pay attention to all the difficulties that we mentioned relatively to cross country comparisons of the relationship between economic performance and labour market institutions, since many variables other than institutions do influence the performance of the economy. But these difficulties are largely relieved in this point because the question is not to observe the influence of institutions on economic performance but rather the impact of the economic slowdown,

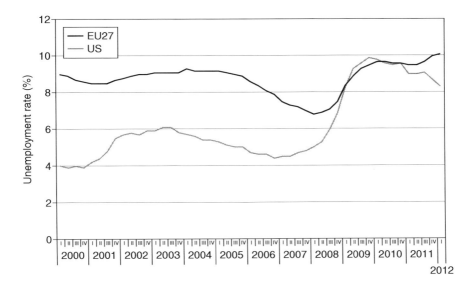

Figure 6.4 Unemployment rates in EU 27 (upper line) and US, seasonally adjusted (source: Eurostat, Statistics in focus, 20/2010).

134 S. Fadda

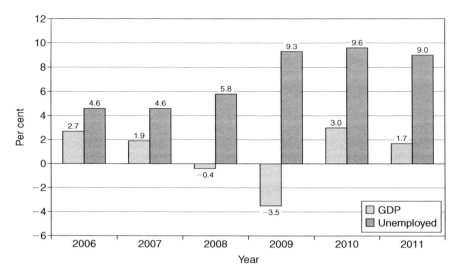

Figure 6.5 GDP growth and unemployment rates in US before and after the crisis (source: OECD data).

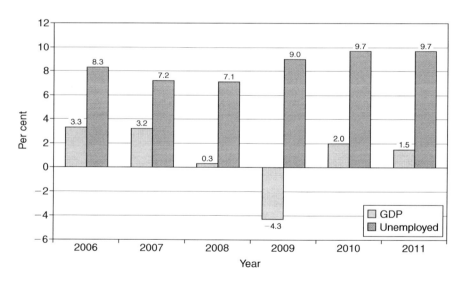

Figure 6.6 GDP growth and unemployment rates in EU before and after the crisis (source: OECD data).

let's say recession, on the labour market. We simply have to consider the reaction of unemployment to the fall of GDP growth rate in different countries. Clearly, structural effects influence this elasticity: the different sectors affected by the fall in the level of economic activity will create different effects on aggregate unemployment simply because of their different labour coefficients and of their different proportions in the composition of GDP. But, once these aspects are accounted for (for instance, the role of the financial sector in the case of UK and Ireland, or the role of the housing sector in Spain) the role played by labour market institutions could be detected. Nevertheless, the problem at this point is given by the complexity of the vector of labour market institutions: it is difficult to disentangle the effect of any single institutional feature, which actually operates together with all the other components of the institutional set up that may compensate or accentuate what its influence would be if considered alone. In fact the labour market institutional set up is an extraordinary combination of a great variety of aspects (some of them have been mentioned in part 2 of this chapter) which makes it difficult to classify and cluster the different countries. Furthermore, the gap between formal legislation and actual practice plus the presence of informal employment are other sources of difficulty. The well known IZA grid is only a simplified approximation which can be used, though, to give an idea of the position of different countries as far as labour market institutions are concerned.

In general terms the higher elasticity of US unemployment with respect to variations in GDP due to the crisis can be explained with less labour market rigidities, as expressed by the variables considered in section 2 above. "Countries with relatively few labour rigidities respond to negative shocks with higher unemployment" (Fitoussy, 2010, Signorelli, 2010), as the cases of US, UK, Canada, Ireland and the Netherlands seem to show.[6] Nevertheless, coming to more details and considering the European evidence, some studies seem to deny this correlation. For instance Eichhorst (2010) after a detailed analysis concludes that

> when analyzing the issue of EPL for regular workers and its role in shaping the outcome of the crisis more generally – i.e. output and employment – a rather ambiguous relationship arises. Indeed the impact of the crisis in terms

Table 6.5 Flexibility models

		Employment protection (core)	
		Strong	*Weak*
Labour market policies	Big	1 (Continental countries, e.g. Germany)	3 ("Flexicurity" countries, e.g. Denmark)
	Small	2 (Mediterranean/Roman/Latin countries, e.g. Spain)	4 (Anglo-Saxon countries, e.g. United Kingdom)

Source: IZA.

of GDP and employment appears to have little to do with the level stringency of employment protection.

But this statement needs two qualifications: first, it refers only to the role of ELP and not to the whole set of labour market institutions, whose role can still be thought as relevant; and, second, it does not distinguish the impact of the crisis on unemployment via changes in GDP from the impact of given changes in GDP on unemployment. Surely, "growth in formal sector jobs is correlated with high economic growth, irrespective of the type of labour markets regulations being applied" (ILO, 1995), but this is not to say that they do not influence the reaction of unemployment to GDP fluctuations. As Blanchard (Blanchard and Wolfers, 2000) says, labour market institutions although potentially able to explain cross country differences today, can hardly be considered able to explain the general evolution of employment over time, but they may significantly influence the ability of economies to respond to adverse shocks.

In fact, as for the impact of GDP fall on unemployment, this has been lower in countries where the institutional set up as a whole (apart from specific EPL) has provided: (a) a greater "internal" flexibility, that is working hours, wage and task adjustments; (b) a higher level of labour market active policies, that is counselling, training and job search assistance; (c) more generous passive labour market policies, in terms of more coverage and higher levels of unemployment benefits, social security and tax relieves (Eichhorst, 2010). The last measures, though, impact more on the level of economic activity through their automatic stabilizing mechanism (ILO, 1995), rather than directly on the elasticity of unemployment to GDP.

Beyond considering the elasticity of unemployment, of paramount importance is to consider the effect of the crisis on labour market structure. In this regard, the ILO (2010) points out the growth of what it calls "vulnerable employment". This notion groups the various jobs which do not meet the qualifications of "decent work". They range from fixed term workers to economically dependent autonomous workers, to workers with informal arrangements, usually without social protection, without rights recognized by collective agreements, with bad working conditions, low pay, low skills and low productivity. The growth of this component can be considered as a main structural effect of the crisis on the labour market. To a large extent this effect is due to a change in labour market institutions, sometimes achieved through structural reforms of labour market regulations, sometimes through actual practices based either on breaking the laws or on their abuse. Clearly the increased international competition associated with the downturn of the world economy has stimulated this kind of evolution in the belief that this might help the countries to become more competitive. Entrepreneurs, on the other hand, try in this way to survive their market and financial difficulties. But surely the decision to introduce greater flexibility of the kind which allows an increasing use of low paid, unskilled and precarious work as a way out of the crisis is a short sighted one.

Unfortunately, all this so-called "flexibility" has impacted on labour productivity. Labour hoarding, the reduction of working hours and the growth of this precarious work are all factors which have contributed to the lowering of productivity per worker.

The proportion in the combination of these three factors is both firm and country specific. It is specific to firms in that it is up to them, when they experience a fall in market demand as temporary, to decide whether to adjust accordingly the labour force or to hoard. The Okun's law implies the decision to hoard. This decision may be influenced by firing and hiring costs which, it has to be noted, are not dependent entirely on institutional factors but also on turnover costs associated with the level of technology, the pace of innovation and the general conditions of the industrial organization and of the supply of human capital. It is also specific to firms in that they can negotiate with the workers working hours reductions instead of employment reductions. Finally, it is firm specific in that it is up to the firm to decide under the pressure of competition, whether or not to use a quota of "precarious work" if that is less costly.

The proportion is also country specific, because labour market institutions are to a large extent determinant of turnover costs and of the possibility of internal numerical flexibility (up to a "zero-hours" reduction in working hours in the case of Italy!). It is particularly on the possibility of using "precarious work", its cost and its conditions, that the institutional set up of each particular country is decisive. If the labour cost (per worker) of precarious work is significantly lower compared to standard work, the firm will be ready (with a short term view) to give up higher per worker productivity in exchange with lower unskilled labour cost.

When this combination of factors occur, per worker productivity either slows down or declines; this in turn will reduce both wage share[7] and competitiveness, triggering a spiral effect which will delay, or rather prevent altogether, the recovery because of insufficient domestic and foreign aggregate demand. Obviously, governments can partially counteract these effects by more spending in passive labour market policies, but a wiser policy should be oriented towards institutional measures aimed at discouraging this perverse combination and at fostering productivity growth, which in the long run would contribute to expand both GDP growth and employment.

The empirical evidence regarding the relationship between employment and productivity after the crisis shows that countries where internal flexibility (as defined above) have helped in smoothing the impact of the crisis on unemployment had to pay this with a productivity slowdown (Marelli *et al.*, 2010). Countries with a "flexicurity" model (high external flexibility combined with strong and effective active and passive labour market policies) had both reduction in employment and increase in productivity. Accordingly, the best choice should be to combine both external flexibility (of the kind necessary to reduce adjustment costs) and internal flexibility with effective active and passive labour market policies.

5   To conclude: Where are we going and where should we go?
    As we have seen, the empirical evidence and the theoretical views on the role

138 S. Fadda

that labour market institutions play in the crises and should play for the recovery are far from univocal. From what we have been considering in this chapter, the following chain of "stylized" facts can be summarized.

Labour market institutional factors have contributed to an increased income inequality and to a reduced labour share in GDP. Out of this evolution a great increase in private indebtedness has come out.

Growing private indebtedness and financial disorder have nourished the crisis which has eventually exploded through a financial bust. The impact of the crisis on the labour market happens through the impact on GDP and through the employment elasticity to GDP variation.

The containment of the unemployment effect is generally due to the presence of higher labour market rigidities. But a deeper analysis shows that what has smoothed the impact of unemployment is not so much the presence of EPL but rather the increase in internal and functional flexibility plus wage moderation, plus the effective active and passive labour market policy.[8]

An important structural effect on the labour market has been the increased presence of "vulnerable work", that is low paid, low skilled and precarious work. This fact, together with the containment of unemployment because of labour hoarding or working time reduction, has generally caused a slow down or a fall in per worker productivity. Labour markets, formal and informal institutions play a key role in this dynamic.

This concludes where we are now, with the addition of a set of fiscal stimuli that have been delivered in several countries in order to speed up the recovery. These fiscal stimuli are different in magnitude according to different countries, beginning with Germany at the top and ending with Italy at the bottom.

6 While fiscal and monetary policy should accompany new financial regulations and converge in stimulating the recovery, great attention should be paid in avoiding the real economy to fall again into those traps which have been the root cause of the recent crises.

In order to do this we suggest that labour market institutions be properly used. Therefore it may be useful to look at the contribution that each particular element of the labour market institutional frame can give to the achievement of five tasks that appear to be necessary to set the recovery on the right path.

The five tasks are:

1   to stimulate aggregate demand through equalized income distribution rather than through private indebtedness;
2   to reduce labour adjustment costs in order to meet the requirements of fluctuations in demand and of restructuring the productive system;
3   to improve skills and human capital accumulation in order to increase productivity;
4   to improve the activity rate and the quality of jobs;
5   to support social dialogue, worker participation and cooperative behaviour among unions, entrepreneurs and government.

Table 6.6

	Tax cuts and fiscal expenditures		Extra credit and similar measures	
	€ bn	% of GDP	€ bn	% of GDP
Belgium	1.2	0.4	2.1	0.6
Denmark	0	0.0	0	0.0
Germany	39.3	1.4	70.3	2.8
Ireland	0	0.0	0	0.0
Greece	0	0.0	23	0.9
Spain	12.3	1.1	54.3	4.9
France	16.9	0.9	41.5	2.1
Italy	−0.3	0.0	0	0.0
Netherlands	6.1	1.0	0.3	0.1
Austria	3.9	1.4	2.5	0.9
Poland	1.6	0.5	5.0	1.6
Sweden	1.1	0.4	8.8	3.0
United Kingdom	22.6	1.4	23.3	1.4
13 largest EU countries	104.8	0.91	231.1	2.9
Imputed EU-27 total	117.3	0.91	258.5	2.0
European Commission	9.3	0.07	15.5	0.1
Imputed grand total	126.6	0.99	274.0	2.1

Source: Table from Bruegel Policy Contribution (2009).

140   S. Fadda

Table 6.7

	1	2	3	4	5
Functional flexibility		+			
Working time flexibility		+			
Numerical external flexibility	−	+			
Possibility of precarious work	−		−		−
Unemployment benefits duration	+			−	
Unemployment benefits coverage	+	+			
Unemployment benefits replacement rate	+				
Union density					+
Coverage of collective agreements					+
Coordination of wage barg. & income policy	+				+
Minimum wages	+				
Job search assistance		+		+	
Counselling			+	+	
Training			+		
Hiring incentives				+	
Help for new start-ups				+	

Taking a taxonomy of labour market institutions it's possible to construct a grid which allows to see their contribution to each of these five targets.

Of course, each element shown in the above rows requires specifications and is in turn divisible into different sub-elements and characteristics. The grid is only a suggested tool for determining the set of labour market institutions which are more appropriate to the needs of a sustainable recovery.

With regard to this, two qualifications must be added. First, all the institutional elements have to be considered in terms of how each complements the other. It doesn't make any sense to consider them separately, because they interact with each other, and the interaction may be such as to turn into positive the effects that separately would be negative, or the other way round. This is also evident when the signs in the same row are positive in some columns and negative in others. The net effect clearly depends on the balance with the other elements, in addition to the specific characteristics of the single institution itself. Second, in addition to the need for general tax and fiscal policy harmonization among different countries, and also for labour standards (concerning, for instance, working time, wage setting, union agreements, precarious work, and so on) a higher degree of international coordination and harmonization is needed in order to avoid a kind of "social-labour dumping" among countries, which would be damaging for all.

To conclude this section it must be added that the programme and recommendations of Europe 2020 are in line with these directions. Differently from the previous Lisbon strategy, guideline 7 for the employment policies of the Member States explicitly states:

> Member States should step up *social dialogue* and tackle labour market segmentation with measures addressing *temporary and precarious employment,*

underemployment and undeclared work. Professional mobility should be rewarded. The quality of jobs and employment conditions should be addressed by fighting *low-wages* and by ensuring adequate *social security* also for those on fixed contracts and the self-employed. *Employment services* should be strengthened and open to all, including young people and those threatened by unemployment with personalised services targeting those furthest away from the labour market. (*Italics added.*)

This is all good, but unfortunately the so called "open method of coordination" doesn't make these recommendations binding for Member States, and it is up to each country to decide whether or not to follow them.

Notes

1 Although this distinction is less sharp than it may seem, see Fadda (2012).
2 And this has actually been made, see the Fraser Institute index of economic freedom.
3
> The analysis suggests that institutionally determined rules, such as employment protection legislation, which some blame for European high unemployment by making firms leery of hiring workers they cannot readily lay off in the future in fact have no effect on employment.... What EPL does is alter the division of the profits from the efficient choice. With EPL the firm pays some of the profit from a layoff to the worker to induce the worker to leave. Absent EPL the firm gets all of the profit from the decision. In this model, institutions alter the distribution of income but not the efficiency of production.
>
> (ibid. page 15)

4 For the difference with the financing through public debt, see Barba and Pivetti 2009.
5 The strong conclusions in this sense drawn by Wallerstein (1999) have been questioned by Golden and Londregan (2005), who stress the importance of other factors, like changes in the supply and demand for skills, or the impact of tax policies.
6 A caveat must be made here, due to the fact that changes in unemployment rate may be influenced by changes in activity rates induced by changes in the rates of unemployment themselves (discouraged worker effect). But, given the differences in activity rates of various countries, we may assume that their changes respond in similar ways to changes in unemployment.
7 Tronti has suggested to me the view that when productivity falls, the labour share raises, due to downward wage rigidity. But we are considering here a fall in productivity due exactly to intensive hiring of low wage labour.
8 The case of Germany is particularly significant in this regard. Its well known missing decline in unemployment during the recession is mainly explained by two peculiar facts: the missing employment increase in the previous boom and the particular incentive to working hours reduction obtained through the "working time accounts" agreed in labour union contracts (Burda and Hunt, 2011): practically a kind of "implicit contract" exchanging overtime work in expansionary phases for working time reduction during recessions.

References

Baker, D., Glyn, A., Howell, D. and Schmitt, J. (2005) Labor market institutions and unemployment: A critical assessment of the cross-country evidence, in David R. Howell (ed.),

Fighting Unemployment: The Limits of Free Market Orthodoxy. Oxford: Oxford University Press.

Barba, A. and Pivetti, M. (2009) Rising household debt: its causes and macroeconomic implications – a long-period analysis, *Cambridge Journal of Economics*, 33.

Blanchard, Olivier and Wolfers, Justin (2000) Shocks and institutions and the rise of European Unemployment: The Aggregate Evidence, *Economic Journal*, 110(1): 1–33.

Bruegel Policy Contribution (2009) *EU Stimulus packages*, Issue 2009/02.

Burda, M. and Hunt, J. (2011) What explains the German labour market miracle in the great recession? IZA discussion paper, 2011, n. 5800.

Burtless, Gary S. (1990) Unemployment insurance and labor supply: a survey, in: W. Lee Hansen and James F. Byers, eds., *Unemployment Insurance* (University of Wisconsin Press, Madison, WI).

Cynamon, B.Z. and Fazzari, S.M. (2008) Household Debt in the Consumer Age: Source of Growth – Risk of Collapse, *Capitalism and Society*, 32.

Eichhorst (2010) The impact of the crisis on employment and the role of labour market institutions, Iza Discussion Paper, 2010, n. 5320.

Fadda, S. (2012) Formal and informal institutions: towards a deeper understanding of a complex relationship. Some cases in the labour market, ASTRIL working paper n. 2, www.astril.org.

Fitoussi, J.P. and Saraceno, F. (2010) Inequality and macroeconomic performance, Document de Travail de l'OFCE, Paris, 2010 n. 13.

Fitoussi, J.P. and Stiglitz, J. (2009) The ways out of the crisis and the building of a more cohesive world, The Shadow GN, Chair's Summary, LUISS University, Rome, May.

Freeman, R. (2007) Labour market institutions around the world, NBER working paper 13242, July 2007.

Glyn, A. (2007) Globalization and profitability since 1950: A tale of two phases? in Shaikh, A. (ed.), *Globalization and the Myths of Free Trade*, Routledge, London.

ILO (1995) *The employment challenge in Latin America and the Caribbean*, Regional office for the Americas, Lima 1995.

ILO (2010) *Global employment trends*, Geneva, 2010.

IMF (2010) *World Economic Outlook*, Washington, DC.

Kumhof, M. and Rancière, R. (2010), *Inequality, leverage and crises*, WP/10/268, International Monetary Fund (IMF).

Marelli E., Signorelli M. and Tyrovicz J. (2010) Crisis and joint employment-productivity dynamics: a comparative perspective for european countries, mimeo.

OECD (1994) *The OECD Jobs Study. Facts, Analysis, Strategies*, 1994.

Onaran, O. (2009) From the crisis of distribution to the distribution of the costs of the crisis: what can we learn from previous crises about the effects of the financial crisis on labor share?, Working Paper n. 195, Political Economy Research Institute (PERI).

Schivardi, F. (1999) *Rigidità del mercato del lavoro, disoccupazione e crescita*, in Banca d'Italia, Temi di discussione n.364.

Schmieder, J.F., von Wacher, T. and Bender, S. (2010) *The effects of unemployment insurance on labour supply and search outcomes*, IAB Discussion paper, n.4.

Signorelli (2010) The labour market impact of financial crises, mimeo.

Taylor, J.B. (2009) *Getting Off Track*, Stanford: Hoover Institution Press.

Vermeulen, P. (2007) Can adjustment costs explain the variability and counter-cyclicality of the labour share at the firm and aggregate level?, European Central Bank, WP n.772, June 2007.

7 Financial crisis, labour markets and varieties of capitalism

A comparison between the European social model and the US model

Pasquale Tridico

1 Introduction

The economic crisis which started in the financial sector in 2007 is still impacting the real economy, driving a decrease in output and employment levels. The crisis is the biggest since the Great Depression of 1929 and several explanations regarding the financial collapse have already been put forward (Obstfeld and Rogoff, 2009; Krugman, 2008; Greenspan, 2007; Skidelsky, 2009; Whelan, 2010, Semmler *et al.*, 2010; FMI, 2008; Bini Smaghi, 2008; Caballero *et al.*, 2008; etc).

The crisis has caused worldwide losses amounting to about €3.5 trillion, according to estimates by the International Monetary Fund (IMF). Just to give an idea, that is a bit less than the GDP of China or Japan, twice the GDP of the United Kingdom, or three times the GDP of India (IMF 2009a). It has driven the global recession we are currently struggling against, causing mass unemployment, high social costs and enormous levels of public debt in many countries.

Some kinds of limited Keynesian policies and fiscal stimuli were implemented both in Europe and the US between 2007 and 2009.[1] Along with these approaches, a great number of bank rescue packages were implemented. However, after the Greek economic crisis in May 2010, governmental policies shifted towards austerity measures, balanced budgets; and, as a result, the consensus which had allowed for partial recovery, monetary liquidity, and the bailout of banks and financial institutions almost dissipated. Fiscal stimuli are no longer unanimously accepted, and the main concerns of industrialized nations became sovereign debt crises, budget sustainability and public spending cuts.

The objective of this chapter is to show how the European Union (EU), which employs different varieties of capitalism, and the United States, which operates based on a competitive capitalist model, are coping with the current economic crisis. Although the EU is fragmented and needs to work towards better and deeper integration among member states, the main features of the European Social Model (ESM) allow for a more sustainable recovery and lessens the social costs. A new index has been developed in this chapter: the Synthetic Vulnerability Index, which shows that the US position is worse than the Eurozone position in terms of social costs, recovery from the current crisis and of exposure to further crises. Nevertheless, current financial reforms, both in the US and EU seem to be insufficient and the recent fiscal austerity measures seem to be moving the economies in the wrong direction.

New levels of government involvement are required in order to keep aggregate demand stable, make full employment possible and create a transparent financial sector, serving the real economy and encouraging productive investments. The rest of the chapter is organized as follows: section 2 introduces briefly the varieties of capitalism argument; section 3 describes the emergence of financialization during post-Fordism; section 4 compares the varieties of financial responses to the crisis in US and EU, section 5 analyses post-crisis differences and tensions between EU and US, builds the Synthetic Vulnerability Index and shows the return of austerity policies, and section 6 concludes the chapter.

2 Varieties of capitalism: economic growth and stability before the financial-led growth regime

In this section I will discuss briefly the growth regime during the the Fordist period. Economic systems of the Fordist regime, in particularly in Western Europe, enjoyed high stability, accumulation, productivity and economic growth. The basic mechanisms of the Fordist model of accumulation are described in Figure 7A.1 of the Appendix.

The prevailing model of development during the Fordist era had three characteristics: first, the Taylorist form of labour organization, organized around a semi-skilled workforce within a framework of particular industrial relations; second, the regime of accumulation which allowed for a sharing of the benefits of productivity gains between workers and firm owners; third, the Keynesian Welfare State, which on one hand provided unemployment benefits, allowing people excluded from the Fordist organization to consume, and, on the other supported a high level of aggregate demand. In Europe this model had different executions, but similar results in terms of GDP performance and social outcomes. Each European country had its own style of development and built a model of capitalism specific to its needs (Gillingham, 2003).

Generally speaking, countries can be classified according to their type of economic system, which can be characterized by particular institutional forms and macroeconomic factors like domestic competition, role of the state, international trade and openness, monetary forms, etc. Following this approach Amoroso (2003) and Jessop (2002) identified four types of economic systems; the Anglo-Saxon model (or competitive capitalism), the Corporative model (Corporative capitalism), the Dirigiste model, and the Social-Democratic model. To these models, Choi Chonj Ju (2004), among others (i.e. Yeager, 2004; Qian, 2003; etc.), added the current model of the Socialist Markets, represented in particular by China and Vietnam.[2]

Bruno Amable (2003) narrated a similar story in his book *The Diversity of Modern Capitalism*, proposing five different ideal types of capitalism, taking into consideration five institutional forms (product market competition, wage-labour nexus, financial sector, social protection and education). He combined the Dirigiste and the Corporative models (forming a Continental European model) and added two new models (the Asian model and the South European model). The Amable (2003) classification is: (1) the Market-based economy (the US and the British economies are the closest to this), (2) Continental European capitalism (lead by Germany and France), (3) the Social-Democratic economies (the Scandinavian economies), (4) South European capitalism, and (5) Asian capitalism.

Table 7.1 summarizes the main characteristics of these socio-economic models, and, in parentheses, lists the notable adherents to the model. The table combines the work of the authors cited above.

For our purposes we will consider the European Social Model as a combination of the German, French and Scandinavian models, despite the fact that many differences still exist among those models.[3] However, these three models have much in common and share similar features, particularly within the financial sector (Sapir, 2005). In general terms, the Eurozone is the aggregation of European countries which fit, to some extent, into the ESM.[4] The UK and Ireland, although EU members, are considered part of the Competitive Capitalism Model (known also as the Anglo-Saxon model or Competitive Market Economies).

The ESM ensured better economic performance in Europe during the Fordist era of accumulation with respect to US. It was able to deliver better GDP performance for a extended period of time, at least until the end of the 1970s (see Figure 7A.2 in the Appendix). After that, the process of financialization, with all its contradictions and instabilities, began and a finance-led growth regime took over; the old Fordist regime went into crisis. Reasons for that are different as explained by many scholars (Lipietz, 1992; Jessop, 2002; Boyer and Saillard, 2002).[5] Under this model of development the EU, or more accurately the Eurozone, was able to outpace the US in social and economic benchmarking areas such as inequality, poverty, public education and life expectancy thanks to a large public program of social expenditures (as Table 7A.1 and Figure 7A.3 in the Appendix display). The US, on the contrary, saw slightly faster GDP growth since the 1980s in comparison to the EU, in particular during the past two decades of financialization, but a concerning drop of important social indicators (inequality and poverty). In my opinion, there are at least two reasons that this does not identify a trade-off between efficiency and equality. First, the EU was also growing over the past 20 years (albeit at lower rates than the US economy), not simply maintaining their social indicators. Second, the current financial crisis affected the US very badly in particular, putting into doubt the US model and its vaunted efficiency (Posner, 2009; Wolff, 2009). For these reasons I argue that the ESM is not only able to produce better social performance but also more efficient and sustainable economic development in the long run than the US model.

Table 7.1 Socio-economic models and their main characteristics

Characteristics models/(leader country)	Competition	Economic regulation	Main economic actors	Relationship between public and private actors	International economic relation	Taxation	Finance
Anglo-Saxon model (USA, UK, Irland)	Promotes free competition	Deregulation; withdrawal of the State from the economy	Firms, corporations, markets,	Residual public sector; market-oriented	Global competition	Low taxes, no or little progressive rate	Deregulation and full liberalization; financing for both consumption and investments
Corporative model (Germany)	Balances cooperation and competition	Decentralized	Tripartite structures (business clubs, trade unions, government)	Public-private partnerships	Protection of strategic sectors in an open economy	High taxation to finance welfare state	Developed finance for investment; extensive credit for small firms; limited finance and credit for consumption; financial regulation, transparency and protection of savings; higher taxes on financial corporations
Dirigiste model (France)	State control; regulated competition	National accumulation and regulation strategy	Private and public sectors	Public-private partnerships under State guide	Protectionism	High Taxes and Collective Recourses	
Social-Democratic model (Scandinavian countries)	State controlled liberalization and competition	Knowledge and innovation as an economic guide for regulation	Public and private firms, ethical corporations	Public-private partnership in order to achieve social cohesion	National actors; moderate free competition; an open economy	High wages; career perspective; high and progressive tax rates	

Source: Adapted from the classifications of Jessop (2002), Amoroso (2003), Amable (2003), and Choi Chonj Ju (2004).

3 Financialization during post-Fordism

After the demise of Fordism, an unstable new regime of accumulation emerged (Jessop, 2002; Boyer and Saillard, 2002). It is characterized by high market financialization, a so-called flexible accumulation regime, and markedly uneven development, with micro-electric, internet, advanced technology, the Knowledge-based Economy driving further cycles of accumulation (Peck and Tickell, 2003; Jessop, 2002). Wages after the 1970s in advanced economies and particularly in US almost stagnated, and profits soared dramatically (Wolff, 2009; EuroMemorandum, 2010). Simultaneously inequality increased sharply (OECD, 2010). In order to keep consumption up, the US maneuvered economic policies: used cheap money which allowed bubbles in the housing sector and private debt soaring; and allowed huge amount of cheap imports from China. This eventually ended up with huge Current Account (CA) deficit: at the eve of the financial crisis in 2007 the US CA deficit was US$700 billion (5 per cent of US GDP), of which 80 per cent depends on Chinese exports (IMF 2009b). US financed the CA debt issuing US bonds which were bought in turn by Chinese. The issue of global imbalances emerged strongly and it is seen as a co-determinant of the current economic crisis (Obstfeld and Rogoff, 2009).

The shape of regulation during post-Fordism changed dramatically to allow for financialization (Lipietz 1992). As Petit (2003: 20) pointed out, with the transition to post-Fordism, institutions are evolving and, in particular, the institutional forms of competition tend to prevail in the emerging regime. On this

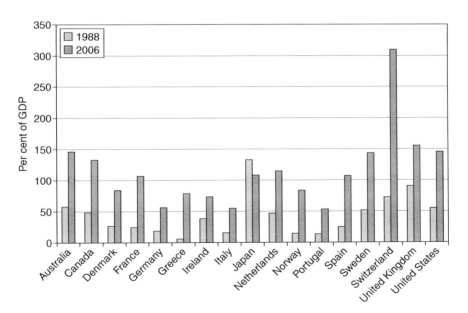

Figure 7.1 Financialization since 1988 (source: World Bank, 2010, Statistical Indicators (online database)).

argument, Boyer (2005) says that in the "hierarchy of the institutional forms," the one leading the way in the advanced economies during the transition period seems to be the finance sector (2005: 4), which shapes all other institutions (2005: 18).[6] Figure 7.1 shows, through the value of market capitalization in the stock exchange, as a percentage of GDP, the consistency of the process of financialization in the past two decades.[7]

Moreover, at the political level, the transition to post-Fordism seems to be assisted by a neo-conservative ruling class. Hence, a comparison with the previous pre-1920s Fordist era seems legitimate, when the liberist model of development was based on an extensive accumulation regime (Aglietta, 1979) with a pressure on labour costs, without government playing a significant role in the economy, without a productivity sharing compromise, and without the Keynesian Welfare State (Basso, 1998). Such a process of financialization was coupled with both an increase of inequality and a decline in the wage shares over the GDP, as Figure 7.2 shows. Biased income distribution and inequality is one of the main factors which gives instability to the current financial-led growth regime, since aggregate demand is weak, and economic growth remain under its real and stable potential path. In general financialization represents a most incoherent set of experiments that cannot be considered a growth regime at all, and its literature tries to impose a coherence to a model that is absent in reality (Engelen et al., 2008; Wolfson, 2003).

Transition to post-Fordist financial-led regimes is identified in the US with Reaganomics and in the UK with Thatcherism. Jessop (2002) argues that new accumulation strategies emerged during that period. They involved multinational

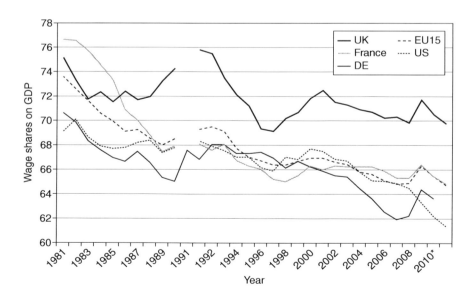

Figure 7.2 Wage shares on GDP, selected countries (source: Euromemorandum 2010).

firms, international financial discipline, a more authoritarian state, and a sort of popular capitalism. The previous Fordist strategy was replaced by an internationally oriented and financially aggressive strategy, deregulated and concentrated dually on Wall Street and in the City of London. Reaganomics and Thatcherism were strategies that aimed to restructure the accumulation system through a new regulation system (Peck and Tickell, 1992), at the expense of the social compromise realized after the Second World War. The result was uneven development (Peck and Tickell, 1992), with regions and countries divided between financial services and technology-oriented ones, and increasing trends in inequalities and income disparities, in particular in the US and the UK, the countries which were more keen on financialization, as Figure 7.3 shows.

A similar transition towards post-Fordism, although less severe than in the US and UK, is exhibited by other continental European countries, such as Germany, France, Italy and Spain (Jessop, 2002), where severe fiscal and monetary policies, along with industrial restructuring, generated precarious jobs and higher inequality in particular since the 1990s (Fitoussi, 1992).

These are the roots of the current financial-led unstable model of accumulation and they put in place the mechanisms which helped spur the current crisis. In particular, when the wage-nexus is compressed and labour becomes extremely flexible, the investment dimension is neglected and replaced by speculative financial investments driven by shareholder interests, and consumption needs to be sustained by fragile financialization and risky financial tools. Failures of the financial-led model of accumulation are evident today because of the crisis, but can be traced to the relatively poor performance of most of the advanced economies

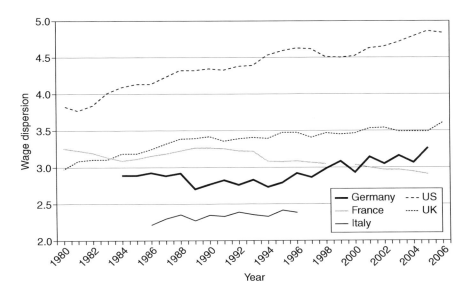

Figure 7.3 Wage dispersion, selected countries (source: Euromemorandum 2010).

during the post-Fordist era, in terms of productivity and GDP growth (see Figure 7A.2 in the Appendix). Petit (2009) refers to the period between 1997 and 2007 as a lost decade of financialized capitalism in terms of productivity gains and growth. Liberalization of finance and globalization did not bring more innovation, since new investments, in which technological progress is usually embedded, lacked substance.

4 Varieties of responses to the financial crisis in the US and EU

The economic crisis of 2007–2009 produced painful outcomes in the labour market and society in general, both in the US and in Europe. In short, it caused a global recession, mass unemployment, high social costs and enormous public debts in many countries (see Figure 7A.4 and Table 7A.3 in the Appendix). In this section I will analyse the responses to the crisis put forward by the US and EU. The US made its response in line with its Competitive Market Economy (CME) model, the EU within the framework of a traditional European Social Model. The latter, however, tends to represent more specifically a Eurozone model (with the exception of Ireland), rather than an EU model since the UK position[8] more often resembles US regulation.

In general, regarding the financial overhaul, the EU (except the UK and Ireland) relies more on the existing institutional governance structures of non-market coordination, while the US, UK and Ireland rely more on the presumed efficiency of financial markets. It is very interesting to see how, at the April 2009 G20 meeting in London, the different types of socio-economic models and their strategies for recovery were clearly divided: the Franco-German axe, supported by Sarkozy and Merkel, called for all-encompassing state regulation and financial restrictions on hedge-funds and tax havens. The Anglo-Saxon strategy, backed by Brown and Obama, aimed mostly at reaching a consensus in order to provide monetary liquidity to the financial system.

The G20 summit, since its first meeting in Washington in November of 2008, has created conditions to change the global financial structures. However, progress has thus far been made only at very superficial levels, such as tax haven limitations and calling for limitations on executive compensation. An interesting step towards a more democratic and global system of financial governance seems to be the creation of a Financial Stability Board (FSB) which should enhance coordination and improve macro and micro prudential supervision.[9] The FSB was established to address vulnerabilities and to develop and implement strong regulatory, supervisory, and other policies in the interest of financial stability. It includes all G20 major economies, the IMF, WB, the Bank for International Settlements (BIS) and the European Commission. The Secretary of the US Treasury Tim Geithner has described it as a fourth pillar in the architecture of global economic governance, along with the IMF, World Bank and WTO.

That said, within the EU many differences exist. These differences can be classified in the following ways:

The European social model versus the US model 151

1 Differences between Eurozone and Non-Eurozone nations;
2 Differences between Member States and the central position of the EU Commission;
3 And, above all, differences between the Eurozone (Germany and France in particular) and the UK.

Tensions and contradictions exist within the EU in general, and this is affecting the final outcomes of financial regulation. Compromises, carve-outs and generic language weaken the new EU regulation (Wahl, 2010).

4.1 US regulation (the Frank–Dodd Act)

In July 2010 a financial reform package was adopted in the US, despite the strong opposition of Republicans and Wall Street lobbies.[10] A lot of compromises and carve-outs weakened the original proposal of the White House and Secretary of Treasury Tim Geithner. The important elements of the US reforms can be synthesized into the following 10 points:

1 New requirements for higher capital and liquidity standards for corporations and banks.
2 The famous "Volcker Rule," which eliminates the dangerous coexistence between investment and commercial banks.
3 Under the Volcker Rule, banks are limited in engaging in proprietary trading.
4 Banks must hold enough capital in reserve to reflect their off-balance sheet, cope with crisis, and avoid illiquidity.
5 A new insolvency regime is introduced, not only for firms but also for banks, and it gives more regulatory and supervisory power to the Treasury.
6 Trade in derivatives is strictly regulated and centralized within a third party clearing authority.
7 Financial firms and hedge funds managers are required to submit swaps to a third authority to back their operations.
8 A new supervision was introduced for Credit Rating Agencies (CRA). The supervisor has the right to examine rating agency operations, data and methodologies. They can be eliminated from a CRA book if they are shown to have been providing bad ratings for long time, and, most importantly, they are prohibited from advising an issuer and rating that issuer's securities in order to reduce/eliminate conflict of interests.
9 US households and consumers, as well as investors, are better protected under the new laws, with a special agency (Consumer Financial Protection Agency).
10 Stronger supervision and oversight from the Fed, with the creation of a Financial Stability Oversight Council that monitors Wall Street's largest firms and financial institutions.

After the US Frank–Dodd Act, a new supervisory architecture system will be in place, with a major role for the Fed and a stronger advisory role for the Treasury.

A *Council of Regulators* is set up to coordinate supervision with the Fed. The Fed wields more prudential supervision over large firms and has an oversight role to play along with other US authorities. This supervision and oversight can be summarized at macro and micro levels. However, the problem remains at operational level, since vigilance, supervision and oversight has to be implemented through the creation of about 20 new authorities.[11]

At the micro level: prudential supervision in US

Banks are now required to hold more capital and liquidity than before. Large hedge funds have to register with the SEC (*Securities and Exchange Commission*)[12] and are regulated by it. Under the Volcker Rule, although this was curtailed by Senate with respect to the initial Obama proposal, proprietary trading is limited. This refers to trading stocks, bonds, currencies, commodities, their derivatives, or other financial instruments with the bank's own capital, rather than that of its customers. In general, proprietary trading is considered to be riskier and is associated with more volatile profits (Conzelman *et al.*, 2010: 4). Moreover, the Volcker Rule introduces the separation between commercial and investment banks.[13] Banks are also required not to bet against their own clients. Commercial banks can no longer make speculative bets for their own profits. Banks will be allowed to invest in private equity and hedge funds, but at a level limited to 3 per cent of their capital. At the same time, a new Consumer Financial Protection Agency, housed in the Fed, was set up to provide consumers with services related to mortgage brokers, debt collectors and credit counsellors. New federal banking regulators have been created, also. At the top of this regulatory and supervision hierarchy sits the Fed, which monitors commercial banks and large firms while the SEC monitors the securities market and the Commodity Futures Trading Commission (CFTC) monitors futures. Insurance is monitored at the state level.

At the macro level: prudential supervision in the US

The Fed is empowered as a systemic regulator in its role of market vigilance and monitoring financial institutions at macro level. The new Council of Regulators chaired by the Secretary of Treasury advises the Fed on systemic risks. It has been created as a new insolvency regime for bank and non-bank firm bankruptcies, with special and extended powers of the Treasury. The new financial architecture was reinforced by the introduction of the newly created Financial Stability Oversight Council, which should reduce the deficit in the US for financial institutions and large firms in particular (Conzelman *et al.*, 2010), thanks in part to the new role of the Fed. The Fed will lead the oversight of large financial institutions whose failures could threaten the financial system. At the same time, the Fed's relationship with banks is controlled directly by the US Congress and the Government Accountability Office (GAO). The GAO can audit: (1) emergency loans made by the Fed (including the ones made after the 2007 financial crisis); (2) the Fed's low-cost loans to banks; and, (3) the Fed's buying and selling of securities to implement interest-rate policy (Conzelman et al., 2010).

4.2 EU regulation and responses

The immediate EU responses to the crisis managed by the European Central Bank (ECB) were delayed in comparison to the Fed's reaction, which put immediately huge monetary liquidity back into in the system and lowered the interest rates (from 5.25 per cent to 2 per cent in 2008 and to 0.25 per cent in 2010). The ECB did the same, but in a more passive way and with some delay (see Table 7A.3 in the Appendix). Moreover, monetary quantitative easy was less consistent and the interest rate was lowered at a slower paces.[14] By contrast, the inadequate response of the ECB was followed by a stronger EU regulatory approach to the crisis. This was mainly the result of the recommendations made by the De Larosière Report (2009),[15] which were adopted by following EU directives and regulations, and by a declaration of support from the EU Commission (2009), the European Council (2009), and the ECOFIN meeting on 9 June 2009. However, as we mentioned above, the EU regulation is weakened by the fragmentation among the EU member states and their different national regulations of financial markets.

At the micro level: prudential supervision in the EU

The new EU regulations for financial supervision of banks, insurance and securities created the European System of Financial Supervisors (ESFS), with 3 functional authorities and regulatory powers over banks, insurance, and securities: the European Banking Authority (EBA), the European Insurance and Occupational Pensions (EIOP), and the European Securities Markets Authority (ESMA).[16] This is a compromise between the UK and the EU commission, plus the France-Germany position. The former did not want to give the EU strong supervisory power. The latter pushed for a stronger role for EU in the financial supervision. The result is a system of oversight which, at the operational level, remains the responsibility of nations. The role of the EBA, EIOP and ESMA is to promote cooperation, financial harmony, a common culture of supervision, and common technical standards for monitoring and control.[17]

The harshest legislation the EU is introducing concerns OTC derivatives (EU, 2010a), securitizations such as Credit Default Swaps[18] and all kind of Alternative Investment Funds (AIF) like hedge funds, private equity funds, real estate funds, commodity funds and infrastructure funds (EU, 2009c). The EU has realized that there is much speculative activity among those funds which need to be regulated. The biggest hedge fund was a fraud (Madoff's fund),[19] and many AIF activities rely on opaque Ponzi schemes. Most OTC derivatives operate wildly in off-shore financial havens across the world, avoiding regulation protections for investors, as EU Commissioner Barnier reported.[20] Only 10 per cent of derivatives traded are standardized and traded on a Stock Exchange; the remaining

90 per cent are traded Over the Counter (OTC), i.e. bilaterally and without control or supervision. At the end of 2009, the volume of OCT trade was around $614 trillion (ten times global GDP) (BIS 2010).

At the macro level: prudential supervision in the EU

The newly created European Systemic Risk Board (ESRB) will be at the center of the new system in the EU, although only with advisory functions[21] (see Figure 7A.5 in the Appendix). European Central Banks play a major role within this Board, helping to define, identify and prioritize all macro-financial risks. Macro-financial stability may need to be pursued through different means than the ECB's price stability objectives Smaghi (2009). This is a possible area of tension between the two institutions, and that is why the ECB, which prioritizes price stability, wants to maintain the leading role.[22] The ESRB deals essentially with macro prudential supervision and reports to ECOFIN. It is also allowed to make warnings and recommendations directly to EU national governments.

5 Tensions, vulnerabilities and austerities among the US and EU

The regulatory overhauls passed after the crisis in the US and EU are different. The differences are just consequences of different perspectives on the crisis, which in turn underlines the different models in which the crisis simultaneously occurred: the ESM and the CME. These differences will likely bring about a new phase of post-financial crisis relations between the US and EU. In fact, the post financial crisis phase brought about both new and old disagreements between the EU and US. These disagreements reflect the basic differences between the economic systems of the EU and US. Varieties of capitalism and the different styles of market economy are issues which have already been explored in the literature, as I mentioned earlier. This affects national problem solving and global answers to the crisis. Institutions are put in place by countries according to each one's own model of capitalism. Hence, finance and financial regulation is an institutional form which reflects a nation's individual economic model.

5.1 Tensions and differences between the EU and US

The most important disagreement, both within the EU and on a global level, concerns a financial transaction tax (FTT). This is an old issue: the first to advance a proposal for a financial activity tax was James Tobin (1978). Now the issue has a twofold significance. First of all, the FTT would serve to finance the huge costs of this crisis. Since the financial sector bears much of the responsibility for this crisis, it is only fair, the advocates of the FTT say, that it pays for the societal costs. The expenditures of governments on stimulus programs to counter the crisis in the real economy was around 3.5 per cent of global GDP. Along with the government money that went to rescuing banks, the total cost is €3.5 trillion at the global level (IMF, 2009a). Second, as in the original opinion of Tobin, it would regulate financial markets, limit speculation and reduce short term and electronic financial activities, which have little to do with investment and saving operations. The FTT is discussed mostly in the EU, in particular among Eurozone nations, with Germany and France the principal supporters. The UK, US and Canada strongly object it and the G20 Pittsburg meeting has already rejected it. Bank lobbies are strongly against the FTT, too. The Obama administration sees a potential compromise in a sort of Bank Levy, which would have a more modest impact on tax collection ($14–19 billion in estimated revenues, against $738 billion in revenues from the FTT).[23] However, in the US many Congress members, in particular after the mid-term election of November 2010 was won by the Republicans, are strongly against a Bank Levy as well. An interesting proposal comes from the IMF, the Financial Activities Tax (FAT), which would tax the profits and remunerations of banks only (IMF, 2009a).

A controversial issue remains over the Basel agreements. On the eve of the financial crisis, the EU had just adopted (in 2006) Basel II, a set of rules regulating the capital requirements of banks, which were very flexible and favourable so that banks would agree to them. The new Basel agreement reached after the crisis (Basel III), in September of 2010, increases banks' capital requirements, limits their liabilities and leverage ratios, and requires higher liquidity standards to meet customers' needs. Moreover, banks are required to fulfil the primary role in the game of securitization; holding higher shares of the securities in the credit risk products. Most importantly, a new definition of "capital" is introduced, according to which equity capital and disclosed reserves only (i.e. liquid and own bank assets) are considered (see Table 7A.4 in the Appendix). This improves the quality and consistency of capital and of leverage. However, while the EU will immediately adopt Basel III as it is suggested in an EU Parliament Proposal of 2010 (EU, 2010b), the US and UK are still devoted to a more flexible definition of capital and continue to refer to Basel II for guidance on most capital requirements. Moreover, the EU (with the exception of the UK) would support even higher standards, with capital requirements set at or near 10 per cent.

Finally, another controversial issue is over Alternative Investment Funds (AIF). The EU recognizes that risks associated with AIF have been underestimated and are not sufficiently addressed by current rules. Many activities of large AIF, particularly those employing high levels of leverage, have greatly contributed to the current financial instability of the UE. Toxic assets related to AIF were implicated in the commodity price bubbles that developed in late 2007.[24] The new legislation tries to regulate not only AIF, but most importantly, AIF managers (AIFM) whose activities in their off-shore headquarters, on behalf of AIM, often avoid regulation. The new EU regulation on these matters is a good step forward (Wahn, 2010). However, the issue of AIF regulation in the EU is very complicated, in particular because of the UK opposition, in line with US position, which prefers to keep looser regulations and protect British interests: at the London stock exchange, 80 per cent of all Hedge funds in the world operate, and the AIF's lobby is very strong. They do not like the idea of stricter supervision, disclosure of strategies, leverage limits, higher costs, or lower risks, which mean lower profits. Since the operational supervisors of the new authorities created by the EU remain at the national level, implementation can be difficult.

Another issue of discordance within the EU, in particular between Germany and the UK, is the case of Credit Default Swaps (CDS). New EU regulations impose stricter supervision and introduce the right to ban short selling and the trade of CDS temporarily when it realizes that there is a speculation. Uncovered or "naked" short selling is banned (European Council, 2010). Such measures would have limited the severity of the Greek crisis in the spring 2010. The ESMA is the newly elected vigilance institution for that. Furthermore, requirements of transparency and information are required at the Stock Exchange where CDS are traded, and individual traders have to disclose their short positions over these assets.[25]

5.2 The Synthetic Vulnerability Index

These disagreements are crucial to the definition of new global financial governance, and show how deep the differences between the EU and the US and UK (and Anglo-Saxon countries in general) (Semmler and Young, 2010). Beyond these differences, and despite the attempts to reform the financial sector, finance and the economy at large still remain vulnerable, both in the EU and US. This is due to a combination of four indicators which are currently in dangerously vulnerable positions: (1) government deficits, (2) unemployment, (3) Current Account deficits (CA), and (4) slow recovery. The average of these four variables was calculated with the Synthetic Vulnerability Index (SVI)[26] in the figure below, for the Eurozone and US. From the SVI, the position of the US appears to be consistently weaker than that of the Eurozone (and in 2010 is –4.8 against –3.975) due in particular to higher government deficits and negative CA balance. 2011 was similar. Moreover, the bilateral position of the EU-US, in terms of import-export merchandise and CA, shows a better position for the EU, in a constant surplus versus the US (see Figures 7A.6 and 7A.7 in the Appendix).

Beside that, another indicator supports the idea that the US is more vulnerable than the Eurozone, and in particular indicates that the US faces higher social costs. That is the recent evolution of the labour market indicators of employment and unemployment. Despite a lower recession in the US as compared to the Eurozone (–2.6 per cent against –4.1 per cent), in the US, the labour market was seriously affected by an unemployment rate which went from 4.6 per cent to 9.8 per cent (+5.2) and employment rate which fell from 72 per cent to 64.5 per cent (–7.5) in 2010 (see Figure 7A.8 in the Appendix). Moreover, in the US, official unemployment seems to be very much underestimated (Feng and Hu, 2010). Many workers get a part-time job while they would like a full time job. Many of them have precarious and unstable job. Around 15 per cent of employees is in a position which can be called "semi-employment" rather than standard employment, and this has

The European social model versus the US model 157

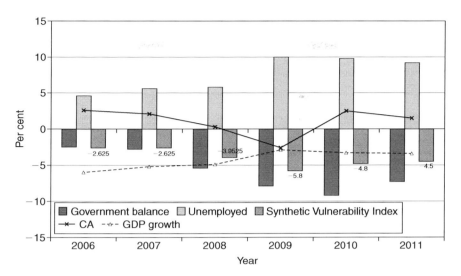

Figure 7.4 US Synthetic Vulnerability Index (source: own elaboration on IMF, 2010 World Economic Outlook (online database)).

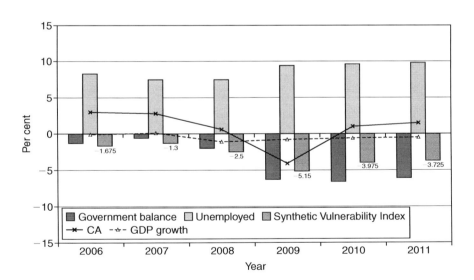

Figure 7.5 EU Synthetic Vulnerability Index (source: own elaboration on IMF, 2010 World Economic Outlook (online database)).

very bad effects on purchasing power and consumption.[27] Poverty and social exclusion is increasing consistently among semi-employed workers. The corresponding figures for the Eurozone look much better, with the unemployment rate rising from 8.6 per cent to 9.6 per cent (+1.2) and employment rate falling from 66.2 per cent to 65.7 per cent (–0.5) (see Figure 7A.9 in the Appendix). Obviously the role of Trade Unions, traditionally stronger in Europe (Nickell, 1997), has been crucial in protecting employment during the recession; beside, the unemployment elasticity to GDP changes seem to be much lower in the EU than in the US. Moreover, the GDP changes (and recovery) in the US seem to be seriously affected by structural problems which shape negatively income distribution and favours mostly the financial sector, which are continuously compensated with short-term finance bonus biases (which do not find any theoretical justification). Wage shares on GDP continue to decline during the crisis, as showed in Figure 7.2 in section 3. Moreover, such a growth seems to be driven mostly by consumption components, which in turn are sustained by the credit. This kind of growth is uneven, unstable and more inclined to generate bubble and burst cycles. It is far from what the International Monetary Fund and the World Bank define "high-quality growth" (HQG). In particular, the IMF defines HQG as "...growth that is sustainable brings lasting gains in employment and living standards, reduce poverty and inequality" (IMF, 1995: 286).

Finally, given the relatively lower percentage of US public expenditure directed towards unemployment policies (0.49 per cent of GDP against the 2.8 per cent of GDP spent by countries in the Eurozone), the human cost of unemployment is much higher in the US than the Eurozone (see Figure 7A.10 in Appendix). All this confirms my argument that the ESM (roughly the Eurozone) is better able to cope with this crisis, allowing fewer social costs and creating better social performance than in the US.

Yet the EU faces a major issue, which the US does not have, i.e. the Euro situation and the contradiction of the European Monetary Union (EMU) having a common monetary policy without: (1) a central budget, (2) a common fiscal policy and, (3) a de facto, no labour mobility within the Eurozone. On the contrary, the US dollar, the federal budget and a labour mobility within the US are the main strengths of American economy vis-à-vis the EMU. The European common currency paradoxically, but perhaps not surprisingly, has divided the EU between core and periphery. This division could be accepted and somehow managed, however it needs to be backed by political decisions which introduce wider common fiscal policies and a central budget (a central budget of around 1 per cent of EU GDP as today, is unacceptably low). It follows that EU imbalances should be treated as an internal issues, managed through Euro-Bonds, ECB policy of buying member state Bonds, and a permanent European Fund such as the Financial Stability Facility which could contribute to manage EU aggregate demand and could work (if not the ECB) as a lender of last resort. In this sense, the Tremonti–Junker proposal of issuing European Union Bonds would go in the right direction.[28]

5.3 The return of austerity

In order to recover from the crisis, governments initially put in place fiscal stimuli and bank rescue packages. These policies were supported by a great consensus among the policymakers, politicians and academics who had begun to look at Keynesian policies in a favourable way. In the US under the Bush administration the TARP (Troubled Asset Relief Program) Act was launched in order to purchase "troubled" assets and equity from financial institutions and to strengthen trust in the financial sector. The Act allowed the Treasury to purchase illiquid, difficult-to-value assets from banks and other financial institutions as a first reaction to the subprime mortgage crisis, for a value of US$700 billion (or 2.3 per cent of US GDP).[29] Similar saving plans were implemented in the UK.

It is, however, debatable whether the policies introduced in the US and the UK over the period 2007–2009 represent orthodox Keynesian policies at all. Certainly, in the UK case, much of this intervention involved direct and indirect handouts to banks with remarkably few strings attached on the assumption that this would enable the latter to rebuild their balances, and encourage them to resume lending to the non-financial sector. In practice, much of this money appears to have leaked out to fund new rounds of speculative activity, whilst the promised "trickle down" has proved limited.

The TARP was followed by Obama's fiscal stimulus, known as ARRA (American Recovering and Reinvestment Act) which entered onto the scene in February 2009 for a value of US$775 billion (or 2.7 per cent of US GDP). The stimulus aims to promote, in the Keynesian tradition, job creation, investment and consumer spending during the recession for a value of (Romer and Bernestein, 2010). In the main EU countries fiscal stimuli were implemented to, for a total around US$300 billion (or 1.5 per cent of EU GDP) (IMF 2009b).

The outcomes of these post 2009 stimuli were quite positive: in the second quarter of 2010, Germany grew at an extraordinary rate of 8.8 per cent, and the UK at 4.8 per cent. Similar stories, although of less magnitude, occurred in other European economies. The US recovered, too, with 1.6 per cent growth for the same period. Nevertheless, after the spring of 2010, policy consensus switched towards austerity measures. After the Greek crisis, governments turned their interests, irrationally, toward budget cuts and policies of contraction (Arestis and Pelagidis, 2010). In the fall of 2010, the new Liberal-Conservative government in the UK announced an austerity plan with cuts in public expenditures and a freezing of public employment wages and jobs for the next three years. A similar plan was announced in the US by President Barack Obama in November 2010, freezing federal pay for the next two years. Chancellor Merkel is proposing similar restrictive plans in Germany, and other continental European countries are preparing financial laws in 2011 very much focused on restrictive fiscal measurements. The objective is to reduce deficits. This seems more like a reaction to the Greek and Irish crises, rather than a rational decision which would help economic recovery (Arestis and Pelagidis, 2010). Such austerity packages have gone hand in hand with a continued lifeline to the banks and financial institutions. Therefore, these austerity packages, one can argue, represents a larger transfer of resources to the financial sector, the costs being borne by society at large, with half-hearted attempts at regulation being combined with renewed speculation. There is a clear link between bank recapitalization and bond vigilantiasm: austerity is imposed both by cutbacks in government spending to pay for the bailouts, and further austerity to fend off even the vaguest threat from bond vigilantes, whose access to funds in part depends on the bailouts.

6 Conclusion

In the same vein as Kindleberger (2005), we can conclude that if there are manias governing financial systems, which are far from rational and efficient, then governments should intervene and regulate. Monetary policy could go further to discourage manias by implementing a financial transaction tax. Beyond that, however, governments need to do something more: guarantee an appropriate level of consumption which could be sustained by an appropriate level of wage in order to maintain an appropriate level of aggregate demand. Finance, regulated under the supervision of the state, should serve productive investments. On the other side, an appropriate level of aggregate demand is guaranteed by a demand management policy which relies on an appropriate level of public investment. However the most recent austerity policies, both in Europe and the US, go just in the opposite direction (Arestis and Pelagidis, 2010)

Lessons can be drawn, obviously, from Keynes and from the Fordist model of production, where finance had a secondary role in the economic system and it was a tool which guaranteed credit for firms and productive investments, while wage, which guaranteed consumption, was the main nexus around which other institutional forms gravitated. Despite the Euro currency crisis, the Eurozone, when treated as a single entity, looks to be in a slightly better position than the US, as the Synthetic Vulnerability Index showed. In fact in the US, deficit issues of Federal States such as California, Nevada and other are not treated separately as one could treat separately similar issues in Greece, Ireland and Portugal. Such a political bias brings commentators to consider European issues more vulnerably than American issues. Beside that, in the EU, institutional forms are more anchored to the wage nexus; unemployment does not increase dramatically as in the US during crisis, and finance is not yet the main institutional form, although the past 20 years in Europe have seen deregulation of finance and liberalization which brought about strong financialization in the economic system and greater systemic risk. The Eurozone, and in particular the countries of the ESM, are able to combine, better than the US, efficiency (GDP growth) and social performance (inequality, poverty, mass education and life expectancy). After the WWII the countries of the Eurozone grew faster than the US and reached better social conditions. Only in the last two decades has the US had slightly faster GDP growth, with further worsening social indicators. However, that GDP growth in the US was led by the kind of financialization which caused the big crash and the Great recession of 2007–2009. In this light, the US model, led by finance, raises many doubts and should be radically reformed. I suggested this has to be done along the lines of the ESM. Despite the fact that GDP recession was deeper in the EU than in the US, social costs are greater than in the EU. Moreover, as we argued in section 5.2, the US recovery seems still be affected by structural problems of income distribution, consumption-driven components and huge compensation in the financial sector. This in the end will generate an unstable economic growth which favours again the top decile of the income distribution and which is keen to cause bubble and burst cycles.

Finally, the EU and US efforts toward financial regulation have to be welcomed, although they still seem insufficient to bring the whole system to a path of stable and sustainable development. In the US, the Frank–Dodd Act is an inferior compromise which would need to be improved in order to give real stability to the system and eliminate, or simply reduce, the systemic risk. Too many carve-outs and ambiguities remain, in particular regarding the oversight role of the Fed towards large firms, the almost unchanged regulation for Rating Agencies and hedge funds, the objections against a financial tax, and the opposition to Basel III. Though it does seem interesting the introduction of the Volcker rule, which separates the dangerous coexistence between investment and commercial banks and limits banks in engaging proprietary trading, occurred in the US. However, complex implementation and creation of new vigilant agencies can still be obstructed by lobby actions and Wall Street deregulation supporters (*The Economist*, 2011).

In Europe, the main difficulties are at the operational level of the new EU financial regulatory systems introduced. Too much fragmentation exists among member states, divisions between Eurozone and non-Eurozone, and most importantly, a very different strategic position between the French–German axe and the British. Such strategic differences pose obstacles to the very important questions, such as a financial transaction tax, hedge fund regulation and the introduction of a sort of Volcker rule. Not to mention the differences over the general framework of the kind of socio-economic model required. Financial stability, financial integration and national supervisory autonomy cannot be achieved simultaneously. The EU must decide what it wants to achieve, knowing that only two out of those three objectives can be achieved simultaneously.

Appendix

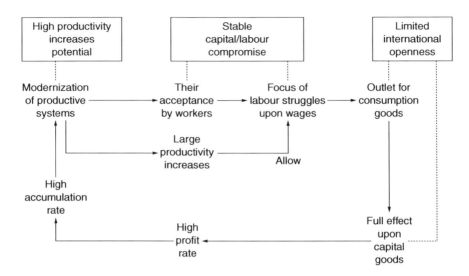

Figure 7A.1 The mechanism of the Fordist Growth Model (source: Boyer, 2000).

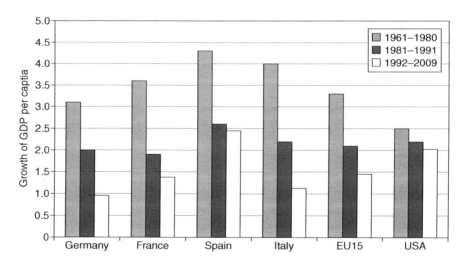

Figure 7A.2 GDP growth in the EU and the US (source: Eurostat).

Table 7A.1 US and Eurozone comparison on main features

	Eurozone 2009	US 2009
World share of GDP	14.8% (EU27: 21%)	20.2%
Global market share in terms of exports (world %)	15% (EU27: 20%)	13%
Population	328 mln: (EU 27: 498 mln)	317 mln
Inequality – Gini coefficient	0.29%	41%
GDP per capita $ ppp	33,452	46,653
Life expectancy at birth	81	79
Poverty (50% of median income) 2006	10%	17.1%
Combined gross enrolment ratio in education (primary, secondary and tertiary levels, % of pop)	95%	92%
Secondary enrolment ratio (% of secondary school-age population)	91%	88%
Primary enrolment ratio (% of primary school-age population)	97%	91%
Expected years of schooling (children)	16	15

Source: IMF, 2010 World Economic Outlook (online database), UNDP (HD Report, online database)

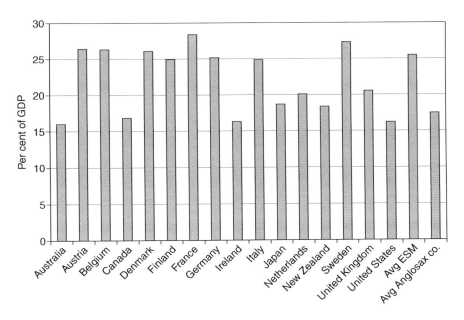

Figure 7A.3 EU and US Social Expenditures (source: OECD 2010, Employment Outlook (online database)).

Table 7A.2 Varieties of capitalism

Varieties of capitalism within the enlarged European Union (17 Eurozone members, with *)			Competitive market economies (Anglo-Saxon model)
European Social model: Austria* Belgium* Finland* France* German* Netherlands* Slovenia* Denmark Sweden Luxemburg* Hungary Czech Rep Greece* Italy* Portugal* Spain*	Hybrid model (mixed between ESM and LME) Cyprus* Malta* Latvia Lithuania Poland Romania Bulgaria Estonia* Slovakia*	Competitive Market Economies (CME) UK Ireland*	US, UK, Ireland, Canada, New Zealand, Australia

Note

Norway and Switzerland are not part of the EU but would fit very well in the ESM (Pontusson 2005). Greece, Italy, Portugal and Spain sometimes classified as Mediterranean model with typical characteristics of the ESM such as consistent Welfare States and Public expenditure, coupled with inefficiency, debt and corruption (which usually are not found in the ESM). Source: adapted from Pontusson (2005), Tridico (2011)

Table 7A.3 Main macroeconomic variables for the US and Eurozone (EU-16)

	2006 US	2006 EU16	2007 US	2007 EU16	2008 US	2008 EU16	2009 US	2009 EU16	2010 US	2010 EU16	2011 US	2011 EU16
GDP (% annual change)	2.6	3.0	2.1	2.8	0.3	0.6	−2.6	−4.1	2.5	1	1.5	1.5
Unemployment (% of the labour force)	4.6	8.3	4.6	7.5	5.81	7.5	10	9.4	9.8	9.6	9.7	9.8
Inflation (HICP nom. change)	3.2	2.2	2.8	2.1	3.8	3.3	0	0.3	2	1.5	2.7	1.7
Government balance(% GDP)	−2.5	−1.3	−2.8	−0.6	−5.4	−2.0	−7.9	−6.3	−9.2	−6.6	−7.3	−6.1
Government debt (% GDP)	61.1	68.3	62.1	66.0	70,6	69.4	83.2	78.7	92.6	84.7	97.4	88.5
Current a/c balance(% GDP)	−6	−0.1	−5.2	0.1	−4.9	−1.1	−2.9	−0.8	−3.3	−0.6	−3.4	−0.5
Central Bank/Fed main interest rates	4.25	2.25	5.25	3.5	2	4	1	2.5	0.25	1.30% (min. 1.19 June 2010)		
Exchange rate 1 Euro over $	1.25$		1.34$		1.36$ (max 1.59$ July 2008)		1.40$					

Source: IMF, 2010 World Economic Outlook (online database), OECD Employment outlook (online database), Fed Statistics (online database), ECB (2010).

166 P. Tridico

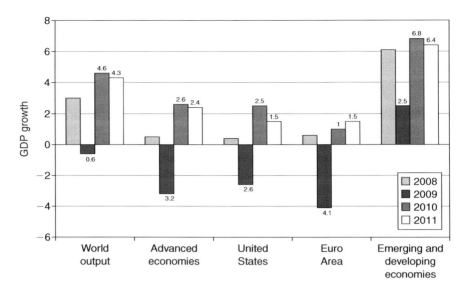

Figure 7A.4 The 2008–9 recession and projections (source: IMF, 2010 World Economic Outlook (online database)).

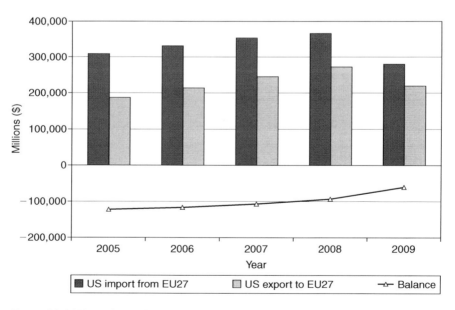

Figure 7A.6 US–EU27 trade balance (source: US International Trade Commission, online database, 2010).

The European social model versus the US model 167

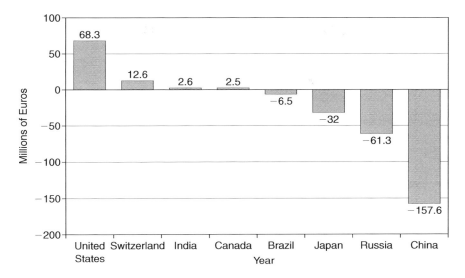

Figure 7A.7 EU current account balance with selected partners (source: Eurostat).

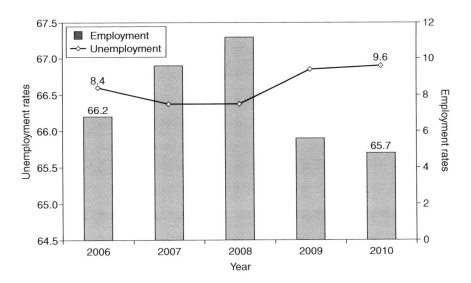

Figure 7A.8 Labour market evolution in the Eurozone (source: Eurostat).

168 P. Tridico

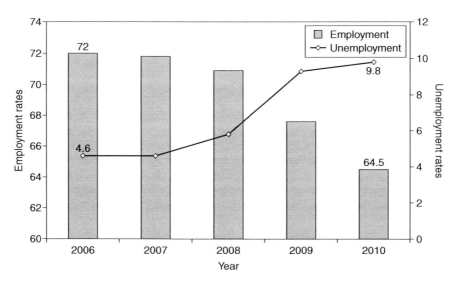

Figure 7A.9 Labour market evolution in the US (source: US Bureau of Labor Statistics).

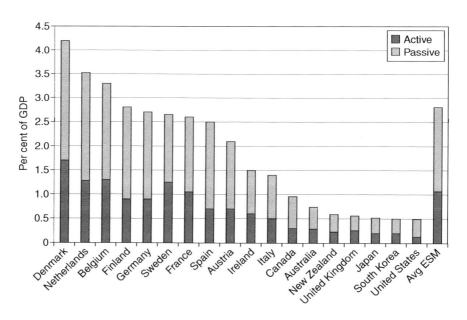

Figure 7A.10 Public expenditure on unemployment, OECD countries (source: OECD 2010, Employment outlook (online database)).

Notes

1 The extent to which those policies reflected orthodox Keynesianism is however very questionable.
2 China and Vietnam represent "Socialist Markets" and seem to be the only two countries which embrace such a model. This represents an evolution and is the result of a reform process which started first in China in 1978 and intensified during the 1990s (Yeager, 2004). This process transitioned China and Vietnam from planned economies to "Socialist Market" economies, characterized by forms of property rights which allow: (1) both private and government investment, without complete liberalization, privatization and political pluralism; (2) integration (though modest) into the world economy; and, (3) government control and monitoring of domestic financial markets.
3 This is more in tune the work of Pontusson (2005), and Soskice and Hall (2001).
4 Distinct varieties of capitalism exist within the EU and Eurozone. The correspondence between the Eurozone and the ESM may be not perfect, but it is a generalization that we need to use in order to compare the ESM to the US. My argument – that considers the ESM superior to the US model – would be even stronger if I were to only consider the European countries which fit into the ESM, i.e. Austria, Belgium, Finland, France, Germany, the Netherlands, Denmark, Sweden, Slovenia, Hungary, the Czech Republic, plus Norway and Switzerland (these last two are not actually EU members). For a detailed classification of the varieties of capitalism with EU member states, see Table 7A.1 in the Appendix.
5 In brief, the causes of the Fordist crisis are: a decrease in productivity, poor labour organization, the internationalization of problems through pressure on labour costs, and the resulting decrease in the demand. These are supply side causes, national and international ones, and exogenous to the core of Fordist economic doctrine.
6 However, both Petit (2003) and Boyer (2005) agree that in the Fordist era, the wage relation was the dominant institutional form and that is what made consistent economic growth possible.
7 Market capitalization (also known as market value) is the share price multiplied by the number of shares outstanding. Listed domestic companies are the domestically incorporated companies listed on the country's stock exchanges at the end of the year. Listed companies do not include investment companies, mutual funds, or other collective investment vehicles.
8 For a detailed overview on the British position, see Turner Review (2009) a UK regulatory Report named after Lord Turner, chairman of the United Kingdom's Financial Services Authority, who chaired the review's research group.
9 The FSB was established after the 2009 G20 summit in London as a successor to the Financial Stability Forum. The latter was founded by G7 countries in 1999 to promote international financial stability, but has had little impact. The FSB is based in Basel, Switzerland. The chairman of the board is Mario Draghi, president of BankItalia.
10 "The Dodd–Frank Wall Street Reform and Consumer Protection Act" was named after the chairmen of the two congressional committees dealing with banking, was signed into law by President Obama on 21 July 2010.
11 See: *The Economist* (2011).
12 A government commission created in 1934 by Congress to regulate the securities markets and protect investors. In addition to regulation and protection, it now also monitors corporate takeovers in the US. The SEC is composed of five commissioners appointed by the US President and approved by the Senate. The statutes administered by the SEC are designed to promote full public disclosure and to protect the investing public against fraudulent and manipulative practices in the securities markets. Generally, most issues of securities offered in interstate commerce, through the mail or on the internet must be registered with the SEC.

13 The coexistence was introduced by Clinton, who repealed the Glass–Steagal Act which had ensured the complete separation between commercial banks, which accept deposits, and investment banks, which invest and take risk, prompting the era of super bank and primed the subprime pump. In 1998 sub-prime loans were just 5 per cent of all mortgage lending. In 2008 they were about 30 per cent.

14 Surprisingly enough in July 2008, two months before the collapse of Lehmann, the ECB increased its interest rate to the high level of 4.5 per cent, even though the crisis had already reached European banks (British Institute Northern Rock was nationalized in February of 2008, and the German IKB went to bankrupt in July of 2007). Since the end of 2008, the interest rate was lowered to 2.5 per cent and then to 1 per cent, although still above the rate of 0.25 per cent set by the Fed.

15 The De Larosière Report, published in February 2009, is the result of the research of the High-Level group chaired by Jacques Larosière, commissioned by the European Commission.

16 See EU (2009b).

17 The opposition to the EU finance regulation of the UK Parliament's Treasury Committee was immediately clear, and in an internal paper it suggested to the UK government to use their veto in the EU Council against it if the initial EU text would not be modified (UK Treasury Committee 2010:5).

18 They are a kind of insurance against credit default, but turned out to be speculative tools on the large scale, thanks to the mistaken evaluation of the CRA (2009a). During the financial crisis, the link between the initial credit and its securities derivatives was lost. Creditors could take more risks, because through CDS they could transfer the risk to somebody else. In the end, nobody knew how many CDS existed and where they were held. CDS were used massively to speculate against the Euro in the Greek crisis (Wahl, 2010).

19 Investors in Madoff's funds lost $60 billion. In 2009, he was sentenced to 150 years in prison for defrauding investors through a massive Ponzi scheme.

20 EU Observer, 16 September 2010. http://euobserver.com/19/30821.

21 The Steering Committee of the ESRB is composed of the seven European System of Central Banks (ESCB) members (including the President of the ECB), the three chairs of the European Supervisory Authorities, a member of the EU Commission, and the President of the Economic and Financial Committee. The General Board of ESRB comprises apart from the Steering Committee members all central bank governors of the EU 27.

22 The primary objective of the ESB is to maintain price stability. This is different from the mandate of the US central bank, as stated in its Statute:

> Fed shall maintain long run growth of the monetary and credit aggregates commensurate with the economy's long run potential to increase production, so as to promote effectively the goals of maximum employment, stable prices, and moderate long-term interest rates.

For the ECB instead, the goal of economic growth secondary to inflation:

> Without prejudice to the objective of price stability, it shall support the general economic policies in the Union with a view to contributing to the achievement of the objectives of the Union as laid down in Article 3 of the Treaty on European Union.
>
> (Article 2 of ECB Statute)

23 The estimate is done with a FTT at 0.1 per cent and a medium reduction of the transaction volume per year (Schulmeister *et al.*, 2008).

24 In its proposal, the EU acknowledges that AIF are covered by a lack of transparency when building stakes in listed companies, conflicts of interest, and failures in fund governance, in particular with respect to remuneration, valuation and administration,

market abuse, misalignment of incentives in management of portfolio companies, weakness in internal risk management, inadequate investor disclosures, pro-cyclical impact of herding and risk concentrations, and direct exposure of systemically important banks (EU 2009c).
25 The German regulation is even stricter on short selling because it bans speculation on falling prices, not only temporarily and in case of threats to stability. The German position is heavily criticized by the UK, which would prefer limited bans, or none at all.
26 The SVI is simply the arithmetic average of those 4 variables all having the same weight. Reasonably, I suppose that governments give to the four issues the same importance and priorities. The lower the worse. As regards Unemployment, which has normally a positive value, it was considered with the opposite sign in order to be consistent with the other variables.
27 Economic Policy Institute Research and ideas for shared Prosperity, Online database, www.epi.org/.
28 Jean-Claude Juncker and Giulio Tremonti made a proposal on the Financial Times for a European Union bond, issued by a European Debt Agency (EDA). Each country can issue European bonds up to 40 per cent of GDP. This would create, over time, a sovereign bond market of similar size to the US one. Initially the EDA would finance 50 per cent of member states' debt issues – but this can be raised to 100 per cent during crises. The proposal also envisions a mechanism to switch between national and European bonds for countries in trouble at a discount rate. This would avoid the problem that secondary markets in many EU sovereign bonds are not sufficient liquid during crises.
29 More than a Keynesian fiscal stimulus TARP was an Act made in order to save, in a direct way, financial institutions. Several commentators and newspapers in the US criticized TARP for being a paradoxical representation of a sort of "financial socialism".

References

Aglietta M. (1979) "A theory of capitalist regulation: the US experience", NLB, London.
Amable B. (2003) *The diversity of modern capitalism*. Oxford University Press, Oxford.
Amoroso B. (2003) "Globalization and Welfare", *Working Paper*, Università di Roskilde.
Arestis P. and Pelagidis T. (2010) "The Case Against Deficit Hawks. Absurd Austerity Policies in Europe". Challenge/November–December.
Basso P. (1998) *Tempi moderni, orari antichi. Il tempo di lavoro a fine secolo*, Franco-Angeli, Milano.
Bini Smaghi L. (2008) "The Financial Crisis and Global Imbalances: Two Sides of the Same Coin." Speech at the Asia Europe Economic Forum, Beijing (December 9): www.bis.org/review/r081212d.pdf.
BIS – Bank for International Settlement (2010): *Semi-annual OTC derivatives statistics*. www.bis.org/statistics/otcder/dt1920a.pdf.
Boyer R. (2005) "Coherence, Diversity, And The Evolution Of Capitalisms: The Institutional Complementarity Hypothesis", CNRS-CEPREMAP, *Discussion Paper* n. 076.
Boyer R. and Saillard Y. (2002) *Regulation Theory: The State of the Art*, Routledge, Oxford.
Boyer R. (2000) "Is a Finance-led growth regime a viable alternative to Fordism? A preliminary analysis", *Economy and Society*, 29: 1, 111–145.
Caballero R., Farhi E. and Gourinchas P.-O. (2008) "An Equilibrium Model of 'Global Imbalances' and Low Interest Rates". *American Economic Review* 98 (March): 358–393.

Chong Ju Choi (2004) "Communitarian Capitalis and the Social Market Economy: an application to China", in John Kidd and Richter F., (eds.) *Development Models, Globalization and Economies*. Palgrave.

Conzelmann T., Rodriguez P.I., Kiiver P. and Spendzharova A. (2010) "Regulatory overhaul in the EU and the US following the financial crisis – what role for accountability?" Paper prepared for the ECPR Standing Group on International Relations Conference, 9–11 September 2010, Stockholm.

De Larosière (2009) Report from The High-Level Group on Financial Supervision in the EU. Brussels, 25 February 2009.

ECB (2010) Monthly Bulletin, June 06/2010, June. Frankfurter.

Economic Policy Institute Research and ideas for shared Prosperity, Online database, www.epi.org/.

Engelen, E., Konings, M. and Ferandez, R. (2008) The Rise of Activist Investors and Patters of Political Responses: Lessons on Agency. *Socio-Economic Review*, 6 (4): 611–636.

EU (2009a) Regulation of the European Parliament and of the Council on credit rating Agencies. 2008/0217 (COD). 14 July 2009.

EU (2009b) Proposal for a Regulation of the European Parliament and of the Council establishing a European Banking Authority. COM(2009) 501 final.2009/0142 (COD).

EU (2009b) Proposal for a Regulation of the European Parliament and of the Council establishing a European Insurance and Occupational Pensions Authority. 23.9.2009 COM. (2009) 502 final. 2009/0143 (COD).

EU (2009b) Proposal for a Regulation of the European Parliament and of the Council establishing a European Securities and Markets Authority. COM (2009) 503 final. 2009/0144 (COD).

EU (2009b) Proposal for a Regulation of the European Parliament and of the Council on Community macro prudential oversight of the financial system and establishing a European Systemic Risk Board. COM (2009) 499 final. 2009/0140 (COD).

EU (2009c) Proposal for a Directive of the European Parliament and of the Council on Alternative Investment Fund Managers and amending Directives 2004/39/EC and 2009/.../EC. 30.4.2009 COM (2009) 207 final. 2009/0064 (COD) C7–0040/09. Brussels.

EU (2010a) Proposal for a Regulation of the European Parliament and of the Council on OTC derivatives, central counterparties and trade repositories. COM (2010) 484/5. 2010/0250 (COD). Brussels.

EU (2010b) Proposal for a Directive of the European Parliament and of the Council amending Directives 2006/48/EC and 2006/49/EC as regards capital requirements for the trading book 38 and for re-securitisations, and the supervisory review of remuneration policies COM (2010) XXX final. Brussels.

EuroMemorandum (2010) *Confronting the Crisis: Austerity or Solidarity*. European Economists for an Alternative Economic Policy in Europe – EuroMemo Group 2010/11.

European Commission (2008) Economic Forecast, Directorate-General for Economic and Financial Affairs, N. 6. Autumn, Brussels.

European Council (2009) Council Conclusions on Strengthening EU Financial Supervision: www.consilium.europa.eu/uedocs/cms_data/docs/pressdata/en/ecofin/108389.pdf.

European Council (2010) Short Selling and certain aspects of Credit Default Swaps, COM (2010) 482. 2010/xxxx (COD). Brussels.

Feng S. and Hu Y. (2010) "Misclassification Errors and the Underestimation of U.S. Unemployment Rates" IZA DP No. 5057 July.

Fitoussi J.P. (1992) *Il Dibattito proibito*, Il Mulino, Bologna.
Gillingham J. (2003) *European integration, 1950–2003. Superstate or New Market Economy?* Cambridge, New York: Cambridge University Press.
Greenspan, A. (2007) *The Age of Turbulence: adventures in a new world*, Allen Lane.
IMF (1995) Gender Issues in Economic Adjustment, IMF Survey, September 25, pp. 286–288.
IMF (2008) "Fiscal Policy for the Crisis", Staff Position Note (by: Antonio Spilimbergo, Steve Symansky, Olivier Blanchard, and Carlo Cottarelli), Washington DC.
IMF (2009a) *Global Financial Stability Report. Navigating Challenges Ahead. October 2009.* Washington, DC.
IMF (2009b) World Economic Outlook. Washington, DC.
IMF (2010) World Economic Outlook (online database).
Jessop B. (2002), *The future of the capitalist state*, Cambridge: Polity Press.
Kindleberger C. (2005) *Manias, panics, and crashes*. New York: Wiley & son.
Krugman P. (2008) *The Return of Depression Economics and the Crisis of 2008.* New York: Norton & Co.
Lipietz A. (1992) *Towards a New Economic Order. Postfordim, Ecology and Democracy*, Polity Press.
Nickell S.G. (1997) "Labour Market rigidities and unemployment: Europe versus North America", *Journal of Economic Perspectives*, n.3.
Obstfeld M. and Rogoff K. (2009) "Global Imbalances and the Financial Crisis: Products of Common Causes" CEPR Discussion Paper No. 7606.
OECD (2010), Employment outlook (online database).
Peck J. and Tickell A. (1992) "Local modes of social regulation? Regulation Theory, Thacherism and uneven development", *Geoforum*, 23 (3), 347–363.
Petit P. (2003) "Large network services and the organisation of contemporary capitalism", *CNRS-CEPREMAP*, WP, n. 2003–14.Aglietta, 1979.
Petit P. (2009) "Financial Globalisation and Innovation: Lessons of a lost Decade for the OECD Economies". CNRS Working Paper, Paris.
Pontusson J. (2005) *Inequality and Prosperity. Social Europe vs. Liberal America.* Cornell University press, Ithaca and London.
Posner R. (2009) *A failure of capitalism*. Cambridge: Harvard University Press.
Romer C. and Bernstein J. (2009) "The Job impact of the American Recovery and Reinvestment Plan". Council of Economic Advisers and Office of the Vice President Elect, White House, Washington, DC, 9 January.
Sapir A. (2005) "Globalization and the reform of European Social models", Bruegel Policy brief. ISSUE 2005/01, NOVEMBER.
Schulmeister S., Schratzenstaller M., Picek O. (2008) A General Financial Transaction Tax. Motives, Revenues, Feasibility and Effects. Vienna: WIFO Publication.
Semmler W. and Young B. (2010) "Lost in temptation of risk: Financial market liberalization, financial market meltdown and regulatory reforms", *Comparative European Politics*.
Skidelsky R. (2009) *Keynes: The Return of the Master*. New York: Public Affairs.
Soskice, D. and Hall, P. (2001) *Varieties of Capitalism*, Oxford University Press.
The Economist (2011) Special Report on International Banking, 14–20 May, London.
Tobin, James (1978) "A Proposal for International Monetary Reform". *Eastern Economic Journal* (Eastern Economic Association): 153–159.
Tridico P. (2011) *Institutions, Human Development and Economic Growth in Transition Economies*. London: Palgrave.

Turner Review (2009) "A regulatory response to the global banking crisis. Financial Services Authority, March, 2009, www.fsa.gov.uk/pubs/other/turner_review.pdf.

UK Treasury Committee (2010) Summary of Treasury Committee opinions on EU Regulatory reform proposals. London.

Wahl P. (2010) "Fighting Fire with Buckets. A Guide to European Regulation of Financial Markets" Weltwirtschaft, Okologie & Entwicklung/World Economy, Ecology & Development. WEED Ass., Berlin.

Whelan K. (2010) *Global imbalances and the financial crisis.* Directorate general for internal policies, European Parliament, Brussels.

Wolff R. (2009) *Capitalism hits the fan. The Global Economic Meltdown and What to Do About It.* New York: Pluto Press.

Wolfson, M. (2010) Neoliberalism and the Social Structure of Accummulation. *Review of Radical Political Economics.* 2003: 35: 3: 255–263.

World Bank (2010) Statistical Indicators (online database).

8 Labour market rigidities can be useful

A Schumpeterian view

Alfred Kleinknecht, C.W.M. Naastepad, Servaas Storm and Robert Vergeer

1 Introduction

With the emergence of supply-side thinking in the 1970s, the claim that high (European) unemployment is caused by 'rigidities' in labour markets became dominant. The usual suspects making labour markets 'rigid' are high minimum wages, high social benefits, strong trade unions, the power of insiders and strong protection against firing. Removal of labour market rigidities tends to weaken the bargaining position of labour and thus can bring down wages. Ultimately, reduction of wages carries the promise of more jobs. Against this, we argue that (1) countries with more flexible labour markets have a low-productive and hence more labour-intensive GDP growth; it is highly doubtful, however, whether this indeed results in lower rates of unemployment; (2) that GDP growth does not differ between countries with 'rigid' versus 'liberalized' labour markets, and (3) labour market rigidities can be useful for the working of what is called the 'routinized' ('Schumpeter II') innovation model. Claims about the beneficial effects of removing labour market rigidities tended to be made under the (often implicit) assumption that this would *not* affect innovation and labour productivity. We give theoretical arguments and quote empirical evidence that it does.

The next section gives illustrations of some key macro-economic variables over the period 1960–2011 for a group of typical 'Rhineland' ('Old Europe') countries that are supposed having rigid labour markets compared to a group of Anglo-Saxon countries that have liberalized labour market regimes. Thereafter we summarize theoretical arguments of why flexibility in labour relations should influence innovation and labour productivity growth, and we discuss empirical evidence.

2 Varieties of capitalism: comparing two groups of countries

The *varieties-of-capitalism* literature distinguishes two types of labour market regimes: (1) *Liberalized Market Economies* (LME) versus (2) *Coordinated Market Economies* (CME). LMEs are characterized by weak protection against dismissal, modest social benefits, weak trade unions, and decentralized wage bargaining systems favouring inequality of incomes. Against a modest protection of labour stands a strong protection of investors. Typical LME countries are the US, Canada, Great Britain, Ireland, Australia and New Zealand. CMEs show rather the opposite: a stronger protection against dismissals, more generous social security systems, stronger trade unions and a tendency towards centralized wage bargaining (enhancing greater income equality). Against the stronger protection of labour, however, stands a weaker protection of investors. Typical CME systems of labour relations can be found in Continental Europe and in Japan (see Hall and Soskice 2001).

In the following figures we give four key economic variables for a group of (rigid) Old Europe countries versus five Anglo-Saxon countries. For ease of comparison, all data are set equal to 100 in 1960.

The figures show the following interesting patterns:

- There is a faster growth of real wages in Old Europe (Figure 8.1). This is not surprising as rigid labour markets in Old Europe leave more power to labour than do 'liberalized' Anglo-Saxon labour markets.
- As a consequence of lower wage growth, input of hours worked is growing substantially stronger under Anglo-Saxon labour market regimes, compared to 'Old Europe' (Figure 8.2).

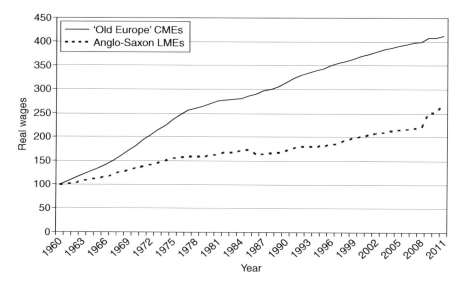

Figure 8.1 Development of real wages, 1960=100 (source: database of the Groningen Growth and Development Centre (www.ggdc.net) & AMECO database).

Notes
Anglo-Saxon countries: Australia, Canada, New Zealand, United Kingdom and United States.
Continental European countries: Austria, Belgium, Denmark, Finland, France, Germany, Italy, Netherlands, Portugal, Spain, and Sweden.
Definition: Real wages = Labour Productivity per hour (GGDC; EKS) * Wage Share at factor costs (Eurostat).

Labour market rigidities can be useful 177

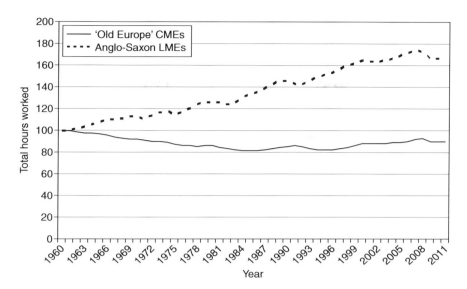

Figure 8.2 Development of total hours worked (1960=100 (source: database of the Groningen Growth and Development Centre (www.ggdc.net).

Notes
Anglo-Saxon countries: Australia, Canada, New Zealand, United Kingdom and United States.
Continental European countries: Austria, Belgium, Denmark, Finland, France, Germany, Italy, Netherlands, Portugal, Spain and Sweden.

- A surprising result emerges from Figure 8.3: GDP growth in both regimes hardly differs (Figure 8.3).
- Figure 8.4 shows the logical consequences from Figures 8.2 and 8.3: If GPD growth is essentially the same, but labour input grows faster in the Anglo-Saxon countries, this means that the Anglo-Saxon countries have substantially lower labour productivity growth, i.e. a slower growth of GDP per hour worked. Choosing a positive frame one can argue that the Anglo-Saxon labour market regime produces more demand for labour; in a negative frame, one can say that Anglo-Saxons have to work more hours for the same GDP growth.

3 Do LMEs have lower unemployment?

A more labour-intensive GDP growth through lower growth of labour productivity may carry the positive message of lower unemployment. There are, however, doubts about whether in 'liberalized' Anglo-Saxon LMEs, unemployment rates are indeed lower. Several studies suggest that the claim that deregulation brings down unemployment rates, lacks robustness (Baker *et al.*, 2005; Baccaro and Rei, 2007; Howell *et al.*, 2007). Vergeer and Kleinknecht (2012a) have submitted the influential model by Nickell *et al.* (2005) to a series of robustness checks. Leaving the data unchanged

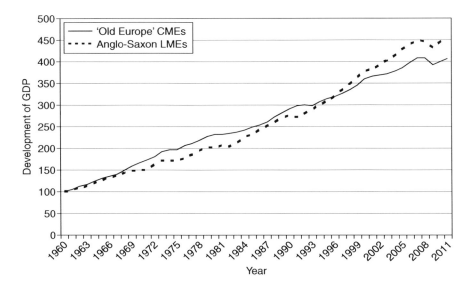

Figure 8.3 Development of GDP (1960=100) (source: database of the Groningen Growth and Development Centre (www.ggdc.net)).

Notes
Anglo-Saxon countries: Australia, Canada, New Zealand, United Kingdom and United States.
Continental European countries: Austria, Belgium, Denmark, Finland, France, Germany, Italy, Netherlands, Portugal, Spain and Sweden.

and applying three small modifications to the Nickell *et al.* model, it turned out that numerous key coefficients changed significance or even sign. Vergeer and Kleinknecht conclude that the claim from NAIRU theory that labour market rigidities cause (high) unemployment is rather shaky. Table 8.1 gives descriptive data on unemployment rates in a number of LME and CME countries. These figures illustrate that, in the long run (1970–2010), it is by no means obvious that either of the two labour market regimes performs remarkably better than the other.

How then to explain that, in spite of a more labour-intensive GDP growth (Figure 8.2), it is doubtful whether LME countries have lower unemployment rates? Possible explanations are an increase of labour supply thanks to generous immigration policies and due to longer working weeks in Anglo-Saxon countries (see Table 8.2). For employers it is cheaper if their personnel work more hours, rather than hiring new people. Labour market institutions in Anglo-Saxon countries give more power to employers; the latter may have used their power forcing employees to work longer. These two arguments may explain why in LME countries we observe an increase in hours worked, but not necessarily lower unemployment rates.

Rather than achieving lower unemployment rates, deregulation seems to have achieved a more unequal income distribution. For example in the US, the share in National Income of the top-10 per cent income earners increased from 33 per

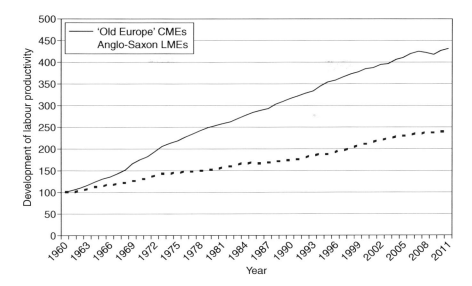

Figure 8.4 Development of labour productivity (1960=100) (source: database of the Groningen Growth and Development Centre (www.ggdc.net)).

Notes
Anglo-Saxon countries: Australia, Canada, New Zealand, United Kingdom and United States.
Continental European countries: Austria, Belgium, Denmark, Finland, France, Germany, Italy, Netherlands, Portugal, Spain and Sweden.

Table 8.1 Average unemployment during 1970–2010 (as a percentage of the working population)

'Flexible' Anglo-Saxon LMEs		*'Rigid' Old-Europe CMEs*	
Canada	7.7	France	7.5
UK	7.2	Italy	7.0
Australia	6.3	Germany	6.2
USA	6.3	Netherlands	6.1
		Sweden	4.7
Average:	6.9	**Average:**	6.3

Source: www.bls.gov/fls/flscomparelf/unemployment.htm

Notes
All unemployment figures follow the US definition and are therefore internationally comparable.

cent in 1976 to 50 per cent in 2007 and the share of the top-1 per cent increased from 8.9 per cent in 1976 to 23.5 per cent in 2007 (Atkinson *et al.*, 2011). Inequality of incomes increased much less in Europe. The real difference between LMEs and CMEs lies first of all in a higher income inequality and not in rates of unemployment.

Table 8.2 Working hours per year, 1990–2010

'Flexible' Anglo-Saxon LMEs		Rigid 'Old Europe' CMEs	
Australia	1,767	Italy	1,840
Canada	1,761	Sweden	1,613
USA	1,720	France	1,509
UK	1,707	Germany	1,478
		Netherlands	1,432
Average	**1,739**	**Average:**	**1,574**
		(Average *without Italy*)	1,508

Source: The Conference Board: Total economy database, January 2012: www.conference-board.org/data/economydatabase/.

4 Why should LMEs have lower growth of labour productivity?

This section summarizes arguments of why deregulation and downward wage flexibility may lead to lower labour productivity growth. We first clarify what is being understood by 'flexibility'. The literature distinguishes three categories (e.g. Beatson, 1995):

1 'Numerical' (or external) flexibility that allows firms to adjust the size of their labour force through flexible hiring and firing;
2 'Wage flexibility' which concerns the responsiveness of wages to economic shocks; and
3 'Functional' (or internal) flexibility that allows firms to reorganize their workforce in internal labour markets through training and HRM policies.

Emphasis on the first two modes of flexibility is characteristic for Anglo-Saxon 'Liberal Market Economies', whereas 'Coordinated Market Economies' (or 'Rhineland' systems) rely more on functional flexibility (see Hall and Soskice, 2001). There is evidence from firm-level data that high *functional* flexibility on internal labour markets may be favourable to innovation and productivity growth (Appelbaum *et al.*, 2000; Bassanini and Ernst, 2002; Michie and Sheehan, 2001, 2003; Kleinknecht *et al.* 2006, Zhou *et al.*, 2011). The policy agenda towards removing labour market rigidities, however, is mainly interested in wage-cost saving *numerical* flexibility and in (downwardly) flexible wages.

Institutional reforms that achieve (downwardly) flexible wages and those allowing for easier firing both work in the same direction: they allow savings on a firm's wage bill. In principle, one might expect that workers accepting a flexible job should earn a positive risk premium that compensates for higher firing risks. Empirical evidence, however, suggests that rather the opposite appears to be the case (Sànchez and Toharia, 2000; Booth *et al.*, 2002; McGinnity and Mertens, 2004; Addison and Surfield, 2005; Picchio, 2006). Such evidence from person-level wage equations is consistent with estimates of firm-level wage equations (Kleinknecht et al., 2006). In other words, flexible workers, on average, earn *less* than regular workers (controlling for other personal characteristics). A possible explanation is the abundant supply of labour in certain segments of the labour market. In the context of this chapter, it does not matter whether lower wage growth is achieved through institutional changes in the wage setting mechanism or through easier firing or through removing other rigidities (e.g. minimum wages or social benefits).

In the following, we discuss three major channels of transmission from removing labour market rigidities to lower innovation and labour productivity growth:

1   Effects on innovative activity;
2   Effects on training;
3   Trust and productivity growth.

The work of Hall and Soskice (2001) suggests that the three channels are complementary.

1 Effects on firms' innovative activity

Three arguments substantiate a causal link from higher wages to higher labour productivity growth. First, one can argue that a price increase of labour (relative to capital) will stimulate the adoption of labour-saving innovations, as proposed by Sylos Labini (1984, 1993 and 1999).[1] Second, in a Schumpeterian perspective, it can be argued that, due to their monopoly rents from innovation, innovators are better able than technological laggards to live with wage increases (or with high adjustment costs due to stricter regulation). Therefore, high real wage growth and labour market rigidities may enhance the Schumpeterian process of *creative destruction* in which innovators compete away technological laggards (Kleinknecht 1998). Or vice versa, de-centralized wage bargaining and (downward) wage flexibility increases the chances of survival for technological laggards. While their survival is favourable for employment (at least in the short run), it is likely to result in a long run decline of the average quality of entrepreneurship and a loss of innovative dynamism. Third, using vintage models, it is easy to demonstrate that more aggressive wage policies by trade unions will lead to the quicker replacement of older (more labour-intensive) vintages of capital by new and more productive ones. A policy of modest wage claims will allow firms to exploit old vintages of capital for longer. This can result in a growing age of capital stock (shown to be one of the reasons behind the productivity crisis in the Netherlands after 1985; see Naastepad and Kleinknecht, 2004).

Against such arguments, there are three counter-arguments. First, labour market rigidity could have negative effects on innovation and productivity by slowing down the reallocation process of labour from old and declining sectors to new and dynamic ones (for a review of the effects of labour market institutions on economic performance, see Nickell and Layard, 1999). Second, the difficult or expensive firing of redundant personnel can frustrate labour-saving innovations at the firm level (Bassanini and Ernst, 2002; Scarpetta and Tressel, 2004). Third, well-protected and powerful personnel could appropriate rents from innovation through higher wage claims, thus reducing incentives for taking innovative risks (Malcomson, 1997). The latter argument might be quite relevant in Anglo-Saxon de-centralized bargaining systems. It appears to be less relevant to rigid 'Rhineland' labour markets that tend to rely on centralized (often industry-level) wage bargaining.

The argument that the difficult firing of personnel will hamper labour-saving innovations might be less relevant for three reasons. First, if firing is difficult, firms have incentives to invest in functional flexibility by means of training, which will allow shifting labour from old to new activities in internal labour markets. In other words, lack of *numerical* flexibility will enhance *functional* flexibility.[2] Second, in many countries, redundant personnel need not be a problem for labour-saving innovations as high percentages leave their firms voluntarily.[3] Third, protection against dismissal may actually enhance productivity performance, as secure workers will be more willing to cooperate with management in developing labour-saving processes and in disclosing their (tacit) knowledge to the firm (see Lorenz, 1999). Workers that are easy to fire have incentives to hide information about how their work might be done more efficiently.

2 Effects on manpower training

Easier firing will lead to shorter average job durations, making the payback period of investment in manpower training shorter. In addition, workers will first of all be interested in acquiring general skills that increase their employability on the external job market, but may be reluctant to acquire firm-specific skills if there is no long-term commitment to their employers (Belot *et al.*, 2002). A similar conclusion emerges from the hypothesis that highly flexible labour reduces the compression of the wage structure (both within and between firms); note that Acemoglu and Pischke (1999) and Agell (1999) argue that wage compression is a reason for the provision of training by firms. Empirical evidence of a correlation between fixed-term employment and a lower probability of work-related training has been provided for the UK by and Booth *et al.* (2002).

3 Trust and productivity growth

Work by Huselid (1995), Buchele and Christiansen (1999), Lorenz (1999), Michie and Sheehan (2001, 2003) and Naastepad and Storm (2006) shows favourable productivity effects of 'high trust' or 'high road' human resource management practices. Long-lasting working relations and strong protection against dismissal can be interpreted as an investment in trust (see also Svensson, 2011), loyalty and commitment which favours productivity growth in four ways.

First, it reduces costs of monitoring and control. For example, Naastepad and Storm demonstrate that firms in low-trust 'Anglo-Saxon' countries typically have much thicker management bureaucracies for monitoring and control, compared to 'Rhineland' countries (2006: 170–191).

Second, it reduces positive externalities, i.e. the leakage of crucial knowledge to competitors which, in principle, discourages investment in knowledge. Third, it favours long-run historical accumulation of (tacit) knowledge in a 'routinized' (Schumpeter II) innovation model (Breschi *et al.*, 2000). The argument about the 'routinized' (versus the 'entrepreneurial') innovation regimes is summarized in Table 8.3 which is inspired by the work of Breschi *et al.* (2000). Fourth, it will favour critical feedback for bosses from the shop floor. Powerful managers have a tendency to select conformists around themselves who hardly contradict them. If this is enhanced by a change of power relations due to easier firing, it can bread problematic management practices.

Table 8.3 makes it clear that continuous accumulation of 'tacit knowledge' (i.e. ill-documented knowledge from experience) in a routinized innovation regime is favoured by *continuity* in labour relations. In other words, a routinized innovation regime gives incentives to reallocation of work within internal labour markets through *functional* flexibility rather than via external labour markets through *numerical* flexibility. The historically *cumulative* nature of knowledge produces path dependencies which give incentives to firms employing protected insiders with long job tenures.

5 Previous empirical findings and hypotheses

Most empirical analyses of the relationship between flexible labour and productivity growth tend to use country or sector data (Buchele and Christiansen, 1999; Nickell and Layard, 1999; Bassanini and Ernst, 2002; Scarpetta and Tressel, 2004; Auer *et al.*, 2005; Naastepad and Storm, 2006). These studies search for relationships

Table 8.3 Stylized comparison of two Schumpeterian innovation models

Schumpeter I model: 'garage business innovation'	Schumpeter II model: 'routinized innovation'
Starters in high tech; niche players	Established firms with professionalized R&D labs
SMEs and young firms	Monopolistic competitors; oligopolists
High entry and exit rates	Stable hierarchy of (dominant) innovators
Properties of the knowledge base: Generally available knowledge → low entry barriers	Dependence on historically accumulated and often firm-specific (tacit) knowledge → high entry barriers
Labour market institutions: Recruitment through external labour markets	Internal labour markets through dependence on accumulated (firm-specific, tacit) knowledge → well-protected 'insiders'

between measures of labour market rigidity and productivity. Most of these studies observe a positive effect of employment protection (e.g. measured by the OECD's *Employment Protection Legislation Index*) on labour productivity growth or innovation indicators. The econometric analysis of Bassanini *et al.* (2009), however, suggests that the net effect of labour market regulation on *aggregate* labour productivity growth is *negative*. The study by Bassanini *et al.* informed the OECD (2007) *Employment Outlook* in concluding that the net effect of labour market regulation on productivity growth is negative, but relatively small. Two other OECD economists, Scarpetta and Tressel (2004), find a large negative impact of employment protection on productivity growth in a subset of OECD countries (those countries featuring sectoral wage bargaining without national co-ordination); however, for all OECD countries taken together, these authors find no impact of employment protection on productivity growth. But this conclusion is not strong because their empirical approach suffers from important limitations and the impact of regulation on aggregate productivity growth is basically imputed or even conjectured – not estimated.[4]

Auer *et al.* (2005) find a positive (though decreasing) relation between job stability, measured as average tenure, and labour productivity. Rather than using measures of EPL strictness, Vergeer and Kleinknecht (2012b) explain labour productivity growth in 20 OECD countries (1960–2004) through changes in wages and in the share of labour in National Income. They find that a 1 per cent extra wage increase (decrease) will result in an increase (decrease) of labour productivity growth by 0.35–0.46 per cent, depending on the specification. Moreover, a 1 per cent rise in the share of capital income in National Income leads to an 0.2 per cent reduction in labour productivity growth. This holds after controls for other factors such as the share of services in the total economy; Verdoorn effects; catching up effects, or past labour productivity growth (path dependency).

A different approach is by Acharya *et al.* (2010) who study patents and patent citations as a proxy for innovation. They argue that stringent labour laws provide firms a 'commitment device' to not punish short-run failures and this would encourage employees pursuing risky and value-enhancing innovative activities. Exploiting time-series variation in changes of dismissal laws, they find that

> innovation and growth are fostered by stringent laws governing dismissal of employees, especially in the more innovation-intensive sectors. Firm-level tests within the United States that exploit a discontinuity generated by the passage of the federal *Worker Adjustment and Retraining Notification Act* confirm the cross-country evidence.
>
> (2010: 1)

Also using patents, Pieroni and Pompei (2008) found a negative effect of labour turnover (as a proxy for external flexibility) on patenting activity at regional level in Italy.

Some studies report firm-level evidence. For example, Michie and Sheehan (2001, 2003) find a positive correlation between 'high road' human resource management practices and innovation in British firms.

Kleinknecht et al. (2006) found negative effects of external flexibility and positive effects of functional flexibility on labour productivity growth in a sample of Dutch manufacturing firms.

Arvanitis (2005) found a positive relationship between functional flexibility and labour productivity for a sample of Swiss companies, but an insignificant effect of external flexibility. Autor et al. (2007) found a positive effect of employment protection on capital investment, skills and labour productivity, but a negative effect on total factor productivity. Lucidi and Kleinknecht (2010) report estimates from 3,000 Italian firms. They show that high shares of flexible workers, a high labour turnover and lower costs of labour (relative to capital) are each related to significantly lower rates of labour productivity growth. Boeri and Garibaldi (2007) found a negative effect of the share of fixed-term contracts on labour productivity growth in a sample of Italian manufacturing firms during the period 1995–2000.

Many of the above arguments (implicitly) assume that easier firing will result in a higher labour turnover. One may object that easy firing being allowed by law does not need to prevent firms from keeping their people for longer. Against this, one can argue that the mere possibility of easy firing may increase mobility. In a firm that is not doing well, employees may search jobs, as soon as they fear lay-offs. Once massive lay-offs take place, competition for jobs in the local labour market may increase dramatically. It is therefore of vital importance for individual workers to start their search process in a very early stage, before others getting aware of the threat of lay-offs. People may therefore leave while their firm might not even have considered firing them.

6 Concluding discussions

What can we conclude about effects of removing rigidities in labour markets? First, long-run GDP growth in *Liberalized Market Economies* (LMEs) does not seem to be systematically higher than GDP growth in *Coordinated Market Economies* (CMEs). It has sometimes been claimed that deregulation of factor markets (and, in particular of labour markets) leads to higher economic growth, pointing to higher growth rates in the US from the 1990s up to 2007. Taking several LMEs together, however, we see little of a superior growth performance (Figure 8.3). It is meanwhile obvious that much of the high pre-2007 growth in the US must have been due to an impressive build-up of debt against the background of a housing bubble (i.e. a kind of 'mortgage Keynesianism'; see Maki and Palumbo, 2001; Palley, 2009; Irvin, 2011). If the Americans take 'deleveraging' serious, we would expect lower growth in the years to come.

Second, compared to CMEs in 'Old Europe', Anglo-Saxon LMEs tend towards a modest wage growth, as their deregulated labour market institutions (including weak trade unions) give weak protection for workers and strong protection for investors. This is related to a strong shift towards higher income inequality in the US compared to Europe.

Third, as can be expected from traditional micro-economics, a more modest wage growth leads to a more labour-intensive GDP growth which is at the cost of a lower growth of GDP per labour hour. Ironically, such a labour-intensive and low-productive GDP growth somehow reminds us of Eastern Europe before 1989. In view of an ageing population and a shrinking working population in most European countries, it is questionable whether a pre-1989 Eastern European style job creation regime is desirable for Europe.

Fourth, while unemployment rates might have looked favourable in the US, notably during the period of credit build-up before 2007, it looks as if, in the long run, unemployment rates in LMEs are not lower than in CMEs (Table 8.1). Several authors have argued that there is no convincing econometric evidence that removal of labour market rigidities, in spite of leading to a more labour-intensive GDP growth, would bring down unemployment rates (Baker *et al.*, 2005; Baccaro and Rei, 2007; Howell *et al.*, 2007). Even a highly cited study by Nickell *et al.* (2005) turns out being based on a non-robust econometric model (Vergeer and Kleinknecht, 2012a). Of course, contributors to the *labour-market-rigidities-cause-unemployment* literature were aware of the limitations of their work and made numerous caveats about the quality (and availability) of data and limitations of their econometrics. Such qualifications, however, did not prevent sweeping conclusions by policy practitioners.

Fifth, above we gave a list of theoretical arguments why deregulated labour market regimes may damage innovation and labour productivity growth. These arguments are most relevant in a 'routinized' innovation regime that relies on path dependent accumulation of (often tacit) and firm-specific knowledge. The US may be strong in IT which is based on an 'entrepreneurial' garage business regime that was not dependent on firm-specific and path dependent historical accumulation of ('tacit') knowledge (at least not in the past). In industries that rely on a 'routinized' innovation regime, however, deregulated US labour markets make such knowledge accumulation harder to do. This may be one of the explanations of why US manufacturers compete so poorly against Japanese and German suppliers.

Finally, we should address a competing hypothesis for our above arguments: the *growth-in-low-productive-jobs* hypothesis as expressed by the OECD (2003). They interpret the finding that 'a weak trade-off may exist between gains in employment and productivity' as arising from newly created jobs at the bottom of the labour market:

> For example, decentralization of wage bargaining and trimming back of high minimum wages may tend to lower wages, at least in the lower ranges of the earnings distribution. Similarly, relaxing employment protection legislation (...) may encourage expansion of low-productivity/low-pay jobs in services.
>
> (Box 1.4, p. 42.)

These low-productive jobs – the OECD's reasoning continues – are created in flexible countries, but *not* in countries with rigid labour markets. In this view, the loss in labour productivity growth through deregulation is mainly a negative by-product of extra jobs created in the low wage segment.

There are two arguments against this interpretation. First, one can argue that, under the *ceteris paribus* assumption, the (extra) hiring of low productive workers should have increased GDP growth in flexible economies, compared to inflexible economies in which these people do not work. Looking at long-run growth, however, there are hardly indications that such extra growth took place (Figure 8.3 above). Second, in a model explaining inter-country differences in labour productivity growth among 20 OECD countries (1960–2004) Vergeer and Kleinknecht (2012b; see also Vergeer, 2010) tested this hypothesis by including, as a right hand variable, the growth of jobs. In other words, they tested whether (above-average) growth of jobs, thanks to admitting low-productive workers into the labour market, would reduce labour productivity growth. Growth of jobs had the expected negative sign but turned out insignificant. This suggests that the slow growth of labour productivity can hardly be explained by low productive workers entering the labour market thanks to deregulation. The productivity growth slowdown takes place primarily in *existing* jobs.

Obvious candidates that explain the latter have been discussed above. Among these are labour-capital substitution, vintage effects, induced technological change or the malfunctioning of Schumpeterian 'creative destruction' as moderate wages protect weaker entrepreneurial talents against being competed away by stronger firms. Moreover, easier hiring and firing will make job durations shorter, thus discouraging training, notably in firm-specific and 'tacit' knowledge. Shorter job durations will also increase various forms of disloyal behaviour such as knowledge leakage or theft and this will force firms to invest into thicker management layers for monitoring and control – which in turn is frustrating for creative people. A major disadvantage of greater personnel turnover is the weak functioning of the 'routinized' innovation model that heavily relies on incremental learning and on path dependent accumulation of (often 'tacit' and firm-specific) knowledge. We conclude that deregulation of labour markets is definitely no free lunch and labour market rigidities have their merits.

Let us end with a note on the crisis in the Eurozone. Mainstream economists propose that Mediterranean countries should make firing of workers easier and cut down social benefits as part of 'structural reforms' that make their economies competitive. Our above results suggest what will happen if this is realized: definitely more labour input, but also a weaker capacity of Mediterranean economies to realize innovation and productivity growth. This is likely to favour creation of low-productive and precarious jobs, rather than enhancing competitiveness through highly productive and qualified jobs.

Notes

1 Note that the dynamic substitution between capital and labour, in this context, differs from the static substitution, with constant technology, implied by neoclassical theory as a response to the relative variation in factor prices. The former, in fact, involves technological change incorporated in new capital goods (Sylos Labini, 1993).
2 See also the discussion by Acemoglou and Pischke (1999) who emphasize that wage compression in rigid German labour markets enhances training for highly educated and for low-educated workers, while in the liberalized US system, mainly highly educated workers receive training.
3 Kleinknecht *et al.* (2006) report that, on average, 9–12 per cent of a firm's personnel in the Netherlands leave voluntarily each year, the exact percentage depending on the state of the business cycle. Nickell and Layard report that this figure amounts to over 10 per cent (1999: 363).
4 The basic but untested idea of Bassanini *et al.* (2009) is that employment protection legislation (EPL) affects industries with high layoffs more strongly than industries where layoff rates are low. Using data for 17 industries in 18 OECD economies (1982–2003), they classify industries into 'binding' and 'non-binding' industries – the second group of industries is the control group. A first problem is that the classification in two groups is by itself far from clear, as it presupposes the existence of unconstrained 'natural' layoff rates prevailing in the absence of employment protection. Second, it is rather unrealistically assumed that the classification into binding/non-binding industries (i) holds true for all years of the period 1982–2003, and (ii) does not vary across countries; all countries are assumed to resemble the US, which they treat as a 'natural benchmark' in this regard (thus neglecting country-specific institutional factors affecting 'natural' layoff rates). A third problem is that country-specific EPL indicators do not change much over time, so that most of the variation in EPL is due to differences *between countries*; this means that within-country variation in EPL cannot 'explain' much of the country-specific productivity-differences across the various industries. Finally, the focus of the analysis is the *difference* in productivity growth rates between EPL binding and non-binding industries, and to calculate the impact of EPL on aggregate labour productivity growth, the authors assume away potential general equilibrium effects of EPL (e.g. the impact of EPL on (a) productivity growth in the non-binding industries, (b) the relative importance, in terms of value added, of binding and non-binding industries, and (c) incentives in physical and human capital formation). All in all, the finding that job protection depresses aggregate labour productivity growth appears not very convincing.

References

Acemoglou, D. and J.-S. Pischke (1999): 'Beyond Becker: Training in Imperfect Labour Markets,' *Economic Journal*, Vol. 109: F112–F142.
Acharya, Viral V., Ramin P. Baghai and Krishnamurthy V. Subramanian (2010): 'Labor laws and innovation', *NBER Working Paper 16484*. Cambridge, MA: National Bureau of Economic Research.
Addison, J.T. and C.J. Surfield (2005): 'Atypical Work and Compensation', IZA Discussion Paper no. 1477.
Agell, J. (1999): 'On the benefits from rigid labour markets: Norms, market failures, and social insurance', *Economic Journal*, Vol. 109: 143–164.
Appelbaum, E., T. Bailey, P. Berg and A.L. Kalleberg (2000): *Manufacturing advantage. Why high-performance work systems pay off*. Ithaca, NY: Cornell University Press.
Arvanitis, S. (2005): 'Modes of labor flexibility at firm level: are there any implications

for performance and innovation? Evidence for the Swiss economy', *Industrial and Corporate* Change, Vol. 14: 993–1016.
Atkinson, A., T. Piketty and E. Saez (2011): 'Top incomes in the long run of history', *Journal of Economic Literature*, Vol. 49: 3–71.
Auer, P., J. Berg and J. Coulibaly (2005): 'Is a stable workforce good for productivity?' *International Labour Review*, Vol. 144 (3): 319–343.
Autor, D.H., W.R. Kerr and A.D. Kugler (2007): 'Does Employment Protection Reduce Productivity? Evidence from US States' *Economic Journal*, Vol. 117: 189–F217.
Baccaro, L. and D. Rei (2007): 'Institutional determinants of unemployment in OECD countries: Does the deregulatory view hold water?' *International Organization*, Vol. 61: 527–569.
Baker, D., A. Glyn, D. Howell and J. Schmitt (2005): 'Labor market institutions and unemployment: a critical assessment of the cross-country evidence', in David Howell, ed., *Questioning liberalization: unemployment, labor markets and the welfare state*, Oxford University Press, pp. 72–118.
Bassanini, A. and E. Ernst (2002): 'Labour market regulation, industrial relations and technological regimes: a tale of comparative advantage,' *Industrial and Corporate Change*, Vol. 11(3), pp. 391–426.
Bassanini, A., L. Nunziata and D. Venn (2009): 'Job protection and productivity' *Economic Policy*, Vol. 24, Issue 58, pp. 349–402.
Beatson, M. (1995): 'Labour market flexibility', *Research Series No. 48*. University of Sheffield, (Employment Department).
Belot, M., J. Boone and J. Van Ours (2002): 'Welfare effects of employment protection', *CEPR Discussion Paper*, no. 3396.
Boeri, T. and P. Garibaldi (2007): 'Two tier reforms of employment protection: a honeymoon effect?', Economic Journal, Vol. 117, 357–85.
Booth, A.L., M. Francesconi and J. Frank (2002): 'Temporary jobs: Stepping stones or dead ends', *Economic Journal*, Vol. 112, 189–213.
Breschi, S., F. Malerba and L. Orsenigo (2000): 'Technological regimes and Schumpeterian patterns of innovation', in: *Economic Journal*, Vol. 110: 288–410.
Buchele, R. and J. Christiansen (1999): 'Labor relations and productivity growth in advanced capitalist economies' *Review of Radical Political Economics*, Vol. 31: 87–110.
Hall, P.A. and D. Soskice (2001): *Varieties of Capitalism*, Oxford University Press.
Howell, D.R., D. Baker, A. Glyn and J. Schmitt, (2007): 'Are protective labor market institutions really at the root of unemployment?', *Capitalism and Society*, Vol. 2: 1–71.
Huselid, M. (1995): 'The impact of human resource management practices on turnover, productivity and corporate financial performance', *Academy of Management Journal*, Vol. 38: 635–670.
Irvin, G. (2011): 'Inequality and recession in Britain and the US', *Development and Change*, Vol. 42: 154–182.
Kleinknecht, A. (1998): 'Is labour market flexibility harmful to innovation?', *Cambridge Journal of Economics*, Vol. 22: 387–396.
Kleinknecht, A., R.M. Oostendorp, M.P. Pradhan and C.W.M. Naastepad (2006): 'Flexible labour, firm performance and the Dutch job creation miracle', *International Review of Applied Economics*, Vol. 20: 171–187.
Lucidi, F. and A. Kleinknecht (2010): 'Little innovation, many jobs: An econometric analysis of the Italian labour productivity crisis', *Cambridge Journal of Economics*, Vol. 34: 525–546.

Lorenz, E.H. (1999): 'Trust, contract and economic cooperation', *Cambridge Journal of Economics*, Vol. 23: 301–316.

Maki, D.M. and M.G. Palumbo (2001): *Disentangling the wealth effect: a cohort analysis of household saving in the 1990s*, Washington, DC: Federal Reserve.

Malcomson, J.M. (1997): 'Contracts, hold-up, and labor markets', *Journal of Economic Literature*, Vol. 35: 1916–1957.

McGinnity, F. and Mertens, A. (2004): 'Wages and wage growth of fixed-term workers in East and West Germany', *Applied Economics Quarterly*, Vol. 50: 139–63.

Michie, J. and M. Sheehan (2001): 'Labour market flexibility, human resource management and corporate performance', *British Journal of Management*, Vol. 12: 287–306.

Michie, J. and M. Sheehan (2003): 'Labour market deregulation, 'flexibility' and innovation', *Cambridge Journal of Economics*, Vol. 27: 123–143.

Naastepad, C.W.M. and A. Kleinknecht (2004): 'The Dutch productivity slowdown: The culprit at last?' *Structural Change and Economic Dynamics*, Vol. 15 (2004), pp. 137–163.

Naastepad, C.W.M. and Storm, Servaas (2006): 'The innovating firm in a societal context: Labour-management relations and labour productivity' in: R.M. Verburg, J.R. Ortt and W.M. Dicke, eds., *Managing technology and innovation*. London: Routledge.

Nickell, S. and R. Layard (1999): 'Labour market institutions and economic performance', in: O. Ashenfelter and D. Card (editors): *Handbook of labour economics* (ch. 46), Elsevier Science.

Nickell, S., L. Nunziata and W. Ochel (2005): 'Unemployment in the OECD since the 1960s. What do we know?', *Economic Journal*, Vol. 115 (January): 1–27.

OECD (2003): More jobs but less productive? The impact of labour market policies on productivity. Chapter 2, in *OECD Employment Outlook 2003*, Paris: OECD.

Palley, T. (2009): *America's exhausted paradigm: macroeconomic causes of the financial crisis and the great recession*, New American Contract Policy Paper. Washington, DC: New America Foundation.

Picchio, M. (2006): 'Wage Differentials between Temporary and Permanent Workers in Italy', *Quaderni del Dipartimento di Economia dell'Universita' Politecnica delle Marche*, no. 257.

Pieroni, L. and F. Pompei (2008): Evaluating innovation and labour market relationships: the case of Italy, *Cambridge Journal of Economics*, Vol. 32 (2): 325–47.

Sànchez, R. and L. Toharia (2000): 'Temporary workers and productivity', *Applied Economics*, Vol. 32: 583–591.

Scarpetta, S. and T. Tressel (2004): 'Boosting productivity via innovation and adoption of new technologies: any role for labor market institutions?', *Policy Research Working Paper Series* 3273, Washington DC.: World Bank.

Storm, S. and Naastepad, C.W.M. (2009): 'Labor market regulation and productivity growth: evidence for twenty OECD countries (1984–2004)', *Industrial Relations*, Vol. 48: 629–654.

Storm, S. and C.W.M. Naastepad (2012): *Macroeconomics beyond the NAIRU*, Cambridge, MA: Harvard University Press.

Svensson, S. (2011): 'Flexible working conditions and decreasing levels of trust', *Employee Relations*, Vol. 34 (2): 126–137.

Sylos Labini, P. (1984): *The Forces of Economic Growth and Decline*, Cambridge, MA: MIT Press.

Sylos Labini, P. (1993): *Progresso Tecnico e Sviluppo Ciclico*, Bari: Laterza.

Sylos Labini, P. (1999): 'The employment issue: investment, flexibility and the competition of developing countries', *BNL Quarterly Review*, Vol. 210: 257–280.

Vergeer, R. (2010): *Labour market flexibility, productivity and employment*, PhD thesis, TU Delft.

Vergeer, R. and A. Kleinknecht (2011): 'The impact of labor market deregulation on productivity: A panel data analysis of 19 OECD countries (1960–2004)', *Journal of Post-Keynesian Economics*, Vol. 33 (2), pp. 369–404.

Vergeer, R. and A. Kleinknecht (2012a): 'Do flexible labor markets indeed reduce unemployment?' in *Review of Social Economy* Vol. LXX (December), pp. 451–467.

Vergeer, R. and A. Kleinknecht (2012b): Does labor market deregulation reduce labor productivity growth? A panel data analysis of 20 OECD countries (1960–2004); unpublished manuscript, TU Delft, March 2012.

Zhou, H., R. Dekker and A. Kleinknecht (2011): 'Flexible labor and innovation performance: evidence from longitudinal firm-level data', *Industrial and Corporate Change* Vol. 20 (3), pp. 941–968.

9 The unemployment impact of financial crises

Enrico Marelli and Marcello Signorelli

1 Introduction

The last financial crisis had significant effects on labour markets in the world: although delayed, in many countries they have shown a high degree of persistence. The response has been differentiated across countries as a consequence of different labour market institutions: where flexible labour markets are dominant the increase in unemployment has been quick and large; on the contrary in other countries – especially where internal flexibility (such as labour hoarding practices or working hours adjustments) has substituted for the external one – the immediate impact has been smaller.

We argue in this chapter that, apart from the mentioned institutional differences, a typical feature of financial crises is that they are likely to lead to larger effects – compared to normal recessions – because the huge falls in production are accompanied by a generalised "systemic" uncertainty. We have proposed a theoretical model in order to econometrically estimate the impact of different types of financial crises on the unemployment rates. Our model is able to detect if the impact of a financial crisis on labour market dynamics goes beyond its effect passing through GDP changes (i.e. the so-called Okun's Law).

The model has been applied to data concerning a large panel of countries in the world and to the period 1980–2005. Our model is also able to distinguish the specific impact of particular types of financial crises: non-systemic banking crisis, systemic banking crisis, currency crisis, and sovereign debt crisis. The detailed theoretical and econometric model is available upon request (see Bartolucci *et al.* 2011): the econometric results confirm the additional effect – with respect to that passing through GDP growth declines – arising from financial crises, probably as a consequence of the increase in the degree of systemic uncertainty. The empirical results are presented in this chapter in a simplified way, i.e. according to alternative numerical simulations under different scenarios of GDP change.

We think that the channels emphasized in our theoretical framework and econometric model – although concerning past financial crises – are also useful to understand the labour market impact of the last financial crisis. Thus, according to our empirical results, it is extremely important that policy and regulatory makers should be fully aware of the impact of financial crises, not only for their effect on unemployment passing through falls in production, but also for the possible existence of an additional significant negative effect on labour demand, caused by the increase in the degree of systemic uncertainty.

The structure of the chapter is as follows. In Section 2 we present the key features of the labour market impact consequent to the last financial crisis and Great Recession. In Section 3 there is a review of the literature on Okun's law and on the role of uncertainty. Our theoretical framework and the operational model are briefly presented in Section 4; they are used in the empirical estimations concerning the impact of previous financial crises. Section 5 concludes, providing some policy hints.

2 The labour market impact of 2007–8 financial crisis and consequent Great Recession

In this section we discuss the evidence on the labour market performance after the 2007–8 financial crisis and the consequent Great Recession, briefly considering the different world regions and then focusing on developed economies, especially the EU-27 countries.

Considering a global perspective, the analysis of labor market performance requires many indicators, all of which differ in their importance according to the level of development of a country (e.g. Brada and Signorelli, 2012). Thus the concept of "working poverty" is more important for less-developed or emerging economies while the unemployment rate is the main indicator in developed countries.

In Table 9.1 some comparative data are presented for the main world regions and for selected years. Comparing the more recent available data (2010) with the initial condition (2007), the world labour market performance worsened in terms of both the unemployment rate (UR) and the employment-to-population ratio (ER), while working poverty continued its previous declining trend. More in detail, the world evolution of the first two indicators was mainly determined by the deteriorated performance in "developed economies and EU".

We recall that the last crisis began as financial crisis at the end of 2007; its deepest impact (with the Lehman Brothers default), was in September 2008, when the real effects initially developed and led to increasing unemployment rates during 2009. The real effects (on production, income, trade, etc.) of financial crises are always lagged and the labour market effects are even more lagged. In the following years top values for the unemployment rates were achieved (especially in the EU) and after a slight contraction they increased again – due to the deceleration in growth rates caused by the sovereign debt crisis – before the end of 2011. Similarly to past crises, a certain degree of persistence of unemployment rate has been shown in many countries, due to phenomena of "hysteresis" (upward shift in the "structural unemployment").

In the next Table 9.2, data on unemployment rates are shown for the EU countries, US, and Japan. Remarkable differences emerge, but a general upward

Table 9.1 Labour market performance in world regions (selected years and indicators)

	Unemployment rate			Employment-to-population ratio*			Working poverty**		
	2000	2007	2010	2000	2007	2010	2000	2007	2010
World	6.3	5.5	6.1	61.2	61.2	60.2	45.9	33.1	30.2
Developed Economies and European Union	6.7	5.8	8.8	56.6	57.1	55.0	–	–	–
Central and South Eastern Europe	10.8	8.4	9.5	52.5	53.5	53.5	13.0	5.5	4.8
East Asia	4.4	3.8	4.1	72.7	71.3	70.4	53.2	25.6	19.1
South East Asia and the Pacific	5.0	5.5	4.8	66.9	66.2	66.7	60.5	38.3	33.0
South Asia	4.4	3.8	3.9	57.2	57.2	54.9	81.2	70.8	68.7
Latin America and the Caribbean	8.6	7.0	7.2	58.5	60.9	61.4	15.1	10.4	9.1
Middle East	10.5	10.3	9.9	41.1	42.6	42.7	8.3	8.0	6.8
North Africa	13.6	10.1	9.6	41.8	43.8	44.2	32.7	28.4	26.5
Sub Sahara Africa	9.2	8.1	8.2	63.3	64.4	64.4	75.7	67.0	63.2

Source: ILO (2012).

Notes
* Calculated on overall population; ** Working poverty (below US$2, share in total employment) as % share in total employment.

shift is very clear in 2009 and 2010 (followed by a prevailing persistence in 2011 and 2012). In particular, the unemployment rate in EU-27 increased from 7.1 per cent in 2008 to 9.7 per cent in 2011 and it is expected to persist at similar levels in 2012. In the US, the unemployment rate started its huge increase an year earlier and, rising from a lower level with respect to EU-27, reached a maximum in 2010 (9.6 per cent) then partly declined in 2011 (8.9 per cent) and is expected to persist around the 9 per cent level in 2012. Finally, the Japanese unemployment rate moderately increased in 2008–9 but remained at a much lower level with respect to EU-27 and the US.

The EU average unemployment rates are the result of remarkable differences across countries (and regions).[1] In 2011 the highest unemployment rates were recorded in Spain (21.7 per cent), Greece (16.6 per cent), Lithuania (15.4 per cent), Ireland (14.4 per cent), Slovakia (13.4 per cent) and Portugal (12.9 per cent), while the lowest rates have been experienced in the Netherlands (4.4 per cent), Austria (4.2 per cent) and Germany (5.9 per cent).

A huge literature exists on the possible "institutional" explanations of the (medium-long run) differences in labour market performance in developed economies (e.g. OECD, 1994; Scarpetta, 1996; Nickell, 1997; Blanchard and Wolfers, 2000; Nickell *et al.*, 2005; Blanchard, 2006; Bassanini and Duval, 2009; Feldmann, 2009; Destefanis and Mastromatteo, 2010; Arpaia and Curci, 2010; Bernal-Verdugo *et al.*, 2012). In addition, a growing number of studies focus on the factors explaining the different impact of last crisis (e.g. Scarpetta *et al.*, 2010; Marelli *et al.*, 2012a and 2012b; O'Higgins, 2012). A complete review and discussion of the above mentioned literature goes beyond the aim of this chapter. We just highlight that, especially during the last crisis, the short-term impact on unemployment has been generally smaller in countries with high employment protection legislation (EPL), low diffusion of temporary contracts, large use of labour-hoarding practices and "internal flexibility".[2] However, the effectiveness of the working-time agreements (and more generally of "internal flexibility") crucially depends on the duration of the recession phase and on the institutional framework in which they are inserted (e.g. Aricò and Stein, 2012; Calavrezo and Lodin, 2012).

In any case, after almost five years from the beginning of the financial crisis (which began with the sub-prime crisis in the US), dramatic problems continue to exist because of the persistence of the impact on labour markets (in particular the transformation of cyclical unemployment in structural unemployment) and the pernicious effects on the weakest segments of the population (e.g. young people).

The diffuse persistence in 2010–12 of high unemployment rates is particularly evident in the Eurozone countries, where the sovereign debt crisis and restrictive fiscal policies caused further declines in GDP growth rates or even new recessions (this happened in several countries at the beginning of 2012).

To assess the incidence of structural unemployment, the long-term unemployment rate (LTUR) is the most used indicator: it refers to the incidence (on the labour force) of people unemployed for more than 12 months. Notice, first of all,

Table 9.2 Unemployment rates in EU countries, US and Japan (2000 and 2007–2012)

	2000	2007	2008	2009	2010	2011	2012*
EU-27	8.7	7.2	7.1	9.0	9.7	9.7	9.8
EU-15	7.7	7.1	7.2	9.2	9.6	9.5	9.7
Euro area (17)	8.5	7.6	7.6	9.6	10.1	10.2	10.1
United States	4.0	4.6	5.8	9.3	9.6	8.9	9.0
Japan	4.7	3.9	4.0	5.1	5.1	4.6	4.8
Austria	3.6	4.4	3.8	4.8	4.4	4.2*	4.5
Belgium	6.9	7.5	7.0	7.9	8.3	7.2	7.7
Bulgaria	16.4	6.9	5.6	6.8	10.2	11.1	11.3
Cyprus	4.8	4.0	3.6	5.3	6.2	7.8	7.5
Czech Rep.	8.7	5.3	4.4	6.7	7.3	6.8	7.0
Denmark	4.3	3.8	3.3	6.0	7.4	7.6	7.3
Estonia	13.6	4.7	5.5	13.8	16.9	12.5	11.2
Finland	9.8	6.9	6.4	6.2	8.4	7.8	7.7
France	9.0	8.4	7.8	9.5	9.8	9.7	10.0
Germany	7.5	8.7	7.5	7.8	7.1	5.9	5.8
Greece	11.2	8.3	7.7	9.5	12.6	16.6*	18.4
Hungary	6.4	7.4	7.8	10.0	11.2	10.9	11.0
Ireland	4.2	4.6	6.3	11.9	13.7	14.4	14.3
Italy	10.1	6.1	6.7	7.8	8.4	8.1*	8.2
Latvia	13.7	6.0	7.5	17.1	18.7	15.0*	13.5
Lithuania	16.4	4.3	5.8	13.7	17.8	15.4	13.3
Luxembourg	2.2	4.2	4.9	5.1	4.6	4.8	4.8
Malta	6.7	6.4	5.9	7.0	6.9	6.4	6.8
Netherlands	3.1	3.6	3.1	3.7	4.5	4.4	4.7
Poland	16.1	9.6	7.1	8.2	9.6	9.7	9.2
Portugal	4.5	8.1	7.7	9.6	12.0	12.9	13.6
Romania	6.8	6.4	5.8	6.9	7.3	7.4	7.8
Slovakia	18.8	11.1	9.5	12.0	14.4	13.4	13.2
Slovenia	6.7	4.9	4.4	5.9	7.3	8.1	8.4
Spain	11.1	8.3	11.3	18.0	20.1	21.7	20.9
Sweden	5.6	6.1	6.2	8.3	8.4	7.5	7.4
UK	5.4	5.3	5.6	7.6	7.8	8.1	8.6

Source: Eurostat online database.

Note
* European Commission, Autumn 2011, Forecasts.

that LTUR was persistently much higher in Europe than in the US, but the gap declined in recent years (Table 9.3). The increase of LTUR was from 2.6 per cent in 2008 to 3.9 per cent in 2010 in the EU-27, while it rose from 0.6 per cent to 2.8 per cent in the US. Secondly, across EU countries differences in LTUR are also noteworthy: in 2010 it was particularly high in Slovakia (9.2 per cent), Latvia (8.4 per cent), Estonia (7.7 per cent), Lithuania (7.4 per cent), Spain (7.3 per cent) and Ireland (6.7 per cent), while the lowest values were recorded in Austria (1.1 per cent), Netherlands (1.2 per cent), Denmark (1.4 per cent) and Sweden (1.5 per cent). Furthermore, the increase over 2008–10 was particularly severe in Lithuania (from 1.2 per cent to 7.4 per cent), Estonia (from 1.7 per cent

Table 9.3 Long term unemployment rates (2000 and 2007–2010)

	2000	2007	2008	2009	2010
EU-27	4.0	3.1	2.6	3.0	3.9
EU-15	3.5	2.9	2.6	3.0	3.8
Euro area-17	4.2	3.4	3.0	3.4	4.3
United States	0.2	0.5	0.6	1.5	2.8
Japan	1.2	1.2	1.3	1.4	1.9
Belgium	3.7	3.8	3.3	3.5	4.1
Bulgaria	9.4	4.1	2.9	3.0	4.8
Czech Republic	4.2	2.8	2.2	2.0	3.0
Denmark	0.9	0.6	0.4	0.5	1.4
Germany	4.1	4.9	4.0	3.5	3.4
Estonia	6.3	2.3	1.7	3.8	7.7
Ireland	1.6	1.3	1.7	3.4	6.7
Greece	6.2	4.2	3.6	3.9	5.7
Spain	4.6	1.7	2.0	4.3	7.3
France	3.5	3.4	2.9	3.4	3.9
Italy	6.3	2.9	3.1	3.5	4.1
Cyprus	1.2	0.7	0.5	0.6	1.3
Latvia	7.9	1.6	1.9	4.6	8.4
Lithuania	8.0	1.4	1.2	3.2	7.4
Luxembourg	0.5	1.2	1.6	1.2	1.3
Hungary	3.1	3.4	3.6	4.2	5.5
Malta	4.5	2.7	2.5	3.0	3.2
Netherlands	0.8	1.4	1.1	0.9	1.2
Austria	1.0	1.2	0.9	1.0	1.1
Poland	7.4	4.9	2.4	2.5	3.0
Portugal	1.9	4.2	4.0	4.7	6.3
Romania	3.5	3.2	2.4	2.2	2.5
Slovenia	4.1	2.2	1.9	1.8	3.2
Slovakia	10.3	8.3	6.6	6.5	9.2
Finland	2.8	1.6	1.2	1.4	2.0
Sweden	1.4	0.9	0.8	1.1	1.5
United Kingdom	1.4	1.3	1.4	1.9	2.5

Source: Eurostat online database.

to 7.7 per cent), Latvia (from 1.9 per cent to 8.4 per cent), Ireland (from 1.7 per cent to 6.7 per cent), Spain (from 2.0 per cent to 7.3 per cent), Slovakia (from 6.6 per cent to 9.2 per cent), and Greece (from 3.6 per cent to 5.7 per cent). Much better changes, in the same period, occurred in Germany, where the LTUR declined from 4.0 per cent to 3.4 per cent, and in the Netherlands and Austria, where it increased slightly from 1.1 per cent to 1.2 per cent and from 0.9 per cent to 1.1 per cent respectively.

Finally, let us compare the evolutions in terms of youth unemployment rate (YUR), i.e. the unemployment rate of people in the 15–24 years range. The YUR in 2011 was 21.4 per cent in the EU-27, 17.3 per cent in the US and 8.2 per cent in Japan (Table 9.4). The YUR also differed among European countries; in the

Table 9.4 Youth unemployment rate (2000 and 2007–2011)

	2000	2007	2008	2009	2010	2011
EU-27	*17.5*	*15.7*	*15.8*	*20.1*	*21.1*	*21.4*
EU-15	*15.2*	*15.2*	*15.7*	*19.9*	*20.5*	*20.7*
Euroarea-17	*16.8*	*15.5*	*16.0*	*20.2*	*20.9*	*20.9*
United States	*9.3*	*10.5*	*12.8*	*17.6*	*18.4*	*17.3*
Japan	*9.1*	*7.7*	*7.3*	*9.1*	*9.3*	*8.2*
Belgium	16.7	18.8	18.0	21.9	22.4	19.9
Bulgaria	33.7	15.1	12.7	16.2	23.2	26.0
Czech Republic	17.8	10.7	9.9	16.6	18.3	18.2
Denmark	6.2	7.5	8.0	11.8	14.0	14.2
Germany	8.7	11.9	10.6	11.2	9.9	8.5
Estonia	24.4	10.0	12.0	27.5	32.9	22.3
Ireland	6.7	8.9	13.3	24.4	27.8	29.2
Greece	29.1	22.9	22.0	25.7	32.8	-
Spain	22.9	18.2	24.6	37.8	41.6	46.4
France	19.6	19.8	19.3	23.9	23.7	23.2
Italy	26.2	20.3	21.3	25.4	27.8	-
Cyprus	9.9	10.2	9.0	13.8	16.7	22.4
Latvia	21.4	10.7	13.1	33.6	34.5	-
Lithuania	30.6	8.2	13.4	29.2	35.1	32.9
Luxembourg	6.6	15.6	17.3	16.5	15.8	14.8
Hungary	12.4	18.0	19.9	26.5	26.6	25.9
Malta	13.7	13.9	12.2	14.4	13.1	13.6
Netherlands	6.1	7.0	6.3	7.7	8.7	7.6
Austria	5.3	8.7	8.0	10.0	8.8	-
Poland	35.1	21.7	17.3	20.6	23.7	25.8
Portugal	10.5	20.4	20.2	24.8	27.7	30.1
Romania	17.2	20.1	18.6	20.8	22.1	23.7
Slovenia	16.3	10.1	10.4	13.6	14.7	15.3
Slovakia	36.9	20.3	19.0	27.3	33.6	33.6
Finland	21.4	16.5	16.5	21.5	21.4	20.1
Sweden	10.5	19.2	20.2	25.0	25.2	22.9
United Kingdom	12.2	14.3	15.0	19.1	19.6	21.1
Norway	9.8	7.3	7.2	8.9	8.9	-

Source: Eurostat online database.

final year (2011) it was particularly low in the Netherlands (7.6 per cent) and Germany (8.5 per cent) but extremely high in Spain (46.4 per cent), Slovakia (33.6 per cent), Lithuania (32.9 per cent), Greece (32.8 per cent in 2010) and Italy (27.8 per cent in 2010). The average increase in the period 2008–10 was remarkable in several countries, with the exception of Germany.

3 Previous research on Okun's law and the role of uncertainty

We have seen in the previous section that unemployment rates significantly increased after the recent financial crises and remained at high levels until five years after the outset of the crisis; this is particularly true in the Eurozone, where the sovereign debt crisis has aggravated the macroeconomic situation and perspectives. In our opinion, two key strands of economic literature are relevant for understanding recent trends: the first one refers to the so-called Okun's law and the second one regards the role played on economic (and labour market) performance by the degree of uncertainty.

Before illustrating the above mentioned strands of literature, we must admit that it is questionable whether the unemployment rate is an appropriate and sufficient labour market indicator. The unemployment rate is a useful indicator in case of particularly bad labour market performance (it can bear macroeconomic implications also because it affects the contractual weight of employees and unions).[3] However, due to the difficulties in correctly defining "full employment", its exclusive use is questionable and the employment rate should be introduced as a complementary indicator. For some investigations, employment indicators are preferable to (or should be at least jointly considered with) unemployment indicators, for the following reasons: (i) there are well-known difficulties and differences in the statistical definitions (across countries and also over time) and in the subjective perception of the unemployment condition, especially regarding the requisite of "active search for a job"; (ii) the unemployment rate also depends on the participation rate (labour supply), which in turn partly depends on the employment rate (job opportunities), i.e. a "discouragement effect" may exist; (iii) considering the importance of the fiscal wedge on labour (social contributions and labour income tax), employment rates are also preferable indicators of the sustainability of national welfare systems; (iv) the Lisbon European strategy, confirmed by the new "Europe 2020" plan, defined total and female employment rates as the crucial objective variables that needed to be improved. In a dynamic perspective, it is easy to show that the change in the unemployment rate is compatible with different dynamics of the employment rate.[4] For example, paradoxically, a reduction in the unemployment rate is also compatible with a fall in the employment rate if the latter is accompanied by a higher reduction in the participation rate (e.g. due to discouragement effect). With these cautionary notes, we can however focus our following discussion on the unemployment rate.

Considering the first strand of literature, a wide research has been devoted to the relationships between unemployment changes and GDP dynamics, especially from a cyclical point of view.[5] Okun (1970) defined a coefficient corresponding to the rate of change of real output associated with a given change of the unemployment rate, focusing on the estimation of "potential" GDP. So, in that seminal paper, unemployment was seen as the exogenous variable and real GDP growth as the dependent variable.

In much empirical research estimating the Okun coefficient, causality is mostly assumed to be in the opposite direction, i.e. changes in output explain variations in unemployment (or employment). Okun's text-book versions explicate a numerical relation between GDP growth (above the "normal" rate g^*_y)

and the unemployment rate (u) changes; a change in output leads to a less than proportional change in unemployment:

$$u_t - u_{t-1} = -\theta(g_{yt} - g_y^*)$$

The intensity of the relation (θ) varies between countries and is unstable over time. It also depends on EPL, labour contracts, and other institutional features. During recessions, "labour hoarding" practices imply that the change in unemployment can be small; in that case productivity may actually decline.[6] During recoveries, productivity gains follow, but employment remains stagnant.

Let us now comment on some key empirical studies. Prachowny (1993) considered the theoretical foundation of Okun's law and derived empirical evidence for the US, supporting the view that the Okun equation is a useful proxy in macroeconomics. Erber (1994) estimated the Okun equation for a number of OECD countries, finding a significant negative correlation between unemployment and growth. Padalino and Vivarelli (1997) found that the Okun equation is valid for G-7 countries and that the growth-employment link in manufacturing is stronger than for the total economy. Blinder (1997) counted the relation between unemployment and growth among the principles of macroeconomics in which "we should all believe", but he also argued that a simple relation between the percentage change of output and the absolute change in unemployment rates is "atheoretical, if not indeed antitheoretical". Baker and Schmitt (1999) estimated the Okun coefficient for a panel of OECD countries and found that: (i) employment intensity of growth was higher in the 1990s than in previous periods, and (ii) foreign growth is a crucial variable for domestic employment dynamics. Lee (2000) estimated the Okun equation for all OECD countries; he stressed that the relationship is not stable over time and differs across countries, but concluded that the impact of growth on employment is still valid. Solow (2000) argued that a good deal of European unemployment was due to lack of demand, thus the use of the Okun equation was appropriate. In short, notwithstanding the various empirical results, many studies suggest that the link between (un)employment and growth is still a useful macroeconomic "rule of thumb".[7]

Many others researches investigated different aspects related to Okun's law.[8] Also a very recent empirical literature refers to it. For example, IMF (2010) examines the role of institutions and policies in explaining changes in Okun's law across countries and over time; Beaton (2010) investigates the stability of Okun's law for Canada and the United States; an asymmetric behaviour in Okun's law over the business cycle has also been detected (in particular, the unemployment rate typically increases by more during recessions than it falls during expansions). In particular, IMF (2010) relates the Okun's coefficients – i.e. the elasticity of the unemployment rate with respect to output – to some key labour market reforms: EPL, unemployment benefits, temporary employment contracts; also wage flexibility (with a more decentralised wage system) may be important. Moreover, the response during recoveries may differ from that during recessions because of: (i) financial crises and stress, (ii) sectoral shocks, (iii) uncertainty, (iv) policies.[9] Gordon (2010) argues that tendency of aggregate hours to grow slowly and productivity to grow rapidly in an output recovery has exhibited a significant change in magnitude over successive business cycles from those predicted by Okun's law. He shows that aggregate hours before 1986 responded to cyclical deviations by almost 2/3 as much, whereas now the response is close to 1.25; on the other hand, productivity no longer shows pro-cyclical fluctuations at all, leaving modern real business cycle literature obsolete.

Finally, Elsby *et al.* (2010) claim that Okun's law performed remarkably well in the first part of the 2007 recession through the first quarter of 2009; however, the last nine months of 2009 witness a departure from the rule since the overall economic activity rebounded but unemployment continued to rise. They attribute this divergence between employment and output to the high level of average labour productivity growth during the period.

Concerning the impact of economic and financial crises, Fallon and Lucas (2002) address the question of how even short-lived crises impact on labour markets. They argue that the financial crises of the 1990s resulted in cuts in real wages though employment was only slightly affected. In sharp contrast, Hall (2010) argues that in the recent crisis the employment situation could not improve because of the poor bargaining ability of the employers. Some other characteristics can be emphasized: for example, Cerra and Sexana (2008) document that large output losses associated with financial crises are highly persistent (only less than 1 percentage point of the deepest output losses is regained by the ten years following a crisis).

Turning now to the second and rather assorted strand of literature, we can state that "uncertainty" is a persisting factor characterizing the functioning of the economic systems and conditioning the behaviour of economic agents. In this context, financial crises produce a certain increase in the degree of (systemic) uncertainty. In particular, many studies investigate, especially from a theoretical point of view, the role of uncertainty (and its changes) in affecting the functioning of economic systems, also through the conditioning of firm's behaviour. Here we only consider a small part of the literature and, in particular, the seminal works and some of the more recent researches.

As for the ground-breaking researches, we just recall Knight's (1921) distinction between risk and uncertainty and Keynes's (1936) considerations on the "weight of argument" and the preference for liquidity. In the more recent literature, many authors consider the role of uncertainty, especially in a post-keynesian perspective (e.g. Dow and Hillard, 1995 and 2002). Vercelli (2002) distinguishes the soft uncertainty from the strong (or hard) uncertainty and explores the interaction between rationality and learning. Sordi and Vercelli (2010) discuss the process of formation and revision of expectations in light of Keynes's epistemological view of the behaviour of "bounded" rational agents under conditions of strong uncertainty.[10] Some researches (e.g. Jones and Ostroy, 1984; Kreps, 1979; Marshak and Nelson, 1962) previously investigated the relationship between uncertainty and flexibility and, in particular, showed how an increase in the degree of uncertainty suggests the adoption of more flexible strategies, i.e. solutions permitting a higher set of options. Bernanke (1983), Pindyck (1991) and Dixit and Pindyck (1993) analyse the effect of uncertainty on investment decisions by considering the role played by irreversibility. For example, if an investment has some characteristic of "irreversibility", due to the existence of "sunk costs", an increase in the degree of uncertainty will probably suggest to delay the realisation of that investment, waiting for a reduction of uncertainty and an increase in the value of the Keynes' "weight of argument".

In other researches the uncertainty is related to some aspects of labour markets (e.g. Malcom *et al.*, 2002). Signorelli (1990 and 1997) analyses the impact of changes in the degree of uncertainty on (desired and actual) labour demand. He considers the firms' hiring decisions as a sort of investment (in "human capital") with a certain degree of irreversibility due to sunk costs (e.g. selection and training costs) and institutional factors (firing costs). An increase in the degree of uncertainty, as showed in some of the literature previously recalled, negatively affects the investment with a certain degree of irreversibility and, consequently, also (desired and actual) labour demand can be affected by changes in the degree of uncertainty.[11]

Financial crises present times of heightened uncertainty, but the intensity depends on the features and extent of the crisis. It is obvious that national financial crises are very different from international financial crises. For example, according to Bordo (2006) and Reinhart and Rogoff (2008a, 2008b, 2009), there were eight episodes of major international financial crisis since 1870.

There is already a literature focusing on the last financial crisis. Hurd and Susan (2010) present household expectations and uncertainty of US households in the aftermath of crisis. Huynh *et al.* (2010) discuss why labour markets' recovery in Asia lagged behind the output growth after the recent crisis. Even papers emphasizing the importance of neo-classical growth models for the prediction of unemployment rates and GDP growth during the financial crisis,[12] find that – due to "uncertainties" ensuing from the crisis – the labor usage per capita could get further worse and will remain below pre-recession levels (see e.g Mulligan, 2010). Hall (2010) argues that while current macroeconomic models predict declines in real GDP and employment correctly, they are unable to show the failure of economies to recover after subsiding of the financial crisis.

All in all, a financial crisis is surely a situation in which the degree of uncertainty increases, thus leading to the mentioned effects on investment, labour demand and also unemployment.

4 Extended Okun's model: an application to previous financial crises

Starting from the standard Okun's law (reviewed in the previous section), we emphasize the need to include a possible supplementary impact on the labour market – additional to that caused by the fall in production predicted by the Okun's equation – arising from financial crises. We argue that such crises produce an increase in "systemic uncertainty" causing (immediately or with short lags) a greater labour market impact.

In our view, therefore, financial crises can have a greater impact on the labour market with respect to simple economic recessions, because of their greater effect in increasing uncertainty and, through this additional channel, in further reducing (desired and actual)[13] labour demand.[14] For example, a firm facing a higher degree of uncertainty (causing less reliable expectations on future budgets and profits) is likely to reduce investment in "employment" (e.g. decreasing or delaying hirings or changing the turnover management), especially if characterized by high sunk costs (i.e. search, selection and training costs) or high degree of irreversibility (due to relevant firing costs).

So, in the proposed theoretical framework changes in unemployment are first explained by changes in GDP (consistently with Okun's Law) but, in addition, we consider a possible supplementary effect peculiar to "financial crises". We interpret this effect as due to an increase in the degree of systemic uncertainty.

We can represent our approach in a schematic way with the help of the Figure 9.1.

While in the traditional approach the econometric investigations emphasise the link between GDP changes and (un)employment changes (possibly including the role of labour market institutions), in our approach we stress the additional effect that financial crises cause on unemployment due to the significant increase of uncertainty.

In order to get robust econometric results, we also suggest to control for many relevant aspects and variables[15]: (i) the "persistence" in the dynamics of the unemployment rate is captured by the lagged values of the dependent variable (unemployment); (ii) the lagged effect of GDP dynamics on labour market indicators (e.g. due to labour "institutions" and labour hoarding strategies) is captured by the lagged values of GDP changes; (iii) the existence of cross country "institutional and structural" differences is controlled by the adoption of country specific parameters.[16]

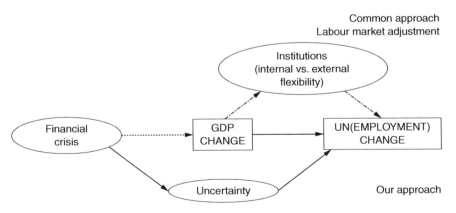

Figure 9.1 Channels of transmission of financial crisis to (un)employment.

The theoretical and econometric[17] model is fully illustrated and discussed in Bartolucci et al. (2011).[18] The estimation refers – for the period 1980–2005 – to an initial large sample of over 200 countries in the world, reduced to a little more than 70 because of data availability.[19]

As to the definition of financial crisis, we use the definition adopted in Honohan and Laeven (2005), that consider as financial crisis the occurrence of: (i) either a "systemic banking crisis" (when a country's corporate and financial sector experiences a large number of defaults and financial institutions and corporations face great difficulties repaying contracts on time) or (ii) a "non-systemic banking crisis" (e.g. a crisis limited to a small number of banks); moreover, we also consider two additional types of crises: (iii) currency and (iv) sovereign debt crises. Data are taken from Laeven and Valencia (2008).

After the estimation of the relevant parameters,[20] in order to better interpret the results under the model previously selected, we computed the expected increase of the percentage unemployment rate – under different scenarios – corresponding to different values of the GDP percentage change; in order to give stability to these predictions, only significant regression coefficients are considered.

The meaning of the presented results is the following. While, for instance, a 5 per cent fall in GDP leads normally to 1.27 per cent increase in the unemployment rate (this is the "standard" effect of a recession without financial crises), in presence of financial crises there is an additional effect, causing a greater increase in unemployment.[21] The additional effect is estimated to be equal to 1.61 per cent in case of a Non-systemic bank crisis, 1.72 per cent with a Systemic bank crisis, etc. The highest effect (with a combination of the two crises at different lags) is 2.72 per cent, i.e. about a 1.5 per cent additional impact on unemployment relative to the "no crises" scenario. Please also note that – in case of Systemic bank crisis – an (hypothetical) positive GDP growth at 5 per cent would not be sufficient to reduce the unemployment rate.

Table 9.5 Simulation results in terms of evolution of the unemployment rate due to an increase of the GDP and presence/absence of specific financial crises

Scenario	GDP increase rate										
	−5.0	−4.0	−3.0	−2.0	−1.0	0.0	1.0	2.0	3.0	4.0	5.0
No crises	1.27	1.10	0.92	0.74	0.57	0.39	0.23	0.07	−0.09	−0.25	−0.41
Crisis 1	1.61	1.44	1.26	1.08	0.90	0.73	0.57	0.41	0.25	0.09	−0.07
Crisis 2	1.72	1.54	1.36	1.18	1.01	0.83	0.67	0.51	0.35	0.19	0.04
Crisis 3	1.95	1.77	1.59	1.41	1.24	1.06	0.90	0.74	0.58	0.42	0.26
Crisis 1 + 2	2.05	1.88	1.70	1.52	1.35	1.17	1.01	0.85	0.69	0.53	0.37
Crisis 1 + 3	2.28	2.11	1.93	1.75	1.58	1.40	1.24	1.08	0.92	0.76	0.60
Crisis 2 + 3	2.39	2.21	2.03	1.86	1.68	1.50	1.34	1.18	1.02	0.86	0.71
Crisis 1 + 2 + 3	2.72	2.55	2.37	2.19	2.02	1.84	1.68	1.52	1.36	1.20	1.04

Legend
"Crisis 1" stands for Non-systemic bank crisis (lag 0). "Crisis 2" for Systemic bank crisis (lag 0). and "Crisis 3" for Systemic bank crisis (lag 1).

5 Conclusions and policy implications

In this chapter we have considered how financial crises normally have deep effects on labour markets, not only because of the consequent recessions – the fall in production reduces labour demand – but also due to the "systemic uncertainty" that further dampens down employment and increases unemployment. As a matter of fact, the results of our empirical estimates concerning past financial crises show that in several cases – especially clear in the event of Systemic and Non-systemic bank crises – there is a significant additional negative impact of the crises on unemployment rates, with respect to the mere impact of GDP changes (i.e. the simple Okun's law).

The general policy implication is that policy makers should be well aware of all the consequences of financial crises, not only for their effects on labour market passing trough the GDP changes but also for a possible additional effect due to the increase in the degree of uncertainty. During financial crises "systemic uncertainty" increases more than in normal recession (without financial crisis) and it negatively affects labour demand, with further negative effects on labour market performance. So, the macroeconomic and social costs of financial crises go well beyond their direct impact (corresponding to GDP decline).

Although our simulations and empirical estimations concerned past financial crises (for the period 1980–2005), the main findings are also helpful in understanding the impact of the most recent "global" crises (2007–8) and the channels leading to higher unemployment in most countries of the world.

In the very first (2008–9) years since the onset of the crisis, macroeconomic policies – including easy monetary policies and huge packages of "fiscal stimuli" (e.g. the Obama package in the US) – have been fundamental to avoid a grave labour market impact similar to that occurred during the Great Depression of 1930s. Afterwards, the situation in the US – and in the world in general – partially improved. However, in Europe the situation of high uncertainty (caused by the 2007–8 financial crisis) was reinforced more recently (2010–12) by the sovereign debt crisis affecting certain Eurozone countries. As a consequence, the increased uncertainty due to the risks of contagion as well as the restrictive fiscal policies, adopted to adjust public finances, are producing prospects of long recession or stagnation in several countries.

We can argue that the current high unemployment in the European context has three main components: (i) a "Keynesian" component, due to the lack of aggregate demand; (ii) a "post-Keynesian" element, caused by a high degree of systemic uncertainty; and (iii) a "structural" component, determining the persistence of the negative effects.

Concerning the first factor, we observe that fiscal stimuli are normally suggested to compensate for the lack of aggregate demand. However, in the current European context the diffuse adoption of restrictive national fiscal policies (for improving debt sustainability) is further depressing the effective demand. The very small fiscal role of the European budget (only 1 per cent of EU's GDP) and the impossibility to adopt adequate fiscal policies at the community level should be stressed.[22] Also the monetary policy – despite certain "non-conventional" measures undertaken by the ECB, such as the purchase of sovereign bonds on the secondary market and the extraordinary (3-years) re-financing operations in favour of commercial banks – has a limited role.

Considering the second element, in order to increase the credibility of fiscal policies and the sustainability of sovereign debts – an indirect way to reduce systemic uncertainty – certain institutional innovations have been introduced in the EU, such as the creation of the European Stability Mechanism (ESM)[23] and the implementation of the "Fiscal Compact". However, it seems unlikely that these innovations alone will be sufficient to reduce the risk of further contagion from the sovereign debt crisis and, especially, to improve the currently feeble GDP and employment growth prospects.

As to the "structural" component and the specific labour market problems, appropriate supply-side policies should be implemented to reduce the high and persistent unemployment rates (in addition to enhancing efficiency in labour markets and competitiveness in product markets). More specifically, active labour market policies should be targeted at the most damaged groups, for instance young people, especially with the aim of contrasting long-term unemployment.

A final policy implication, derived from both our empirical results on past financial crises and the evidence of the last multifaceted crisis, highlights the need for a better "regulatory system" and governance at the world level, or at least in the Eurozone, in order (i) to create sustainable conditions for a virtuous model of growth (able to create more and better jobs) and (ii) to contrast financial crises that – as we have discussed in this chapter – provoke huge economic and social costs, because of both economic recession and increased uncertainty.

Notes

1 For an empirical investigation of the crisis's impact on regional labour markets in Europe, see Marelli *et al.* (2012a).
2 An analysis of the different types of flexibility can be found in Eichhorst *et al.* (2010).
3 In addition, the information supplied by long-term unemployment (and the long-term unemployment rate) remains crucial in assessing labour market performance, since it is an indicator of the degree of persistence.
4 The employment rate may be defined as the complement to one of the unemployment rate (divided by 100) multiplied by the participation rate:

$$ER = \frac{E \times 100}{P_{20-64}} = \left(\frac{LF - U}{LF}\right) \times \frac{LF \times 100}{P_{20-64}} = \left(1 - \frac{UR}{100}\right) \times PR \tag{1}$$

where LF is the labour force (= employment (E) + unemployment (U)); UR is the unemployment rate (= unemployment × 100/labour force); ER is the employment rate (= employment × 100/population 20–64); and PR is the participation rate (= labour force × 100/population 20–64). Starting from equation 1, the unemployment rate may be defined as the complement to one of the ratio between employment rate and participation rate (the result multiplied by 100):

$$UR = \left(1 - \frac{ER}{PR}\right) \times 100 \qquad (2)$$

5 In a little different strand of literature, Cook and Hiromi (2005) investigate why output in developing economies may fall even as labour input remains constant during financial crises. They distinguish between formal and informal labour markets and explain this fall in output in terms of reallocation of resources from formal to informal sectors of the economy. However, it needs to be mentioned that data availability on informal labour is a missing link for carrying out such empirical studies.
6 As for the joint employment-productivity dynamics in recession, see Marelli et al. (2012b).
7 There also exists a significant literature with a critical position: for example, Flaig and Rottman (2000) criticised the Okun coefficient literature because it neglects the influence of relative prices. Indeed, they argued that the employment intensity of growth is clearly related to real labour cost; consequently, estimating a simple Okun equation is not appropriate, due to incorrect specification.
8 For example Weber (1995); Kaufman (1988); Sögner and Stiassny (2002); Knotek (2007); Huang and Lin (2008).
9 From a methodological standpoint, IMF (2010) proposes a dynamic version of Okun's law, in which the change in unemployment depends on the lagged values of the change in output, of the change in unemployment itself and some control variables (including a dummy to indicate a state of recession). An employment version of Okun's law is also estimated.
10 In particular, the authors argue that a lower "weight of argument" (i.e. a high degree of uncertainty) may be interpreted as an index of potential learning, and thus the higher the potential learning, the higher the degree of intertemporal flexibility sought by a rational agent.
11 As for an application to the Italian case in a long run perspective of structural change, see Signorelli and Vercelli (1994).
12 While there are some studies showing that the last financial crisis was the outcome of labor market imbalances and not the vice versa (see, e.g. Jagnathan et al., 2009), most of the literature has consensus that the causality runs from crisis to labour markets (see, e.g. Elsby et al., 2010; Hall, 2010 and Mulligan, 2010).
13 We do not investigate here this distinction (see, Signorelli, 1990 and 1997).
14 Two additional aspects – affecting GDP growth – are not investigated here. The first one refers to the fact that the further reduction in labour demand will reduce available income and consumption with further negative effects on GDP dynamics. The second one refers to the possible reduction of the propensity to consume due to the increase in saving in presence of higher uncertainty.
15 The traditional econometric investigations of Okun's law consider a simplified equation as the following:

$$\Delta u_{it} = \alpha_i + \Delta y_{it} \beta_i + \varepsilon_{it}$$

where the focus is on the β Okun's coefficients (dependent on labour market institutions).
16 The model to be estimated can be represented as follows:

$$\Delta u_{it} = \alpha_i + \sum_{t=0}^{L_1} \Delta y_{i,t-1} \beta_{i1} + \sum_{t=0}^{L_1} r_{i,t-1} \gamma_{i1} + \sum_{t=0}^{L_2} d_{i,t-1}^{(c)} \delta_1^{(c)} + \varepsilon_{it}$$

where $d_{it}^{(c)}$ is a dummy equal to 1 when a crisis of type c is observed for country i in period t; and $r_{i,t}$ is another dummy variable equal to 1 if there is a recession.

17 It belongs to the class of linear mixed effect models; for a review on this family of models see McCulloch et al. (2008).
18 In Bartolucci et al. (2011) the results of the initial estimations are fully reported; they are available upon request.
19 To investigate the severity of financial crisis for economies at different development levels, we initially identified five income groups (Low income, Lower middle income, Upper middle income, High income–non OECD, High income–OECD).
20 The α's, β's, γ's, δ's specified in previous endnotes, together with the choice of an optimal number of lags for each type of crisis: see again Bartolucci et al. (2011).
21 This important result is obtained – we repeat – after controlling for many aspects, like the lagged impact of GDP changes, the inertia of the dependent variable (i.e. the unemployment rate), country specific factors, etc.
22 In this context, two new European financial instruments (Eurobonds) have been proposed: (i) "project Eurobonds" for up to 6 per cent of European GDP, reflecting the idea of J. Delors, useful for realising large-scale European investments in infrastructure, R&D and human capital, thus favouring innovation, economic growth and net job creation; (ii) "stability Eurobonds", transforming a part of the national debts in the Eurozone countries, for example for an amount up to 60 per cent of national GDP, into "Eurozone guaranteed bonds", with the aim of reducing interest rates (on such bonds) and the risk of speculative attacks.
23 This will be the permanent mechanism designated to assist the individual countries, while in the 2010–12 period there was also a provisional fund ("European financial stability fund"), already used to help Greece, Ireland and Portugal.

References

Aricò F.R. and Stein U. (2012), "Was short-time work a miracle cure during the Great Recession? The case of Germany and Italy", *Comparative Economic Studies*, 54(2).

Arpaia A. and Curci N. (2010), "EU labour market behaviour during the Great Recession", Directorate General Economic and Monetary Affairs, European Commission. *European Economy – Economic Papers*, 405.

Baker D. and Schmitt J. (1999), "The Macroeconomic Roots of High Unemployment: the Impact of Foreign Growth", *Economic Policy Institute*, www.epinet.org.

Bartolucci F., Choudhry M.T., Marelli E. and Signorelli M. (2011), "Financial Crises and Labour Market: Beyond the Okun's Law", paper presented at the *16th World Congress, International Economic Association*, Tsinghua University, Beijing, July 4–8, 2011; and also at the *EACES International Workshop, University of Perugia*, November 10–11, 2011.

Bassanini A. and Duval R. (2009), "Unemployment, institutions, and reform complementarities: Re-assessing the aggregate evidence for OECD countries", *Oxford Review of Economic Policy* 25(1): 40–59.

Beaton K. (2010), "Time Variation in Okun's Law: A Canada and U.S. Comparison", Working Paper n. 7, *Bank of Canada*.

Bernal-Verdugo L.E., Furceri D. and Guillaume D. (2012), "Labor market flexibility and unemployment: new empirical evidence of static and dynamic effects", *Comparative Economic Studies* 54(2).

Bernanke B. (1983), "Irreversibility, Uncertainty and Cyclical Investment", *Quarterly Journal of Economics*, 85–106.

Blanchard O. (2006), "European unemployment: the evolution of facts and ideas", *Economic Policy* 21(45): 5–59.

Blanchard O. and Wolfers J. (2000), "The role of shocks and institutions in the rise of European unemployment: the aggregate evidence", *Economic Journal* 110(462): 1–33.

Blinder A.S. (1997), "Is there a core of practical macroeconomics that we should all believe?", *American Economic Review*, 87: 240–246.

Bloom N. (2009), "The Impact of Uncertainty Shocks," *Econometrica*, Vol. 77, No. 3, pp. 623–685.

Bordo M. (2006), "Sudden Stops, Financial Crises, and Original Sin in Emerging Countries: Déjà Vu?", *NBER Working Paper*, 12393.

Brada J.C. and Signorelli M. (2012), "Comparing Labor Market Performance: Some Stylized Facts and Key Findings", *Comparative Economic Studies* 54(2).

Calavrezo O. and Lodin F. (2012), "Short-time working arrangements in France during the crisis: an empirical analysis of firms and employees", *Comparative Economic Studies* 54(2).

Cerra V. and Saxena S.C. (2008), "Growth Dynamics: The Myth of Economic Recovery", *American Economic Review*, 98(1): 439–457.

Choudhry M.T., Marelli E. and Signorelli M. (2012), "Youth Unemployment and the Impact of Financial Crises", *International Journal of Manpower*, n. 1.

Cook, D. and Hiromi N. (2005), "Dual Labor Markets and Business Cycles", Working Paper Series 2006-36, *Federal Reserve Bank of San Francisco*.

Destefanis S. and Mastromatteo G. (2010), "Labour-market performance in the OECD: some recent cross-country evidence", *International Journal of Manpower* 31(7): 713–731.

Dixit A. and Pindyck R. (1993), *Investment under Uncertainty*, Princeton University Press.

Dow S.C. and Hillard J. (1995), (eds.), *Keynes, Knowledge and Uncertainty*, Edward Elgar, Cheltenham (UK) and Northampton, MA (USA).

Dow S.C. and Hillard J. (2002), (eds.), *Keynes, Uncertainty and the Global Economy. Beyond Keynes*, Volume Two, Edward Elgar, Cheltenham (UK) and Northampton, MA (USA).

Elsby M., Hobijn B. and Sahin A. (2010), "The Labor Market in the Great Recession," *NBER* Working Paper No. 15979.

Eichhorst W., Feil M. and Marx P. (2010), "Crisis, what crisis? Patterns of adaptation in European labor markets", *Applied Economics Quarterly* 56(61) Supplement: 29–64.

Erber G. (1994), "Verdoorn's or Okun's Law?", *German Institute for Economic Research* Discussion Paper n. 98, Berlin.

Fallon P.R. and Lucas R.E.B. (2002), "The Impact of Financial Crises on Labor Markets, Household Incomes and Poverty: A Review of Evidence", *The World Bank* Research Observer 17(1): 21–45.

Feldmann H. (2009), "The unemployment effects of labor regulation around the world", *Journal of Comparative Economics*, 37(1): 76–90.

Flaig G. and Rottmann H. (2000), "Input Demand and the Short- and the Long-Run Employment Thresholds. An Empirical Analysis for the German Manufacturing Sector", *CESifo* Working Paper, n. 264.

Gordon R.J. (2010), "Revisiting and Rethinking the Business Cycle: Okun's Law and Productivity Innovations", *American Economic Review: Papers & Proceedings*, 100: 11–15.

Hall R.E. (2010), "Why Does the Economy Fall to Pieces after a Financial Crisis?", *Journal of Economic Perspectives*, 24(4): 3–20.

Hurd M.D. and Susann R. (2010), "Effects of the Financial Crisis and Great Recession on American Households," *NBER* Working Paper No 16407.

Honohan P. and Laeven L.A. (2005), *Systemic Financial Distress: Containment and Resolution*, Cambridge University Press, Cambridge (UK).

Huang H.-C. and Lin S.-C. (2008), "Smooth-time-varying Okun's Coefficients", *Economic Modelling*, 25:363–375.

Huynh P., Kapsos S., Kim K.B. and Sziraczki G. (2010), "Impacts of Current Global Economic Crisis on Asia's Labor Market", ADBI Working Papers 243, *Asian Development Bank Institute*.

ILO (2012), *Global Employment Trends 2012 – Preventing a deeper jobs crisis*, International Labour Organization. Geneva.

IMF (2010), "Unemployment Dynamics During Recessions and Recoveries: Okun's Law and Beyond", Chapter 3 in *World Economic Outlook: Rebalancing Growth*, Washington.

Jagannathan R., Kapoor M. and Schaumburg E. (2009), "Why are we in a Recession? The Financial Crisis is the Symptom not the Disease!", *NBER* Working Paper No. 15404.

Jones R.A. and Ostroy J.M. (1984), "Flexibility and Uncertainty", *Review of Economic Studies*, 13–32.

Kannan P. and Fritzi K.-G. (2009), "The Uncertainty Channel of Contagion", *IMF* Working Paper 09/219, Washington: International Monetary Fund.

Kaufman R.T. (1988) "An International Comparison of Okun's Law", *Journal of Comparative Economics*, 12: 182–203.

Keynes J.M. (1936), *The General Theory of Employment, Interest and Money*, Macmillan, London.

Kinght F.H. (1921), *Risk, Uncertainty and Profit*, Houghton and Mifflin, Boston.

Knotek E.S. (2007), "How Useful is Okun's Law?", *Federal Reserve Bank of Kansas City Economic Review* (Fourth Quarter), pp. 73–103.

Kreps D.N. (1979), "A Representation Theorem for Preference for Flexibility", *Econometrica*, 47.

Laeven L.A. and Valencia F. (2008), "Systemic Banking Crises: A New Database", *IMF* Working Paper, 224, Washington, DC.

Lee J. (2000), "The Robustness of Okun's law: Evidence from OECD Countries", *Journal of Macroeconomics*, 22(2): 331–356.

Malcolm Sawyer M. and Shapiro N. (2002), "Market Structure, Uncertainty and Unemployment", in Dow S.C. and Hillard J. (eds.), *Keynes, Uncertainty and the Global Economy. Beyond Keynes*, Volume Two, Edward Elgar, Cheltenham (UK) and Northampton, MA (USA).

McCulloch C.E., Searle S.R. and Neuhaus J.M. (2008), *Generalized, Linear, and Mixed Models*, Wiley, Hoboken.

Marelli E., Patuelli R. and Signorelli M. (2012a), "Regional unemployment in the EU before and after the global crisis", *Post-Communist Economies* 24(2).

Marelli E., Signorelli M. and Tyrowicz J. (2012b), "Crises and joint employment-productivity dynamics: a comparative perspective for European countries", *Comparative Economic Studies* 54(2).

Marshak T. and Nelson R. (1962), "Flexibility, Uncertainty and Economic Theory", *Metroeconomica*, 42–58.

Moosa I.A. (1997), "A Cross-Country Comparison of Okun's Coefficient," *Journal of Comparative Economics*, Vol. 24, No. 3, pp. 335–356.

Mulligen C.B. (2010), "Aggregate Implications of Labor Market Distortions: The Recession of 2008–09 and Beyond", *NBER* Working Paper No. 15681.

Nickell S. (1997), "Unemployment and labor market rigidities: Europe versus North America", *The Journal of Economic Perspectives*, 11(1): 55–74.

Nickell S., Nunziata L. and Ochel W. (2005), Unemployment in the OECD since the 1960s. What do we know? *Economic Journal* 115(500): 1–27.
OECD (1994), *OECD Jobs Study*, OECD, Paris.
O'Higgins N. (2012), "This time it's different? Youth labor markets during 'The Great Recession'", *Comparative Economic Studies* 54(2).
Okun A.M. (1962), "Potential GNP: Its Measurement and Significance", *American Statistical Association*, proceedings of the Business and Economics Statistics Section, Alexandria, Virginia.
Okun A.M. (1970), "Potential GDP: its Measurement and Significance", in Okun A. (ed.) *The Political Economy of Prosperity*, Washington D.C.
Padalino S. and Vivarelli M. (1997), "The Employment Intensity of Growth in the G-7 Countries", *International Labour Review*, 136: 199–213.
Pindyck R. (1991), "Irreversibility, Uncertainty and Investment", *Journal of Economic Literature*, September.
Prachowny M.J.F. (1993), "Okun's Law: Theoretical Foundations and Revisited Estimates", *The Review of Economics and Statistics*, 30: 331–336.
Prati A. and Sbracia M. (2002), "Currency Crises and Uncertainty About Fundamentals," *IMF* Working Paper 02/3, Washington: International Monetary Fund.
Reinhart C. and Rogoff K. (2008a), "This Time Is Different: A Panoramic View of Eight Centuries of Financial Crises", *NBER* Working Paper, 13882.
Reinhart C. and Rogoff K. (2008b), "Banking Crises: An Equal Opportunity Menace", *NBER* Working Paper, 14587.
Reinhart C. and Rogoff K. (2009), "The Aftermath of Financial Crises", NBER Working Paper, n. 14656.
Scarpetta S. (1996), "Assessing the role of labour market policies and institutional settings on unemployment: a cross-country study", *OECD Economic Studies*, 26: 43–98.
Scarpetta S., Sonnet A. and Manfredi T. (2010), "Rising youth unemployment during the crisis: how to prevent negative long-term consequences on a generation?", *OECD Social, Employment and Migration Working Paper*, 6.
Signorelli M. (1990), "Incertezza, flessibilità e domanda di lavoro: un tentativo di chiarificazione concettuale", *Economia & Lavoro*, 3.
Signorelli M. (1997), "Uncertainty. Flexibility Gap and Labour Demand in the Italian Economy", *Labour*, 11, 1, 141–175.
Signorelli M. and Vercelli A. (1994), "Structural Changes in the Post-War Italian Economy", in *Economic Performance: a look at Austria and Italy*, B. Boehm and L. F. Punzo (eds.), Physica-Verlag, Heidelberg.
Signorelli M., Choudhry M. and Marelli E. (2012), "The Impact of Financial Crises on the Female Labour", *European Journal of Development Research* 24(3).
Sögner L. and Stiassny A. (2002), "An Analysis on the Structural Stability of Okun's Law: A Cross-Country Study", *Applied Economics*, 14, 1775–1787.
Solow R.M. (2000), "Unemployment in the United States and in Europe: A Contrast and the Reasons", *CESifo Working Paper*.
Sordi S. and Vercelli A. (2010), "Heterogeneous Expectations and Strong Uncertainty in a Minskyian Model of Financial Fluctuations", *DEPFID Working Papers*, n. 10.
Vercelli A. (2002), "Uncertainty, Rationality and Learning: A Keynesian Perspective", in Dow S. C. and Hillard J. (eds), *Keynes, Uncertainty and the Global Economy. Beyond Keynes*, Volume Two, Edward Elgar, Cheltenham (UK) and Northampton, MA (USA).
Weber C.E. (1995), "Cyclical Output, Cyclical Unemployment, and Okun's Coefficient: A New Approach." *Journal of Applied Economics*, 10(4): 443–445.

Index

Page numbers in *italics* denote tables, those in **bold** denote figures.

abstract forms of crisis 52
accumulation 42, 43, 52; differential 41, 42, 44, 45
accumulation regime 13, 103–4, 114; finance-dominated 98, 104, 108–13, 148–9; flexible 147; Fordist 144
Acharya, V.V. 184
Africa, unemployment *194*
aggregate demand 144, 160
AIG 4, 100
Alternative Investment Funds (AIF) 153, 155–6
Amable, B. 144–5
American Recovering and Reinvestment Act 159
Anglo-Saxon economic model 144, 145, *146*
arbitrage 52; liquidity 13
Arvantis, S. S. 185
Asian capitalism 145
asset-back securities (ABS) 3, 36, 37, 69, 105
Auer, P. 184
austerity measures 2, 12, 14, 54, 143, 144, 159–60
Australia: collective bargaining centralization *132*; financialization **147**; house prices 2; as Liberalized Market Economy (LME) 176; social expenditure **163**; trade union density *130*; unemployment *179*; unemployment expenditure **168**
Austria: collective bargaining centralization *132*; collective bargaining coverage *130*; current account **81**; debt ratios *108*; employment protection legislation (EPL) *129*; social expenditure **163**; trade union density *130*, **131**; unemployment 195, *196*, *197*, *198*; unemployment expenditure **168**
autonomization of finance 52
Autor, D.H. 185

Baker, D. 91, 126, 200
Bank of England 4, 60, 71–2
Bank for International Settlements (BIS) 70, 150
bank money 53
banking: originate and distribute model (ODM) 62, 68, 70, 74–5, 104–5; originate and hold model 62; shadow 13, 52, 55, 75, 104
banks: bail-outs 2, 101, 143, 160; bonus system 101; capital reserves requirements 151, 152, 155; default 3–4, 37; interbank lending 3, 100; liquidity crisis 3–4; liquidity standards 151, 152; non-systemic crisis 204, 205; securitization techniques 66; solvency problems 3–4; systemic crisis 204, 205; *see also* central banks
Barba, A. 128
Bartolucci, F. 204
Basel accords 73, 74, 75, 155, 161
Bassanini, A. 184
Bear-Stearns 4, 100
Beaton, K. 200
Belgium: collective bargaining centralization *132*; collective bargaining coverage *130*; current account **81**; debt ratios *108*; employment protection legislation (EPL) *129*; social expenditure **163**; trade union density *130*, **131**; unemployment *196*, *197*, *198*; unemployment expenditure **168**

Index

Berle, A. 64
Bernanke, B. 202
Black, W.K. 55
Blinder, A.S. 200
Boeri, T. 185
bonus systems 3, 101
Bordo, M. 202
Boyer, R. 148
Bretton Woods system 66
Brown, G. 150
Brunnermeir, M. 70
budget deficit 82, 89, 90, 93–4, 101; *see also* structural budget deficit rule
Bulgaria: debt ratios *108*; unemployment *196*, *197*, *198*
business cycle 113, 201; convergence 80, 82
business sector, debt 111, **112**

Canada 155; collective bargaining centralization *132*; financialization **147**; house prices 2; social expenditure **163**; trade union density *130*; unemployment *179*; unemployment expenditure **168**
capital: accumulation *see* accumulation; circuits of 49, 55; fictitious 50, 52; financial 55; functioning 51, 52; human 103, 138; money as 51, 52; productive 40, 49, 50, 52, 55; as property 51, 52, 53
capital account surplus/deficit 81
capital flows 99, 104, 109–10, 112
capital reserves 151, 152, 155
capitalism 19–39; Asian 145; commercial 42; competitive 143, 144, 145; consumer 60; Continental European 145; corporative 144; crisis of 12–13; crisis-tendencies of 40, 41, 52; debt 60; efficiency arguments for 25–7; instability and unevenness 24–7; laissez-faire 27, 31–2; money-manager 45, 55, 60, 61; periodization of 44; political 42, 48, 55, 56; rational 42, 48, 55, 56; variegated 43, 44; varieties of (VoC) 12, 14, 40, 42–4, 91, 144–5, *164*; welfare state 27–31
capitalists 21, 22, 23
Carchedi, G. 49–50
Carney, M. 46
central bank money 53
central banks 4, 80, 100, 113; independence 86; as lender of last resort 47; *see also* Bank of England; European Central Bank; Federal Reserve
Cerra, V. 201

Chick, V. 74
China 9, 47, 54; US trade deficit with 9
Chinese Minsky moment 46
Chinloy, P. 68
Choi Chonj Ju 144
Cifuentes, A. 73
collateralized debt obligations (CDO) 3, 37, 69
collateralized mortgage obligations (CMOs) 71
collective bargaining: centralization 131; coverage 130–1
commercial capitalism 42
commodity circulation 50
Commodity Futures Trading Commission (CFTC) 152
commodity money 53
communism 27, 29
communist political parties 28
competitive capitalism 143, 144, 145
Competitive Market Economy (CME) model 145, 150, 154
competitiveness policies, EMU members 95–6
computerization 32, 33, 37
Congress of Industrial Organizations (CIO) 28
consumer capitalism 60
Consumer Financial Protection Agency 151, 152
consumption: appropriate level of 160; debt-driven 1, 13, 99; norms 113
consumption credit 1, 2, 6, 37, 99, 107, 110, 113
consumption inequality 6
contagion effects 46, 48, 51, 53, 54, 205
Continental European capitalism 145
contracts, labour 14, 23, 131, 195, 200
Coordinated Market Economies (CME) 11, 175, 176; GDP growth 177, **178**, 185; hours worked **177**; labour productivity **179**, 180; unemployment 178, *179*, 186; wages 176, 185
corporative capitalism 144
corporative economic model 144, 145, *146*
corruption 55
cost–benefit analyses 26
credit 12, 40; creation 65; excess 53; self-regulating 72–6; theory of 50
credit card debt 36
credit consumption 1, 2, 6, 37, 99, 107, 110, 113
credit–debt relations 51
credit default swaps (CDS) 3, 37, 153, 156

Credit Rating Agencies (CRA) 3, 4, 62, 151, 161
criminal activity 12, 38–9
criminovation 40
crisis-management 12, 40, 41, 49
critical political economy 41
culture-economy interaction 25
currency: dollar as global 10–11; international 11
current account (CA) balance, EU **167**
current account (CA) deficit 99, 110, 113, 156; EMU members 81, 82, 92, 109; US 8–9, 10
current account (CA) imbalances, EMU members 80–2, 92–3, 109
current account (CA) surplus 99; EMU members 81, 82
cyclically adjusted budget deficit *see* structural budget deficit rule
Cyprus, unemployment *196, 197, 198*
Czech Republic, unemployment *196, 197, 198*

De Larosière Report (2009) 153
debt: business sector 111, **112**; financial sector 111, **112**; household 13, 35, 36, 99, 107, *108*, 111–12, 112–13, 127, 128; mortgage 35, 36, 46; public 8, 47, 53, 80, 82, 83, 128; sovereign 7, 47, 53, 109, 143, 193, 195, 199, 205, 206
debt capitalism 60
debt default 3–4, 12, 37, 112–13
debt servicing 98
debt-driven consumption 1, 13, 99
debt-financing 66
debt-to-GDP ratios 84, 107, *108*
debt-to-income ratios 113
default correlation 3
deflation 110
demand: aggregate 144, 160; for labour 32
democratic deficit 11
demonetized financialization 67
Denmark 6; collective bargaining centralization *132*; collective bargaining coverage *130*; debt ratios 107; employment protection legislation (EPL) *129*; financialization **147**; house prices 2; social expenditure **163**; trade union density *130*, **131**; unemployment *196, 197, 198*; unemployment expenditure **168**
deregulation: financial 1, 5, 47, 48, 61–2, 67, 74, 98, 99, 104, 105, 127, 160; labour market 126–7, 177–9, 186, 187

derivatives 52, 64, 66, 74–5, 110, 151, 153–4
developing countries 11, 109
Dirigiste economic model 144, 145, *146*
Dixit, A. 202
dollar: exchange standard 53; as global currency 10–11
Draghi, M. 85

East Asia, unemployment *194*
Eastern Europe 100
ECOFIN 153, 154
Economic and Monetary Union (EMU) 13, 79–97, 158; balanced structural budget 89–90; competitiveness policies 95–6; and convergence criteria 82; crisis, nature of 79–82; current account imbalances 80–2, 92–3, 109; economic partnership programmes 84; excessive deficit procedure (EDP) 83, 84, 85; and fiscal compact 13, 82–4, 86, 89, 206; fiscal policy 80, 93–4, 110, 158; government debt ratios 83; inflation rates 82, 95–6; Keynesian medicine for 92–6; structural budget deficit rule 83–4, 86–90; structural reforms 85, 86, 90–1; and Treaty on Stability, Coordination and Governance 82–5; *see also* Eurozone
economic/financial crisis (2007–9) 1, 11–12, 40–56; behavioural explanations 61; EU 7–8, 150–1, 153–6; institutional explanations 60–1; and labour market 127–41, 193–8; overviews 2–4, 99–102; root of 1, 4–7; structural explanations 60; and unemployment 193–8; US 8–10, 143, 145, 150, 151–3, 154–6
Economist, The 47
efficiency 25–7
Eichhorst, W. 135–6
Elsby, M. 201
employment: full 45, 89; precarious 136–7, 140; temporary 200; undeclared 141
employment protection legislation (EPL) 125, 129, 135–6, 141n3, 184, 188n4, 195, 200
employment rate 156, 199
employment services 141
employment-to-population ratio (ER) 193, *194*
'entrepreneurial' garage business innovation 183, 186
Epstein, G. 98
Erber, G. 200

Estonia: debt ratios *108*; unemployment *196*, *197*, *198*
euro 53, 109
Euro-bonds 158, 208n22
Euromarket 66
Europe 2020 plan 199
European Banking Authority (EBA) 153
European Central Bank (ECB) 4, 7, 60, 79–80, 85, 94–5, 153, 154; independence 94; as lender of last resort 95; monetary policy 80, 95
European Commission 150, 153
European Council 153
European Financial Stability Facility (EFSF) 101
European Insurance and Occupational Pensions (EIOP) 153
European Securities Markets Authority (ESMA) 153, 156
European Social Model (ESM) 6, 11, 14, 143, 145, 150, 154, 158, 160, 161
European Stability Mechanism (ESM) 206
European System of Financial Supervisors (ESFS) 153
European Systemic Risk Board (ESRB) 154
European Union (EU): current account balance **167**; Economic and Monetary Union *see* Economic and Monetary Union; and economic/financial crisis 7–8, 150–1, 153–61; fiscal stimuli 159; GDP 7, **134**, 143–4, 145, 158, 160, 161, **162**; single market 7–8; Stability and Growth Pact 79, 80, 83–4; Synthetic Vulnerability Index **157**; Treaty on Stability, Coordination and Governance in the Economic and Monetary Union 82–5; unemployment 133, **134**, **157**, 160, *194*, 195, *196*, *197*, *198*; and US trade balance **166**; varieties of capitalism 14
Eurozone 8, 13, 53, 54, 60, 101–2, 109–10, 145, 150, 160, 161, *163*, 187; labour market evolution **167**; macroeconomic variables *165*; sovereign debt crisis 205; unemployment 158, 195, 199; *see also* Economic and Monetary Union (EMU)
evolutionary political economy 12, 40, 41–2
exchange rates: crises 109; fixed 65, 66, 80; floating 80; nominal 81, 92; real 81, 92, 109; stability 82; volatility 106, 112
export-led growth 1, 5, 13, 99, 114

Fadda, S. 1–16, 123–42
Fallon, P.R. 201
Fannie Mae 4, 100
Federal Reserve (Fed) 4, 38, 127, 151, 152, 153
feudalism 20–1, 39
fiat money 53
fictitious capital 50, 52
finance, circuits of 53
Financial Activities Tax (FAT) 155
financial arbitrage 52
financial capital 55
financial crises: unemployment impact of 192–211; *see also* economic/financial crisis (2007–9)
financial innovation 1, 2–3, 6, 13, 45, 47, 51, 52, 54, 60–78, 104
financial instability hypothesis 44, 45, 46, 49, 54–5, 61–2, 70
financial liberalization 67, 99, 110, 260
financial markets 63–4; privatization of 66–7; volatility of 106
financial regulation 60–1
financial sector 104–5, 148; debt 111, **112**; deregulation of 1, 5, 47, 48, 61–2, 67, 74, 98, 99, 104, 105, 127, 160; globalization of 1, 5, 13, 109, 110, 114
Financial Stability Board (FSB) 150
Financial Stability Facility 158
Financial Stability Oversight Council 151, 152
financial transaction tax (FTT) 154, 155, 160, 161
financialization 1, 5–6, 7, 9, 54, 98–9, 102–7, 127, 145, 160–1; demonetized 67; during post-Fordism 147–50; transformations brought about by 13, 52–3, 104–7
financial-led growth 1, 7, 11–12, 148, 149–50
Finland: collective bargaining centralization *132*; collective bargaining coverage *130*; current account **81**; employment protection legislation (EPL) *129*; social expenditure *163*; trade union density *130*, **131**; unemployment *196*, *197*, *198*; unemployment expenditure **168**
firing and hiring 124, 137, 180, 181, 182, 185, 187
fiscal compact, EMU 13, 82–4, 86, 89, 206
fiscal crisis 101
fiscal policy 24, 80, 102, 205–6; EMU 80, 93–4, 110, 158; expansionary 47; restrictive 205

Index

fiscal stimuli 143, 159, 205
Fisher, I. 46
Fitch 4
fixed exchange rates 65, 66, 80, 81
floating exchange rates 80
Fordist regime 144, 145, **162**
Foucault, M. 102
France 145, 155; collective bargaining centralization *132*; collective bargaining coverage *130*; current account **81**; debt ratios *108*; employment protection legislation (EPL) *129*; financialization **147**; house prices 2; investment-to-profits ratio **106**; labour share **129**; social expenditure *163*; trade union density *130*, **131**; unemployment *179*, *197*, *198*; unemployment expenditure **168**; wage dispersion 149
Frank–Dodd Act 151, 161
fraud 40, 55
Freddie Mac 4, 100
freedom 21, 23
frictional unemployment 126
Friedman, M. 38
full employment 45, 89

G7 countries 11
G20 countries 11, 150
'garage business innovation' *183*, 186
Garibaldi, P. 185
GDP 133, 187; change 14, 192, 203; Coordinated Market Economies (CME) 177, **178**, 185; EU 7, **134**, 143–4, 145, 158, 160, 161, **162**; labour markets and 175; labour share in 124, 128, **129**, 138; labour-intensive growth 14, 186; Liberalized Market Economies (LME) 177, **178**, 185; potential 199; ratio of debt to 107, *108*; and unemployment **134**, 135, 136, 199–204, 205; US **134**, 135, 158, 160, **162**, 185; wage share of 131
Geithner, T. 150, 151
Germany 7, 8, 54, 101, 145, 155; austerity measures 159; collective bargaining centralization *132*; collective bargaining coverage *130*; current account **81**; debt ratios *108*; employment protection legislation (EPL) *129*; financialization **147**; investment-to-profits ratio **106**; labour share **129**; social expenditure **163**; trade union density *130*; unemployment 141n8, *179*, 195, *196*, *197*, *198*; unemployment expenditure **168**; wage dipersion **149**

Gini coefficients 6
global Minsky moment 46
globalization 108, 131; financial 1, 5, 13, 109, 110, 114; trade 109
GM 100
gold standard 53, 66
Goldman Sachs 4, 64
Goldsmith, R. 60
Gordon, R.J. 201
government debt *see* public debt
government intervention 23–4, 25, 38
Great Depression 46, 61, 63, 205
Greece 86, 102, 109; collective bargaining centralization *132*; current account **81**; debt ratios *108*; economic crisis 7, 8, 101; employment protection legislation (EPL) *129*; financialization **147**; labour market reforms 85; trade union density *130*; unemployment 195, *196*, *197*, *198*
Greenspan, A. 5, 68, 72
growth: export-led model of 1, 5, 13, 99, 114; financial-led model of 1, 7, 11–12, 148, 149–50; high-quality (HQG) 158; and labour productivity 14
growth-in-low-productive-jobs hypothesis 186–7

Hall, R.E. 201, 202
hedge funds 3, 37, 68, 114, 150, 151, 152, 153, 155–6, 161
hedging finance 45, 47, 51
high-quality growth (HQG) 158
Hirchleifer, J. 65
hiring and firing 124, 137, 180, 181, 182, 185, 187
Hirsch, F. 10–11
hoarding: labour 136, 138, 192, 195, 200, 203; of money 50
Honohan, P. 204
hours worked 136, 137, 138, 176, **177**, *180*, 192
household labour 34
household production 44
households: debt 13, 35, 36, 99, 107, *108*, 111–12, 112–13, 127, 128; purchasing power 127, 128; savings rate 128
housing sector 127; prices 2, 35–6, 99, 107
human capital 103, 138
human resources management (HRM) 14, 184
Hungary 100; debt ratios *108*; trade union density *130*; unemployment *196*, *197*, *198*
Hurd, M.D. 202

Huynh, P. 202
hysteresis 193

immigration, US 19, 31, 32–3
income distribution 1, 6, 13, 37, 107, 148, 158, 161, 178–9; equalization of 138; polarization of 98, 99, 108–9, 113–14
income inequality 1, 5, 6, 9, 12, 13, 108, 128, 138, 148, 175, 178–9, 185
income tax 94
inequality 113–14, 145; consumption 6; income 1, 5, 6, 9, 12, 13, 108, 128, 138, 148, 178–9, 185; wealth 6, 12, 114
inflation 80, 109, 110; above target 88; below target 88
inflation rates 82
inflation targeting 95
informal labour 44
innovation: financial 1, 2–3, 6, 13, 45, 47, 51, 52, 54, 60–78, 104; firm 14, 175, 181–2, 183, 186, 187
insider trading 55
insolvency regime 151
institutional political economy 12, 40, 41–2
interbank market 3, 100
interest rates 4, 80, 82, 153; real 95
International Labour Organization (ILO) 131, 136
International Monetary Fund (IMF) 11, 100, 113, 143, 150, 158, 200
investment 50, 89–90; behaviour 105–6; financial theory of 48; operating surplus 106; public 9
Ireland 53, 109, 150; collective bargaining centralization *132*; and Competitive Capitalist Model 145; current account **81**; debt 107, *108*; economic crisis 101–2; employment protection legislation (EPL) *129*; financialization *147*; house prices 2; as Liberalized Market Economy (LME) 176; social expenditure **163**; trade union density *130*; unemployment 195, *196*, *197*, *198*; unemployment expenditure **168**
Italy: collective bargaining centralization *132*; collective bargaining coverage *130*; current account 81; debt ratios *108*; employment protection legislation (EPL) *129*; financialization **147**; house prices 2; labour share **129**; social expenditure **163**; trade union density *130*; unemployment *179*, *196*, *197*, *198*; unemployment expenditure **168**; wage dispersion 149

Ivanova, M.N. 47, 49

Japan: collective bargaining centralization *132*; as Coordinated Market Economy (CME) 176; financialization **147**; investment-to-profits ratio **106**; labour share **129**; social expenditure **163**; trade union density *130*; unemployment 195, *196*, *197*, *198*; unemployment expenditure **168**
Jessop, B. 12–13, 40–59
JP Morgan 64

Kalecki, M. 48
Keynes, J.M. 24, 25, 201
Keynesian economics 30
Keynesian medicine, for EMU ills 92–6
Keynesian Welfare State 144
Kleinknecht, A. 14, 175–91
Knight, F.H. 201
knowledge, tacit 14, 182, 183, 186
Krugman, P. 38

labour: adjustment costs 138; contracts 14, 23, 131, 195, 200; demand for 32; firing and hiring 124, 137, 180, 181, 182, 185, 187; hoarding 136, 138, 192, 195, 200, 203; household 34; informal 44; productive 21, 22, 23; reproductive 44; supply of 32, 178, 181; unproductive 22, 23
labour force participation 127
labour market 4–5; in Coordinated Market Economies (CME) 175, 180; deregulation 126–7, 177–9, 186, 187; Eurozone **167**; and financial crises 127–41, 193–8, 202, 203; flexibility 1–2, 5, 6, 14, 90–1, 110, 124, 136, 137, 138, 175, 180, 182, 192; and GDP growth 175; and labour productivity 183–5; in Liberalized Market Economies (LME) 175; reforms 13–14, 85, 124–6; rigidities 14, 126, 138, 175–91; US 32–3, **168**; women in 32, 34, 35
labour market institutions 13–14, 123–42
labour productivity 6, 14, 37, 136, 137, 138, 175, 177, 181, 187; Coordinated Market Economies (CME) **179**; and economic growth 14; and labour market regulation 183–5; Liberalized Market Economies (LME) **179**, 180–3; and trust 182–3; and wages 184
labour share in GDP 124, 128, **129**, 138

Index

labour unions *see* trade unions
Laeven, L.A. 204
laissez-faire capitalism 27, 31–2
Langley, P. 75
Latin America and Caribbean, unemployment *194*
Latvia: debt ratios *108*; unemployment *196*, *197*, *198*
Lazonick, W. 105
Lee, J. 200
Lehman Brothers 4, 64, 100
lender of last resort 47, 95, 158
leverage 53
Levy, J. 48
Liberalized Market Economies (LME) 175, 176; GDP growth 177, **178**, 185; hours worked **177**, *180*; labour productivity **179**, 180–3; unemployment 177–80, 186; wages 176, 185
Lipietz, A. 5–6
liquidity 13, 62, 63–76
liquidity arbitrage 13
liquidity crisis 3–4, 45
liquidity standards 151, 152
Lisbon European strategy 199
Lithuania: debt ratios *108*; unemployment 195, *196*, *197*, *198*
Lucas, R.E.B. 201
Lucidi, F. 185
Luxembourg: collective bargaining centralization *132*; current account **81**; trade union density *130*; unemployment *196*, *197*, 198

Maastricht Treaty 8; convergence criteria 82
McCarthyism 29
McCullery, P. 45
Macdonald, N. 68
Madoff, B. 39
Magnus, G. 45–6
Malta, unemployment *196*, *197*, 198
manufacturing 32
Marelli, E. 14, 192–211
market completion 68, 72
market failures 42
market liquidity 69
markets 20, 21; perfect 72; *see also* financial markets
Marx, K. 40, 41–2, 44, 49–52, 53, 54, 55
Marxian moment 48
Marxism 29
Merkel, A. 150, 159
Merrill Lynch 4

Mexico: mass emigration to US 32–3; remittance flow to 32, 33
Michie, J. 184
Middle East, unemployment *194*
minimum wages 1
Minsky, H. 13, 42, 44–5, 46, 48, 49, 50, 51, 54–5, 61–2, 70, 71, 74
Minsky meltdown 45
Minsky moment 40, 44, 45–7, 51, 54, 71
monetary crises 51, 52
monetary policy 24, 110, 160, 205, 206; ECB 80, 95; expansionary 127
money 12, 40, 51, 65, 67; bank 53; as capital 51, 52; central bank 53; commodity 53; fiat 53; as means of (deferred) payment 51; state 53; world 53
money-manager capitalism 45, 55, 60, 61
Moody's 4
Morgan Stanley 4
mortgage debt 35, 36, 46
mortgage default correlations 9
mortgage financing 3
mortgage-backed bonds (MBB) 3
mortgage-backed securities (MBS) 3
mortgages 105; sub-prime 4, 62, 68, 99–100, 105, 159
multinational companies 5

Naastepad, C.W.M. 175–91
neo-conservatives 6, 148
neo-institutionalism 103
neo-liberalism 2, 5, 12, 27, 31, 40, 47, 53, 54, 61, 91, 99, 102, 103, 108
Nesvetailova, A. 13, 60–78
Netherlands: collective bargaining centralization *132*; current account **81**; debt ratios 107, *108*; employment protection legislation (EPL) *129*; financialization **147**; house prices 2; labour productivity 181; social expenditure **163**; trade union density *130*; unemployment *179*, 195, *196*, *197*, *198*; unemployment expenditure **168**
New Deal 12, 28, 29, 30
New Keynesianism 103
New Zealand: collective bargaining centralization *132*; as Liberalized Market Economy (LME) 176; social expenditure **163**; trade union density *130*; unemployment expenditure **168**
Nickell, S. 186
nominal exchange rates 81, 92
non-accelerating inflation rate of unemployment (NAIRU) 89, 178

non-accelerating wage rate of unemployment (NAWRU) 89
non-financial business sector 105–6
non-systemic banking crisis 204
North American Free Trade Agreement (NAFTA) 32–3
Northern Rock Bank 4
Norway: collective bargaining centralization *132*; financialization **147**; house prices 2; trade union density *130*; unemployment *198*

Obama, B. 150, 159
Occupy Wall Street movement 23
OECD Jobs Study 13
off-balance-sheet assets 55, 69, 73, 74, 151
offshore finance 68, 104, 153
Okun's law 14, 137, 192, 198–204, 205
Onaran, Ö. 106
optimal currency areas (OCA) 80
Orghangazi, Ö. 105
O'Sullivan, M. 105
output, potential 88–9
output gap 89
outsourcing 32
Over the Counter (OTC) derivatives 152–3

Padalino, S. 200
Pakistan 100
Palley, T. 45
patenting activity 184
Pederson, V. 64
perfect markets 72
petty commodity production 44
Pieroni, L. 184
Pindyck, R 202
Pivetti, M. 128
Poland: debt ratios *108*; unemployment *196*, *197*, *198*
political capitalism 42, 48, 55, 56
Pompei, F. 184
Ponzi finance 13, 39, 44, 45, 46, 47, 51, 71, 153
Portugal 109; collective bargaining centralization *132*; current account **81**; debt ratios *108*; employment protection legislation (EPL) *129*; financialization **147**; trade union density *130*; unemployment 195, *196*, *197*, *198*
potential output 88–9
poverty 45, 145, 258; working 193, *194*
Prachowny, M.J.F. 200
precarious work 136–7, 140

price bubbles 2
prices, housing sector 2, 35–6, 99, 107
Prince, C. 70
private financial markets 66–7
private property 20, 21
production 21; capitalist 52; household 44; petty commodity 44; subsistence 44
productive capital 40, 49, 50, 52, 55
productive labour 21, 22, 23
productivity *see* labour productivity
profit 37, 42, 48, 50, 51, 55–6; predatory 55; rate 51
property: capital as 51, 52, 53; private 20, 21; rights 125
proprietary trading 152
public debt 8, 47, 53, 80, 82, 83, 128
public investment 9
public ownership 20
purchasing power 127, 128, 158

quantitative easing 153

Ramskogler, P. 103
Rasmus, J. 46
rational capitalism 42, 48, 55, 56
Reagan, R. 5, 30–1, 148, 149
real economy 12, 13, 47, 49, 50, 54, 100, 127, 143, 144, 154; crisis-tendencies in 48; expansion of 53
real exchange rates 81, 92, 109
real interest rates 95
Regulation Theory 103, 104
Reinhart, C. 202
remittance flows, US–Mexico 32, 33
Renminbi 53
reproductive labour 44
risk 3, 13, 52, 105; management 68–9, 76; optimization 65, 68; trading 62, 64, 65, 69
Rogoff, K. 202
Romania: debt ratios *108*; unemployment *196*, *197*, *198*
Roosevelt, F.D. 28–9
'routinized' innovation 14, 175, 183, 186, 187
Rueff, J. 10–11

Sarkozy, N. 150
saving 9–10
saving glut theory 10
savings 89–90, 128
Sawyer, M. 13, 79–97
Scarpetta, S. 184
Schmitt, J. 200

Schumpeterian innovation models 14, 175, *183*
scientific finance 67–8
securitization 4, 47, 48, 55, 60, 62, 63, 65, 66, 68, 71, 72, 73, 74, 75, 105, 153, 155
self-regulating credit 72–6
service sector, US 32
Sexana, S.C. 201
shadow banking 13, 52, 55, 68, 75, 104
shareholder power 105
Sheehan, M. 184
Signorelli, M. 14, 192–211
single market 7–8
slavery 20–1, 39
Slovakia: debt ratios *108*; unemployment 195, *196*, *197*, *198*
Slovenia, unemployment *196*, *197*, *198*
social democracy 31
social dialogue 138, 140
social expenditure **163**
social security 136, 141, 176
Social-Democratic economic model 144, 145, *146*
socialism 20, 27, 29
Socialist Markets 144
socialist political parties 28
Solow, R.M. 200
solvency crisis 3–4, 45
Sordi, S. 201
South Asia, unemployment *194*
South East Asia 9; unemployment *194*
South European economic model 145
South Korea, unemployment expenditure **168**
sovereign debt 7, 47, 53, 109, 143, 193, 195, 199, 205, 206
Spain 109; collective bargaining centralization *132*; current account **81**; debt ratios *108*; employment protection legislation (EPL) *129*; financialization **147**; house prices 2; labour share **129**; trade union density *130*; unemployment *196*, *197*, *198*; unemployment expenditure **168**
speculation 12, 40, 42, 52
speculative finance 45, 51
Stability and Growth Pact 79, 80, 83–4
Stand and Poor's 4
state money 53
stock markets 37, 111
Stockhammer, E. 13, 98–119
Storm, S. 175–91
structural budget deficit rule, EMU 83–4, 86–90

structural unemployment 89, 126, 193, 195
structured investment vehicles (SIVs) 69
student debt 36
sub-prime mortgage market 4, 62, 68, 99–100, 105, 159
subsistence production 44
supply, of labour 32, 178, 181
surplus 21, 23
Susann, R. 202
Sweden: collective bargaining centralization *132*; collective bargaining coverage *130*; employment protection legislation (EPL) *129*; financialization **147**; house prices 2; social expenditure **163**; trade union density *130*, *131*; unemployment *179*, *196*, *197*, *198*; unemployment expenditure **168**
Switzerland: collective bargaining centralization *132*; debt ratios *108*; financialization *147*; trade union density *130*
Synthetic Vulnerability Index 14, 143–4, 156–8, 160
systemic uncertainty 14, 201–2, 203, 205

tacit knowledge 14, 182, 183, 186
Taft–Hartley Act 29, 30
tax havens 150
taxation 25; Financial Activities Tax (FAT) 155; financial transaction tax (FTT) 154, 155, 160, 161; income tax 94; progressive, EMU members 94; US 30
technological change 108
temporary employment 200
Tett, G. 69
Thatcher, M. 5, 30–1, 148, 149
Tobin, J. 154
toxic assets 3, 37, 47, 53, 155
trade 53; globalization of 109; US–EU **166**
trade deficit 81; EMU members 92–3; US–China 9
trade unions 22–3, 28, 30, 125–6, 158; in Coordinated Market Economies (CME) 176; density 109, 126, 129–30, 131; in Liberalized Market Economies (LME) 175; power of 129
training 14, 182
Tressel, T. 184
Tridico, P. 1–16, 90
Troubled Asset Relief Program (TARP) 159
trust, and productivity growth 182–3

uncertainty 201–2, 203, 205
underemployment 141
unemployment 2, 7, 26, 27, 89, 101, 110, 138, 141, 156, 175; Africa *194*; benefits 124–5, 136, 144, 200; Coordinated Market Economies (CME) 178, **179**, 186; East Asia *194*; EU 133, **134**, **157**, 160, *194*, 195; Eurozone 158; expenditure on **168**; and financial crises 192–211; frictional 126; and GDP **134**, 135, 136, 199–204, 205; global 131; and labour market deregulation 127, 175, 177–9; and labour market rigidity 186; Latin America and Caribbean *194*; Liberalized Market Economies (LME) 177–80, 186; long-term rate (LTUR) 195, 196, *197*; Middle East *194*; South East Asia *194*; structural 89, 126, 193, 195; US 133, **134**, 135, 156, **157**, 158, 186, 195, *196*; voluntary-search 124; world *194*; youth 197–8
United Kingdom (UK) 53, 102, 145, 150, 155; austerity measures 159; collective bargaining centralization *132*; collective bargaining coverage *130*; debt ratios 107, *108*; employment protection legislation (EPL) *129*; financialization **147**; house prices 2; investment-to-profits ratio **106**; labour share **129**; as Liberalized Market Economy (LME) 176; social expenditure **163**; trade union density *130*, *131*; unemployment *179*, *196*, *197*, *198*; unemployment expenditure **168**; wage dispersion **149**
United States (US) 12, 14, 53, 54, 143–4, 145, *163*, 205; American Recovering and Reinvestment Act 159; anti-communist witch hunts 29; austerity measures 159; and China trade deficit 9; collective bargaining centralization *132*; collective bargaining coverage *130*; Commodity Futures Trading Commission (CFTC) 152; Consumer Financial Protection Agency 151, 152; Council of Regulators 152; current account (CA) deficit 8–9, 10; debt (household 35, 36, 113, **128**; public 8); debt-to-GDP ratios *108*; and economic/financial crisis 8–10, 143, 145, 150, 151–3, 154–61; employment protection legislation (EPL) *129*; and EU trade balance 166; Financial Stability Oversight Council 151, 152; financialization **147**; Frank–Dodd Act 151, 161; GDP **134**, 135, 158, 160, **162**, 185; Government Accountability Office (GAO) 152–3; house prices 2, 35–6, 99; household debt 35, 36, 113, **128**; immigration 19, 31, 32–3; income inequality 6, 9, **128**, 178–9, 185; investment-to-profits ratio **106**; labour market 32–3, **168**; labour share **129**; as Liberalized Market Economy (LME) 176; macroeconomic variables *165*; manufacturing jobs 32; Medicare liability 8; New Deal 12, 28, 29, 30; New Left 30; rightist coalition 29–30; Securities and Exchange Commission (SEC) 152; service sector 32; social expenditure **163**; Social Security system 8, 28; stock markets 111; Synthetic Vulnerability Index **157**; Taft–Hartley Act 29, 30; taxation 30; trade unions 22–3, 30, *130*, *131*; Troubled Asset Relief Program (TARP) 159; unemployment 133, **134**, 135, 156, **157**, 158, 186, 195, *196*, *197*, *198*; unemployment expenditure **168**; wage dispersion **149**; wages 9, 31, 32, 33–4, 36, 108, 113; welfare-state capitalism 28–30
unproductive labour 22, 23

value-at-risk (VAR) models 69
variegated capitalism 43, 44
varieties of capitalism (VoC) 12, 14, 40, 42–4, 91, 144–5, *164*
Vercelli, A. 201
Vergeer, R. 175–91
Vermeulen, P. 124
Vivarelli, M. 200
Volcker Rule 151, 152, 161

Wade, R. 74
wage bargaining: centralized 176, 182; decentralized 175, 181, 200
wage dispersion **149**
wage labour 21
wage setting 125–6
wages 21, 102, 107, 110; appropriate level of 160; contraction 5, 6; Coordinated Market Economies (CME) 176, 185; flexible 180–1, 181, 200; growth **176**, 181, 185, 186; indirect 2; and labour productivity 184; Liberalized Market Economies (LME) 176, 185; and market pressures 125–6; minimum 2; moderation 5, 8, 114, 126, 138; real 176; reduction 175; share of

wages *continued*
 GDP 131; stagnation 9, 12, 33–4, 36, 37, 113; US 9, 31, 32, 33–4, 36, 108, 113
Washington Mutual 4
wealth: distribution of 6, 37; inequality 6, 12, 114
Weber, M. 40, 42, 55
Weberian moment 48
welfare state 144
welfare state capitalism 27–31
Winters, B. 62
Wolff, R. 12, 19–39
women: household labour 34; labour market participation 32, 34, 35
women's liberation movement 32

working class 12, 33, 99, 102, 113; indebtedness 12, 13, 36, 99, 107
working hours 136, 137, 138, 176, **177**, *180*, 192
working poverty 193, *194*
World Bank 103, 150, 158
world money 53
world system theory 10, 11, 44
World Trade Organization (WTO) 150
World War II 29

youth unemployment 197–8

zero output gap 89
Zhou Xiaochuan 11